# THE REPO MARKET SHORTS SHORTAGES AND SQUEEZES

Scott E.D. Skyrm

# Also by
## Scott E.D. Skyrm

## The Money Noose

*Jon Corzine and the Collapse of MF Global*

Brick Tower Press (2013)

## Rogue Traders

Brick Tower Press (2014)

## More Rogue Traders

Brooklyn Writers Press (2020)

**BROOKLYN**
WRITERS PRESS

Library of Congress number registration submitted.

ISBNs:
978-1-952991-28-8 (Hardback)
978-1-952991-27-1 (e-Book)

Cover Design: Andy Semnitz

The Brooklyn Writers Press is a registered DBA of the Brooklyn Writers Co. LLC

Printed in the United States of America

# CONTENTS

# History

# The Basics

# Shorts, Shortages and Squeezes

# Risk, Scandal, Panic and Regulations

# The Modern Market

# INTRODUCTION

I started my career working for the Bank of Tokyo, located at 100 Broadway in downtown New York City. It was right across from Trinity Church and around the corner from Wall Street and the New York Stock Exchange. It was the heart of the financial markets at the time. I had just graduated from Lehigh University with two degrees in economics, and I was eager to see how I could do on Wall Street, one of the most competitive industries in one of the most competitive cities in the country.

I had literally talked my way into the job. I'd had many job interviews over the summer, but nothing seemed to fit: support areas, junior analysts, personal assistants. None of that would do it for me. I wanted to work on the trading floor. Ironically enough, I remember after a job interview at Nomura, the HR person literally told me that she liked me for the job, but felt that I'd spend too much time hanging around the trading floor.

In October 1989, I met with the Head of Bank of Tokyo Securities, a local government bond dealer and subsidiary of The Bank of Tokyo. It was a small operation, maybe 15 people. I was hired as an "assistant" on the trading desk, which numbered maybe three traders and three salespeople. And, naturally, a Japanese "home staff" guy to oversee the Americans.

In February 1990, the Repo trader and settlements manager, two positions that were combined into a single person, went on vacation. He had a split role at the company, financing the firm's Treasury positions in the morning and watching over the securities settlements in the afternoon. Today, there could never be a combined trader and operations person, but bond market regulation was much lighter back then.

In order to cover the Repo trading and settlements, the firm chose me to do the settlements and Adam from the operations group to finance the trading positions. Adam had been with the company for a few years and had impressed management. This was his shot at a back-up role on the trading floor. Everything went well the first day; it was all as smooth as possible with no problems.

For those not familiar with the Repo market, it's an early morning market. These days, the market opens at 7:00 AM New York time. Back then, the market opened around 8:00 AM. The second day, Adam didn't show up. As the hours ticked by, the head trader said, "Scott-san, where is he?" I didn't know. There was no phone call. There was nothing. He then said, "Scott-san, can you do the Repo?"

In my head, my answer was, "I don't know." But the answer that came out was, "Yes. I can do it!" I figured it out and got it done. There were no problems. Every day since then, I've been in the Repo market.[1] Repo trader, Repo salesman, Repo desk manager, Repo economist. I believe I've done it all. Just about every role there is in the short-end of the market. I've experienced it all. And Repo is all I've done since that inauspicious beginning.

---

[1] I wonder if Adam showed up that day what I'd be doing now.

I started working on this book about 25 years ago. Back then, I thought I knew a lot about the Repo market. Looking back, I still had a lot to learn. This is a much richer and thorough book than it would have been years ago.

There have been tremendous changes in the financial markets since I started my career. The market is nothing like it was back then. The Repo market is forever changed: the Treasury market's surpassing $31.5 trillion, electronic trading, the financial crisis, Dodd-Frank regulation, globalization of markets, rise of hedge funds, debt ceiling crises, quantitative easing, ZIRP (Zero Interest Rate Policy), the collapse of many broker-dealers and banks, rogue traders, the list goes on.

This book is one part textbook (Don't give up yet!), one-part stories, one part history, and one part a journey through the financial markets over the past thirty years. I tried very hard to keep it interesting and not too dry. However, remember, there's still important content that needs to be included to make it useful. There's important market infrastructure that needs to be understood in order to understand larger parts of the Repo market.

The book doesn't have to be all about U.S. Treasurys, but that's mostly what it's about. U.S. Treasuries are the foundation of the Repo market. However, these days there are Repo transactions in just about any financial instrument: federal agencies, municipal bonds, corporate bonds, foreign government bonds, emerging markets bonds, mortgage loans, etc.

This is the story of the modern financial markets, starting with the development of a new financial instrument and a journey through market panics, regulation, trading scandals, booms and busts.

I will warn you in advance: I was trained in economics, so I often look at the markets through the lens of supply and demand. In one way, this book is a study of a market. You will see how supply and demand interacts and how pricing is created. Repo is a true market. Repo rates are determined by the interaction of supply and demand. Supply is the number of securities outstanding and the amount of those securities available in the marketplace. Demand is the amount of cash in the market. It's also the number of shorts in the market – the traders who have sold Treasury securities short and must borrow them.

Repo stands for "Repurchase Agreement," which means that if I loan a security to you, you agree to give it back. The opposite of that is officially called a Reverse-Repurchase agreement. It's the opposite of a Repo. If I borrow a security from you, I agree to return it back to you. In basic terms, Repo is a collateralized loan. One party borrows cash and holds a security as collateral. In case you didn't realize, most people already have a collateralized loan of one kind or another. When you buy a house with a bank loan, the bank holds the title to the property until you pay off the loan; the house is the collateral for the loan. It's the same in the Repo market. When you buy a house, the bank requires a down payment, which is really margin on the loan, and if you stop paying interest, the bank forecloses on the loan and takes away the house. Same in the Repo market. But more on that later.

The size of the Repo market is estimated to be $6.0 trillion in Reverse-Repo and $5.6 trillion in Repo. It's at its all-time peak. That makes it one of the largest markets in the world. Globally, the size of the Repo market is estimated to be $15 trillion. By contrast, the U.S. stock market capitalization is $27.7 trillion, and the total size of the Treasury market is $31.5 trillion.

Repo is the oil that lubricates the engine of the financial markets. It keeps it running smoothly; it's the plumbing of the financial system. You might even say it's the oil that lubricates the engine of the entire economy.

Here are some important characteristics of the Repo market:

In one respect, Repo is a popular instrument for short-term cash investments for institutional investors, with "short-term" meaning from overnight through one year. It's an ultra-safe investment. It's an investment collateralized with a Treasury security at a competitive market rate of interest.

In another respect, Repo is a mechanism for market participants to cover short sales of U.S. Treasurys. This is a big part of the Repo market and arguably the most interesting part.

In another respect, it provides collateralized funding for large leveraged investors. OK, let's just get this said up front. Yes, the Repo market is the way hedge funds can highly leverage their trading positions. More on this later. Actually, a lot on this throughout the book.

In another respect, the Repo market makes the U.S. financial markets the most efficient in the world. The efficiency achieves the lowest cost of funding for the U.S. government. And the efficiency does not stop there. It reverberates throughout the economy. A more efficient Treasury market means better pricing for mortgage-backed securities, municipal debt (like your state or local government), corporate debt, and any other debt you can think of. Efficiencies drive costs lower, and lower costs benefit everyone.

Let's begin.

# Early History

You may not have heard of the Panic of 1907, but it's pretty important in the financial markets. Few people know it's one of the largest economic and stock market contractions of all time. Even fewer people know that the event that triggered the creation of the Federal Reserve was sparked by a stock squeeze.

In the early 1900s, the economy was humming along just fine. Ford Motor Company gave us the creation of the assembly line and the Wright brothers gave us the first airplane. In April 1906, a major earthquake in San Francisco sparked a fire that burned most of the city. In order to help rebuild, capital began flowing West, out of New York City and into the Bay Area.

By October 1907, the stock market had been declining all year long. Economic conditions were not great, but still not terrible. A man named F. Augustus Heinze and his family owned a majority of the shares of the United Copper Company. Heinze had made his fortune in the copper industry, and had recently moved to New York from Butte, Montana. Heinze's brother, Otto, didn't like the decline in their family's fortune and devised a plan to corner the shares in United Copper. Otto believed that much of the downward pressure on the company's shares was due to short selling. Naturally, short sellers need to borrow the stock in order to deliver the shares that were sold, and the Heinze brothers suspected their brokers were loaning shares to speculators. Otto's plan was simple – buy more United Copper shares and then stop letting their brokers loan their securities into the market. The short sellers would be forced to buy the shares back and the price would skyrocket. But in order to get the money to finance their stock purchases, they needed a loan.

Back in those days, banks did not lend money to stock speculators. That business was left to the trust companies. Trust companies were not banks. In one way, they were the original non-bank financial institutions, the original shadow banks. They were officially financial institutions that were state chartered, and the state charter had much lighter regulatory requirements, including lower reserve requirements and the ability to write uncollateralized loans. Since banks did not write uncollateralized loans, the New York Stock Exchange brokers went to the trust companies. It was a good business for everyone. Brokers were able to get loans to leverage both their own trading positions and the positions of their clients.

Otto Heinze went to his preferred trust company, Knickerbocker Trust, and arranged the financing. On October 14, 1907, he bought every share he could, driving the price from $39 a share up to $52 a share. The next day, October 15, the Heinze brothers recalled all of their stock that was loaned through the brokers to the short sellers. At this point, all they had to do was wait for the price of the stock to take off as the short sellers were forced to buy back their shares. The next day, the price of United Copper didn't rally. In fact, it began to decline. As it turned out, the number of shorts were not very deep, and no one had problems borrowing the shares. By the end of the day on October 16, the stock had dropped to $10.

The Heinze brothers were ruined and Knickerbocker Trust was teetering on insolvency, having made loans on a $30 stock that was now only worth $10. One-third of the value of the collateral (the stock) was wiped out. As word got out about the trouble with the Heinze brothers, United Copper, Knickerbocker Trust, people began to panic. Depositors lined up at the doors of Knickerbocker Trust when they opened the next day to withdraw their deposits. When people couldn't get their money back, panic spread to the other trust companies and then to the banks.

Over a period of three weeks from October through November 1907, a national panic swept through the country. The trust companies were no longer able to supply loans to the stock brokers. The rate for an overnight loan used to finance stock positions shot up from 9.5% to 70%, and that was for brokers lucky enough to get a loan! There was just no money available. Stock prices fell even further. The stock market dropped over 50% within just a few weeks.

In short, J.P. Morgan himself put together a consortium of the largest New York industrialists and captains of industry. They personally made loans to New York Stock Exchange brokers, which stemmed the panic and helped to stabilize the market. However, the so-called Panic of 1907 would forever change the banking system.

Many European countries had already established semi-private, quasi-governmental central banks. Central banking was in fashion and the new thing in banking. However, the U.S. banking system was still behind the times. A new system was needed to address the peaks and troughs of the financial markets. It was clear the country could not rely on New York big wigs to bail out the financial system every time there was a panic or crisis. The U.S. needed a central bank.

The Federal Reserve System was created by Congress on December 23, 1913, and began operating on November 16, 1914. Twelve regional banks were set up across the country to provide liquidity to their regions. The state of Missouri was lucky enough to be granted two district banks in their state (St. Louis and Kansas City) because, well, the Speaker of the House was from Missouri. All federally chartered banks were required by law to become members. State banks, savings and loans, thrifts, and credit unions all had the option of becoming members.

The United States finally had a central banking system ready to provide liquidity to the banks and prevent future panics.

The modern use of Repo financing, though not yet called a Repo, began shortly after the U.S. entered World War I in 1917. Part of the Fed's official mandate was to "provide an elastic currency," which, as we know, includes providing liquidity to the banking system. During its first few years, injecting cash into the financial system exclusively involved the rediscounting of commercial paper. The Fed loaned money to banks and received commercial paper as collateral. Then, with the growing issuance of Liberty Bonds by the U.S. government, banks began presenting these new government securities to the Fed for rediscounting. When the Fed rediscounted the first Liberty Bond, the Repo market was born.

However, it was still not time for the Repo market to emerge. Banks were required to keep a certain portion of their deposits as reserves at the Fed. Any cash in excess of the "required reserves" were a bank's excess reserves. Those excess reserves could be deposited at the Fed or loaned to other banks in an inter-bank market, dubbed the federal funds market.

Federal funds were first traded in New York in the summer of 1921. During the first years of the Fed, banks could transfer funds between each other in two ways: from their clearinghouse account or from their account at their Federal Reserve Bank. A clearinghouse transfer took at least one day to clear, while the Fed account cleared on the same day. If a bank needed funds in their clearinghouse account, they could borrow the funds from another bank in their Federal Reserve Bank account. The next day, when the clearinghouse funds arrived, the overnight loan in their Federal Reserve Bank account was paid off.

Participation in the federal funds market was limited to banks who held funds at the Federal Reserve Banks. The Fed liked the federal funds market because it provided members with a way to borrow bank reserves without tapping the discount window. Trading in fed funds eventually included wire transfers and other payment methods. Non-banks were prohibited from engaging in the federal funds market, which is still the case today.

The fed continued to use Repo transactions to manage the quantity of reserves, kind of like the original open-market operations. At first, all 12 district banks executed Repo within their districts. This was eventually consolidated and centralized into the Federal Reserve Bank of New York. The Fed added Banker's Acceptances (BAs) to the list of collateral they accepted in rediscounting, which also helped create a secondary market for banks' BAs.

As time went on, it became clear the Repo market was the primary tool for the Fed to manage liquidity in the financial system.

The 1930s saw many changes to the banking system. The Banking Act of 1933, also known as Glass-Steagall, regulated the stock market, separated securities dealers from banks, and established the Securities and Exchange Commission (SEC). Though the SEC regulated many securities markets, government securities were considered exempt. That meant that federal securities laws did not apply. The thinking at the time was to let those markets operate free of government regulation, which would allow the Treasury and municipalities to sell debt at a lower cost. Oh, and one more thing. There was a clause known as Regulation Q, which prohibited banks from paying interest on savings accounts. Keep in mind, the unregulated government securities market and Regulation Q will be important years later in the development of the Repo market.

The inter-dealer Repo market was given a big boost with the passage of the Treasury-Federal Reserve Accord of 1951. In this act, the Fed was given the mandate to control inflation and officially began using Repurchase Agreements as a tool to inject liquidity (cash) into the financial system. At the same time, a Repo market began developing outside of the banking system.

As interest rates began to rise in the post-war period, leaving your cash at a bank that paid near zero percent interest was not such a good investment. Corporations and municipalities had millions of dollars to invest, but could not get a decent return on the short-term cash. They wanted a rate, because any rate was better than nothing. At the same time, securities dealers on Wall Street began holding trading positions. Previously the role of the broker-dealer was as a pure middleman. That's the broker part of broker-dealer. When a client wanted to sell a bond, the firm's salesmen scoured the market to find a buyer. If they could find a buyer, the trade was done: end-user seller to end-user buyer, and the Wall Street firm just stood in the middle. That changed in the 1950s. Some broker-dealers, like Bear Stearns and Salomon Brothers, realized they could make money buying bonds for their own trading account. And, they could even make money betting on the direction of interest rates. Yes, they still brokered buys and sells between institutional customers, but there was some easy money to be made by taking a little market risk. And they did.

In order to finance their trading positions, these Wall Street firms naturally had funding facilities at their clearing banks, but those facilities were relatively expensive. Then, along came corporations and municipalities looking to invest their excess cash. They were so desperate to get a good rate of return that it turned out to be a cheap funding source for the Wall Street firms.

Thus, the private sector Repo market was born. At this point, it wasn't just the Fed doing Repo with banks; now there were securities dealers trading with corporate clients. Just when customers were looking to invest cash, securities dealers needed cash. And it was a reliable source of cash. It was the perfect marriage of supply and demand. And the Repo market took off.

However, a small flaw developed in this market that had dire consequences years later. No one added the coupon accrued interest to their Repo transactions. Coupon accrued interest is the interest that accrues on a bond between semi-annual coupon payment dates. Basically, a bond accrues a little bit of interest each day. The value of a bond increases each day by that small amount of one day's worth of coupon interest.

In the 1950s Repo market, in order to keep things simple, Repo transactions were priced with just the principal amount of the trade. The bond's Repo price was calculated by simply multiplying the bond's par amount by the market price. No one added on the accrued interest. Picture this: It's the 1950s and you don't have a mainframe computer, calculator, or even a phone that makes basic calculations. Yes, there were hand calculations and tables that the back-office used to calculate yields and bond prices, but can you imagine how long that takes? At the time, it made back-office work just a lot easier by leaving the coupon accrued interest off of the trade. This had dire consequences down the road.

As the U.S. financial system continued to grow in the 1960s, more and more corporate clients wanted the new overnight Repo cash investment. Broker-dealers, corporations, and municipalities could not access to the federal funds market, but they could book a Repo and get a market rate of interest. The overnight Repo rate traded slightly below the federal funds rate. The combination of the federal funds rate for banks and the Repo rate for non-banks established the dual overnight rates of the U.S. financial system.

Then, there was another big Repo market development in 1966: The first use of Matched Sales. At times, there were surges in bank reserves and the Fed needed to drain liquidity from the financial system. The Fed booked Matched Sales by selling U.S. Treasurys to Primary Dealers and buying the securities back the next day or some date in the near future.

There is a subtle and distinct difference between Matched Sales and a Reverse-Repo transaction. Matched Sales are an outright sale of securities with an outright purchase booked at a future date. Under a

Reverse-Repo with the Fed, the Fed loans securities to Primary Dealers for a day or more. The end result is the same: The Fed is draining liquidity by putting securities into the market. Why Matched Sales instead of Reverse-Repo? At the time, Fed lawyers believed there were potential legal problems with the Fed borrowing cash from securities dealers. But selling them securities and buying back those securities in the future was legally OK.

There was one more important development that occurred at this point. Up until this time, the inter-dealer Repo market was primarily used for funding dealers' long positions or for corporate clients to invest cash. No one was using Repo to cover short positions. Back then, short positions were covered through a "box loan" at the security firm's clearing bank. If a securities dealer was short a Treasury, the security would remain uncovered and they left a long position of another U.S. Treasury in their "box" (securities account) as collateral. After the securities settlement system closed, the clearing bank swapped the long position for the short position through the bank's Securities Lending Department. This was the predecessor to the "bonds borrowed/bonds loaned" transaction that became popular with securities lending groups from the 1980s through 2000s. At the end of the 1960s, the total size of the Repo market stood at $4.9 billion

The 1970s was a decade marked by runaway inflation and the Fed's attempt to control that inflation. Early in the decade, short-term interest rates spiked in 1973-1974, reaching a high of 14% as the U.S. went off the gold standard and was hit with an oil embargo. Where banks were now allowed to pay 3.00% interest on savings accounts, overnight Repo rates were trading between 10% and 20%. Institutional investors were obviously attracted to the high rates in the

Repo market and flocked to get in. Many more large corporations amended their investment rules to allow them to invest in Repo, bringing even more cash investors into the market.

Where securities dealers' short positions were still being covered by the Securities Lending Group at the clearing bank, the standard cost was a 50 basis point fee. The securities dealer borrowed the short positions 50 basis points lower than the rate they received on their long Treasury position. It was a good deal that kept margins high for the clearing bank. But by the late 1970s, securities dealers realized they could borrow securities directly from each other and avoid the 50 basis point fee. Here is where the Specials market was born. Securities dealers began calling around the Street or used inter-dealer brokers to find specific securities to cover their short positions. Depending on the demand for that specific security, the Repo rate for a Special traded at a premium to the General Collateral Repo rate.

As the Treasury market grew, more and more trading positions were financed in the inter-dealer Repo market. Some securities dealers even discovered that Repo could be a business. They borrowed securities from the Street and loaned them to cash investor customers. Thus, the Repo Matched-Book was born. Repo transactions were not just used to finance the firm's inventory or to invest client cash, securities firms began to act as an intermediary between the borrowers and lenders. The size of the Repo market hit $45 billion at the end of the 1970s.

By the early 1980s, the Repo market was the largest single securities market in the world. And the fact that government securities were all still exempt from federal securities laws made it even more attractive. Back then, people assumed that fewer rules and regulations meant lower costs and better returns. Everyone was getting in. Not just the money-center banks and securities firms in New York, but also the regional banks and broker-dealers, small corporations, and local municipalities.

The stage was set for tremendous growth, a kind of coming-of-age for the Repo market. U.S. government debt continued to grow, and more and more long positions were funded while more and more short positions were covered in the inter-dealer market. By 1981, the size of the repo market stood at $111 billion. By 1986, it had crossed $200 billion.

But three flaws still existed. There was no regulation. With all the growth in the market, there were no calls to regulate Repo financing, securities dealers, or government bonds. The securities rules set up in the 1930s mainly targeted individual investors, the stock market, and banks. For years, there was never an outcry to regulate the government bond market. Large, sophisticated investors buying and selling AAA-rated, risk free, government bonds was not high on the to-do list. And free markets were much more a rallying cry in the 1980s than it is today.

Then, and this is a big one, it was still market convention to price Repo transactions without including the coupon accrued interest. Accrued interest was basically just ignored by the Repo market.

Third, there was uncertainty in terms of the legal status of Repo. What happened if a Repo counterparty went bankrupt or became insolvent? Was Repo a secured loan or a sale with an agreement to repurchase? No one really knew and it was never tested. Even the bankruptcy court was unsure whether a Repo was a collateralized loan or a sale and buy-back.

However, an event was about to occur that would transform the Repo market forever and create the modern Repo market: Drysdale Securities.

# Drysdale and the Dawn of The Modern Repo Market

David Heuwetter was the head trader at Drysdale Government Securities and had a great trading idea. It was really more of a scheme to take advantage of the difference in the market convention between outright Treasury purchases and Repo trades. Still at this time, when someone bought and sold a U.S. Treasury outright, the securities settled with the coupon accrued interest added to the purchase price. That is, when you bought a U.S. Treasury, you had to pay for the amount of interest which had already accrued on the security since the last coupon payment date.

When interest rates were low, the accrued interest was small, even negligible. However, in the early 1980s, interest rates shot up above 10%, which meant there was a lot of interest accruing on bonds each day.

Heuwetter realized he could short-sell U.S. Treasurys outright and deliver the securities to the buyer and receive the price plus the accrued interest. Then, when he borrowed the securities in the Repo market, he only had to pay the purchase price. He was getting the full use of the accrued interest on the bonds at no cost. In order to maximize the amount of cash he collected, he concentrated on shorting Treasurys that were at least halfway through the semi-annual coupon payment date. With years of declining bond markets (rising interest rates), he had made a lot of money shorting the Treasury market. By February 1982, he had accumulated $4.5 billion in short positions and had $2.5 billion in long positions. As one Wall Street trader later remarked, "It was the most astonishingly leveraged operation that I have ever seen."[2]

Overall, it was a pretty good trading strategy. He made money in two out of three possible scenarios. If bond prices went down, he made a lot of money. If the market stayed the same, he earned free interest on the cash. If the Treasury market rallied, he risked a pretty big loss. And guess what? Between February 1982 and May 1982, the Treasury market reversed its decline and started to rally. This was the one chance in three that he wasn't hoping for.

When the May 15, 1982, coupon interest payments were due on a Monday, Drysdale was wiped out and didn't have enough money to make the payments. That Sunday evening, Heuwetter called Drysdale's clearing bank, Chase Manhattan, and informed them that "we may have a problem" meeting the $160 million interest payment due the next day. Could Chase possibly lend Drysdale $200 million to tide them over? What he didn't tell them was that, yes, the market rally had wiped them out, but the problem was even worse than that. Drysdale had conducted its Repo trading mostly through Chase's Securities Lending Department. As it turns out, Drysdale's counterparties believed they were trading with Chase and not Drysdale. They believed Chase was not acting "as agent" for Drysdale, and instead, Chase was the principal on the trade. So, if Chase would not accept responsibility for the $160 million in coupon interest payments, the problem might be even worse.

---

[2] Little did he know what was coming over the next 40 years!

Up until then, no one had ever defaulted on a Repo transaction. The government securities market operated under the assumption that the buyer in a Repo was entitled to liquidate the trade in the event of a default, but there was no law on the books, and it was never tested in court. At the same time, there was really nothing differentiating a Repo from a collateralized loan, so everyone in the market was unsure whether or not they could liquidate the Drysdale/Chase Repo trades.

The lack of clarity with the bankruptcy status left Chase with a major dilemma. If the bank refused to pay the coupon interest to the Street and that action contributed to any of those securities dealers going bankrupt, a future court ruling against Chase could expose them to significant liability. However, if Chase made the coupon payments for Drysdale, they were taking a large loss and would line up as a creditor of Drysdale in bankruptcy court. It was a lose/lose situation.

Following Drysdale's collapse, both the government securities market and Repo market were frozen. Though Chase initially covered the payments and took over Drysdale positions to liquidate them, there still was no resolution of the Repo property rights and accrued interest pricing, and it weighed on the market. Then, the issue came up again just three months later when another firm, Lombard-Wall, collapsed in August 1982. Once again, Lombard-Wall had Repo transactions with the Street, but this time, there was no large bank to cover their losses. Immediately following the bankruptcy, Lombard-Wall's Repo trades went into bankruptcy court; their Repo counterparties were not allowed to liquidate them. That was, of course, the worst-case scenario for the securities market. Picture you might be long or short a few hundred Treasury bonds, but you won't know for sure for a few weeks. On top of that, interest rates were swinging around wildly!

The government securities and Repo markets were frozen. Again! The Fed called together the heads of the 20 largest banks and securities dealers for a meeting at the Fed's New York office. Not only was there pressure on Chase from the dealer community, but now it was also coming from the Fed itself. Though the Fed would later announce their only involvement was hosting a meeting, the concept would be quite similar to the future meetings for Long Term Capital Management in 1998 and Lehman Brothers in 2008. The next day, Chase relented and, as they say, the rest is history. In most textbooks, that's where the story ends, but in the context of the Repo market, it was just the beginning.

One week after Drysdale's collapsed, the executive committee of the Primary Dealers Association met to discuss a new convention for Repo and proposed including accrued interest on Repo trades. The Association formally adopted the rule on June 14, 1982, and by October 1982, the New York Fed ordered accrued interest to be included on the pricing of all Repo trades, moving to full accrual pricing as the standard market practice. But the story still did not end.

Since there were still no laws on the books defining Repo and no court cases to establish precedence, the legal status of Repo remained in question. The key issue was the treatment of Repo during a bankruptcy or a default. If Repo was technically a collateralized loan, then securities held by a creditor would be part of the bankruptcy proceedings, meaning the securities could be tied up for months or even years. If a Repo was technically a sale and a repurchase transaction, then the securities could be immediately liquidated in the event of a default. It was a major issue that would have ramifications going forward. On one hand, a Repo looked like a single transaction (a collateralized loan) since the buyer had the right to the coupon payments and the right to substitute collateral. On the other hand, a Repo was also a pair of transactions (one sell and one buy) where the buyer took title of the securities, could sell them or pledge them to another party, and had the right to return identical securities (i.e. U.S. Treasury 10 Year Notes). Since all of these factors were true, they argued, Repo trades should be free from the automatic stay provisions in a bankruptcy and could be immediately liquidated.

In September 1982, the Federal Bankruptcy Court of New York ruled that a Repo was a separate sell and buy transaction, meaning it was not a collateralized loan. The court recognized that allowing prompt liquidation was necessary to continue the orderly functioning of the market. Then, two years later in 1984, Congress passed an extension of the federal bankruptcy laws so that Repo transactions in Treasurys, federal agencies, bank CDs, and BAs were exempt from the automatic stays in bankruptcy by law.

# BROKER-DEALER BANKRUPTCIES AND THE BEGINNING OF TRI-PARTY

Surprisingly, it took the bankruptcies of an assortment of small government bond dealers in the 1980s to create the Tri-Party Repo market. Before the 1980s, all Repo trades settled DVP (delivery versus payment) and were mostly traded between securities dealers and money-center banks. As more customers entered the Repo market in the 1970s and 1980s, they routinely gave their cash to the securities dealer to hold in a safekeeping account. Safekeeping accounts are sometimes called hold-in-custody (HIC) and also unaffectionately known as "trust me" Repo. Back then, cash investors had plenty of faith in their securities dealers, trusting them to hold the cash, hold the securities, and price the securities accurately. Of course, at the time, there were few alternatives. These days, there are rules and regulations governing the HIC transactions, but back in the 1970s and 1980s, there was virtually no regulation. In fact, only 25% of all bond dealers were under any regulation at all. Both the Treasury market and government bond securities dealers were basically unregulated. And, maybe, given that, it comes as no surprise that those firms were abusing the cash and collateral they gave customers in the hold-in-custody Repo accounts.

The lightly regulated system lasted for many years, but eventually abuses began to surface. The municipal bond market was the first to suffer from the effects. In 1975, after the SEC brought several cases against municipal bond firms for excessive mark-ups, misrepresentations, high-pressure sales techniques, and churning customer accounts, the industry set up the Municipal Securities Rule Making Board (MSRB) as a solution through self-regulation. The municipal bond market was finally under rules, albeit rules they made for themselves. But still, there were no changes in the government bond market.

Back then, government bond firms operated with minimal capital, no mark-to-market on trading positions, and Repo transactions with customers that were often mis-marked and under-collateralized. Though the Repo market had been functioning well for years, there were no industry standards and no standardized Master Repurchase Agreement. Overall, the only regulation in the government securities market was for the 36 Primary Dealers that had supervision from the Federal Reserve.

Lombard-Wall was one of those small, unregulated government bond dealers. With the spike in interest rates in the early 1980s, they had begun offering hold-in-custody Repo as a cash investment for savings & loans, municipalities, and pension funds. In conjunction with their municipal bond underwriting, they offered "Flex Repo" to clients, where excess cash generated from a bond underwriting would stay in an HIC account and could be withdrawn as needed, sometimes lasting as long as several years. The firm collapsed on August 17, 1982, when it came to light that they had under-collateralized many of their safekeeping Repo transactions. After the bankruptcy was announced, Lombard-Wall filed a stay provision in bankruptcy court, which was a temporary restraining order so that Repo counterparties could not sell their collateral without court approval. One month later, the court ruled that Repo was not a collateralized loan and the Repo counterparties had the right to liquidate their trades. This was good news for the Street – the dealer community – but customers who had left both their securities and their cash at Lombard-Wall had no ability to liquidate their trades and get their cash back.

Lion Capital was another small broker-dealer based in New York that filed for bankruptcy two years later in May 1984. Their fraud was even worse than Lombard-Wall. Whereas Lombard-Wall had mis-priced securities, Lion Capital had taken the securities out of the customer accounts and used them to pledge as margin to fund their own trading operations. Lion Capital's customers lost $40 million worth of securities that were missing from their safekeeping accounts.

E.S.M. Government Securities was established in 1976 as a small municipal bond dealer in Fort Lauderdale, Florida. They were known for living the high life, driving Mercedes and Jaguars, and the principals paid themselves salaries as high as $500,000 a year. E.S.M. had dozens of municipalities as clients, mainly because they were known for offering the highest rates on hold-in-custody Repo. They advertised that the Repo investments were backed by U.S. Treasury securities. The problem was that they were not. So, if you thought all the potential safekeeping frauds were already covered, you'd be wrong. These guys were pledging the same collateral to more than one client, so when they collapsed, there was only a small amount of actual securities in the safekeeping accounts. All total, their customers lost about $300 million, and those customers included Home State Savings Bank in Cincinnati, which took losses of $150 million. It set off a bank run on Ohio Savings & Loan, and American Savings and Loan

Association in Miami lost $55.3 million, while the City of Beaumont, Texas, lost $20 million.

Other bankruptcies followed, including RTD Securities, Inc., and Bevill, Bresler, & Schulman Group. Except for Drysdale, all the customer losses were from the Repo transactions and due to collateral held (or not held) in safekeeping accounts. Between 1977 and 1985, failures of government bond dealers resulted in about $1 billion in losses.

After Drysdale, Lombard-Wall, Lion Capital, RTD Securities, E.S.M. Government Securities, and Bevill Bresler & Schulman, there were calls for regulation in the government securities market and a strong desire to end the Wild West days of unregulated government securities. Congressional hearings on the safety of the market were held in 1985. At the same time, dealers were working on self-regulation to bring all government securities under an organization called the Public Securities Rulemaking Board, similar to the MSRB except for U.S. Treasurys and Agencies. However, years after those failures, little progress was made and they were unable to even standardize or clean up the Repo market practices. The Government Securities Act (GSA) of 1986 was passed and signed by President Reagan, which required government securities dealers to register with the SEC or be regulated as subsidiaries of banks. The Secretary of the Treasury had the authority to make rules for custody, the proper use of customer securities, net capital ratios, and the allowable leverage for Repo transactions.

Not surprising, customers were still unwilling to invest their cash in hold-in-custody Repo after 1984. The Street had a major problem: HIC Repo was an easy source of funding for dealers and a good investment for cash customers. The Street needed a safer way of transacting safekeeping Repo, and they realized an agent was needed to stand in between the cash provider and the securities provider.

Throughout the early 1980s, Salomon Brothers had been pioneering a type of Repo transaction where they could automatically sweep very small pieces of collateral from their own account into a customer's HIC Repo account. Instead of writing trade tickets for each individual piece of collateral, the clearing bank would just sweep them into the customer account. It was a huge time saver.

After the HIC Repo problems, a few securities dealers approached the Bank of New York and Chemical Bank to replicate the Salomon Brothers sweep accounts. Except this time, the clearing bank would act as a joint custodian on the transaction, working as an agent for both Repo counterparties. The clearing banks agreed to provide a service to verify that there was sufficient collateral to meet the amount of the loan, to hold and verify the securities in the account, and to maintain proper margin. Sometime between 1985 and 1986, the Tri-Party Repo market was born.

As its name suggests, Tri-Party Repo is an agreement between three parties. There's the seller of the securities (the securities dealer), the buyer of the securities (cash investor), and the clearing bank (the bank that holds both the securities and the cash). The cash investor liked the transaction because they have better security. They knew the securities were priced and margined correctly by the clearing bank. For the securities dealer, Tri-Party minimized settlements and ticket processing. It gave them more time to allocate collateral throughout the day, and it made it easier to finance smaller pieces. The clearing bank did most of the work. They handled the risk management, pricing the collateral, and accommodated collateral substitutions. They managed the settlement risk, cleared the trades, provided valuation, and the position reporting. And, on top of that, they get paid a fee. Sounds like everyone wins!

When there was a problem with HIC Repo, the market figured out a way to reduce investor risk. It brought cash investors back to the Repo market. Tri-Party Repo grew to become a major source of funding for the securities dealers and a major cash investment option for customers. From the mid-1980s, the Tri-Party market grew from zero to over $3.7 trillion today.[3] Of that, $3.3 trillion are government securities – U.S. Treasurys and federal agencies. That is an incredible amount of growth in 35 years. After the Financial Crisis in 2008, cracks started to appear in the system, but that's a story for a later chapter.

---

[3] Federal Reserve; February 2022

# Shadow Banking

It is often overlooked how important the bankruptcies of Drysdale and Lombard-Wall were to the financial markets. And not just for the Repo market, as global financial markets were all affected. Repo property rights were established, Repo contracts were tested in court, and bankruptcy rules were finalized. This was big! Repo legally became repurchase transactions as opposed to collateralized loans, because the court realized the importance of being able to quickly liquidate securities positions in a bankruptcy. Imagine if the judge had ruled that Repo was a collateralized loan. In the case of a default or bankruptcy, the Repo transactions would be tied up in bankruptcy court for years. That's great for the lawyers, but not so much for everyone else.

The new legal status of Repo led to the creation of a whole new industry which forever changed the world's financial markets. The Repo market became the plumbing that greased the global financial markets. That industry? It's the one awkwardly called "shadow banking." That's right, there would be no shadow banking industry without the ability to quickly liquidate Repo contracts.

The term shadow banking is thrown around as the perennial risk factor to the financial system. The hidden risk lurking in the shadows. There's no real definition of a shadow bank, but a shadow bank is basically a financial institution that performs banking functions. A shadow bank can be anything from an REIT (Real Estate Investment

Trust) to a mortgage finance company to a hedge fund to a broker-dealer.

Think of what banks do. In the simplest terms, a bank takes in deposits and makes mortgage loans. The mortgage loans are the bank's investments. The deposits are the bank's funding. Anyone with a savings or checking account is lending money to a bank. The bank borrows money from the depositors and loans money to the homeowners.

Mortgage REITs are a great example of shadow banking. The REIT buys mortgage-backed securities (MBSs) and borrows money to finance the purchases in the Repo market. The mortgage-backed securities are just like a bank writing a mortgage loan, except they're a security, and the Repo transactions are just like the deposits. But the REIT is not a bank. It's a shadow bank.

Let's take it one step further. Consider a hedge fund that owns a corporate bond and borrows money via a Repo to finance it. They own an asset and borrow money. They're also just like a bank. Instead of a bank writing a corporate loan, the hedge fund owns the company's corporate bond. A hedge fund can even own a collateralized debt obligation (CDO) and finance it in the Repo market. Sounds a little risky? We will get there eventually!

From a high-level view, when you think of Repo in the shadow banking world, think of it like a bank deposit. Because it's legally a repurchase transaction as opposed to a collateralized loan, it means that if there's any sign of trouble, the Repo trades can be liquidated, just like depositors lining up at the front doors of a bank – or trust company – waiting to withdraw their money.

Perhaps when the courts made Repo transactions so easily liquidated, it made the business model work too well. Suppose you kept your money in a savings account at a bank and when you went to withdraw your cash, the bank said, "We will give you your cash as soon as we sell some mortgage loans. Maybe next week." No one would like that. They'd never deposit their money at that bank again.

Now, picture a bank that's financing CDOs for a hedge fund through Repo transactions. Suppose the floor dropped-out from under the CDO market, like it did in 2007, and the bank issued a margin call to the hedge fund. Suppose the hedge fund told the bank, "We will give you your cash as soon as we sell some CDOs. Maybe next week." That doesn't work. But the Repo counterparty has an out. No need to wait. Once there is technically a default or bankruptcy, the bank can take over the hedge fund's positions and liquidate them. Then they cross their fingers that they had taken enough margin to cover the losses on the forced sale!

That brings up a good question. Why are there runs on banks and shadow banks? The question is easily answered when you look at what banks and shadow banks have in common. They lend long and borrow short. It's the age-old business model flaw of the banking system. They are lending money long-term and borrowing money short-term. A bank writes a 30-year mortgage loan to a homeowner and borrows money from their depositors to cover the loan. Remember, the depositors can show up any day and withdraw their money. Unfortunately, this same bank business model flaw extends to the shadow banks. They also lend long and borrow short. Just like a bank, a REIT's MBS portfolio might have an average weighted maturity of, say, seven years. Their Repo funding transactions might have maturities from overnight to three months. The REIT is lending money for seven years and borrowing money, at best, for three months.

Regardless of your feelings about banks, broker-dealers, hedge funds, and REITs leveraging themselves to magnify their profits and losses, the fact remains that leverage is a widely-used investment tool at all levels of the game. Much of the credit – or blame, depending on your perspective – for making this leverage possible goes to David Heuwetter. Without the special treatment of Repo in a bankruptcy, allowing the Repo counterparty to immediately liquidate Repo transactions, there would be significantly less leverage in the markets today. Again, depending on your perspective, that reality can be looked at in two distinctly different ways. Leverage has enabled financial efficiencies and brought down the costs of financial services on an immense scale. It has also brought down more than its fair share of financial stalwarts, including Long Term Capital Management, Bear Stearns, Lehman Brothers, and MF Global.

Shadow banking is a huge part of the financial markets today, but the Fed was not originally designed for an economy with shadow banking. In 2020, 68.1% of U.S. mortgage loans were originated by non-banks; they were instead initiated by mortgage loan companies. What do you need a bank for? Remember in the movie,[4] "If I write a loan on a Friday afternoon, it's sold to a big [investment] bank by Monday lunch."

The financial system changed very little from 1914 to 1980, but think about how much it changed from 1980 to today. The Federal

---

[4] *The Big Short,* Michael Lewis.

Reserve was originally designed to provide liquidity to banks. That's it. Back then, a financial institution could be a bank, trust company, credit union, or Savings and Loan. I can't even list all of the different types of financial institutions there are today. Back then, the financial instruments were mortgage loans, corporate loans, stocks, bonds, and commercial paper. Did I miss anything? Once again, I can't even list all of the different types of financial instruments today.

Given the growth of the financial system over the past 40 years, there's been a lot of growing pains in the financial markets. The Fed had to change to keep up. Since I started in the business, there has been the creation of mortgage-backed securities, the 1990 Savings and Loan crisis, various 1990s trading scandals, rogue traders, broker-dealers consolidated into banks, and then everything else imaginable securitized into asset-backed securities. Then, there was the internet stock boom, computerization of markets, September 11, the housing boom and bust, not to mention the Liquidity Crisis of 2007, the Financial Crisis of 2008, new bank regulation, huge U.S. Treasury debt issuance, the Repo market blow-up of September 2019, and the COVID crisis of March 2020. It almost sounds like a Billy Joel song!

What's next? There's always another crisis around the corner, and it seems the financial system gets stress-tested about every ten years or so. Recall the birth of the Fed, which was a reaction to the Panic of 1907. Bankers provided liquidity when trusts companies were over-extended. Think of the trust companies as the shadow banks today. In that case, the Panic of 1907 was not too different from the Liquidity Crisis 2007 and the Financial Crisis 2008. Except these days, everything is on a much larger scale. Drysdale led to the creation of the modern Repo market, and that market experienced many crises over the next 40 years.

# Classic Federal Reserve

Officially, the Fed's mandate is to promote "maximum employment and price stability." And, at times, it also serves as the "lender of last resort." Price stability is another name for inflation. It doesn't mean there's supposed to be no inflation; economists generally agree that a little bit of inflation is a good thing. According to Alan Greenspan, the former Federal Reserve Chairman, "Price stability is the state in which expected changes in the general price level do not effectively alter business or household decisions." In fact, the Fed really likes a 2% inflation rate, which is loosely attributed to a 1950s Harvard economist named Sumner Slichter, who was dubbed a "limited inflationist."

Full employment is a little different. Generally, when the unemployment rate gets down to around 4%, we're at full employment. But employment also depends on the labor force participation rate. That's how many people consider themselves in the workforce – there are those with a job and those who are looking for a job. It's easier to have a low rate of unemployment if there are fewer people in the workforce, so the headline rate can sometimes be deceiving.

The Fed stimulates the economy by lowering interest rates and they slow down the economy by raising interest rates. If inflation or economic growth is running too high, they raise rates. If unemployment is high and growth is slow, they decrease interest rates. When inflation and unemployment are low and economic growth strong, it's a "Goldilocks economy" – just right! Basically, we don't want the economy moving too fast or too slow. The worst-case scenario is when both unemployment and inflation are high – the so-called stagflation – that plagued us in the 1970s.

The Fed can't control long-term interest rates. There are just too many factors that affect long-term rates. But the Fed *can* control short-term rates, and they do. The Fed's main policy tool is to set the level of overnight interest rates. That's where the federal funds rate comes in. In the past, the Fed set a target *rate* for fed funds, like 1.00%. Recently, it set a target *range*, like between 1.00% to 1.25%.

When the Fed lowers the fed funds rate, it's called an ease – easing monetary policy. When the Fed raises rates, it's called a tightening. Here's a little bit of trivia. A tightening used to be referred to as a snugging. Something akin to turning a screw a little tighter. Tightenings have been described in different ways by different Fed chairmen. William McChesney Martin started the analogy that it's the Fed's job to take away the punch bowl just as the party gets going. Fed Chairman Paul Volcker liked the term snugging. Back in April 1987, he called for a tightening as "some slight snugging" of interest rates. Chairman Alan Greenspan used the term to imply unannounced changes in monetary policy, which was back before the central bank specifically announced interest rate targets.

When it comes time to change the federal funds rate, the Fed usually moves in 25 basis point[5] or 50 basis point increments, or decrements. A 25 basis point change is a pretty normal policy change,

---

[5] The fed funds rate was at a 1/8 target range for much of the 1980s. They brought the target range back in December 2008, when they eased from a 1.00% target rate to a 0.0% to 0.25% target range.

such as from 1.00% to 1.25%. If the Fed feels they need to move rates more aggressively, they'll move by 50 basis points. For example, from 1.00% to 1.50%. At times when the Fed moved by more than 50 basis points, it meant there was a real crisis at hand. A 1.00% move – a full point – signals there are big problems out there.

Changes in monetary policy are decided by the Federal Reserve Open Market Committee, or FOMC for short. The group meets eight times a year, approximately every six weeks. It's composed of board members, who are political appointees, and the twelve regional Federal Reserve bank presidents, who vote on a rotating basis.

Before 1994, the Fed used Repo operations both to *signal* and to *implement* monetary policy. That's right, here's where the Repo market comes in! Though the Fed was officially targeting the fed funds rate, it used Repo operations to add and drain reserves from the banking system.[6] It was the job of the New York Federal Reserve Bank to create the "conditions in reserve markets that will encourage fed funds to trade at the target rate" by conducting open market operations (OMO). Basically they were supposed to keep the fed funds rate within or close to the target rate.

Back then, the Fed used System RP, Customer RP, and Matched Sales to both signal policy changes and manage the everyday liquidity. The Fed set a target rate for fed funds, but the Fed never announced the rate. They never said, "The target rate is now 5.25%." Instead, they intervened in the market to imply the target rate. It was up to the

---

[6] Yes, the Discount Rate was a symbolic change in policy, and bill and coupon passes affected the market on a longer-term basis, but Repo operations were the day-to-day tools for keeping the fed funds rate in the right place.

market to figure out what the Fed was doing. It kept many economists occupied.

Let's say there was a slight shortage of liquidity (cash) in the system and the fed funds rate was trading a little high at 5.3125% (5 5/16%), instead of the target rate of 5.25%. The Fed would enter the market, announce an operation, and borrow securities from the market. By taking securities out of the market, it put cash into the market. Securities come out and cash goes in. Now, let's say the fed funds rate was trading at 5.1875% (5 3/16%) with the same target rate of 5.25%. The Fed would execute the opposite transaction. Because there was a little excess liquidity in the system, they would loan securities into the market, taking cash out. These Open Market Operations are more fine-tuning of overnight rates, but there were plenty of times when the actual fed funds rate deviated from the target rate by much more than a sixteenth.

When the Fed wished to add or drain reserves, they announced the operations during a 15-minute window. Originally, the window was officially between 11:30 AM and 11:45 AM. But in practice, it was really a 5-minute time-frame between 11:30 AM and 11:35 AM. Every day at 11:30 AM, the market would grow quiet while everyone waited to see what the Fed was going to do. In market speak, it was called "Fed Time." In December 1996 the Fed pushed the timeframe an hour earlier to 10:30 AM, and then again in April 1999 to 9:30 AM.[7]

The Fed added liquidity in two different ways. A System RP, or system Repo operation, was to move overnight rates lower. System RPs implied a large operation and could sometimes signal a policy

---

[7] Of course, the Fed could be flexible with its timing. The Fed can enter the market earlier or later depending on market conditions.

change. A typical operation was between $2 billion and $10 billion. However, if the Fed had only a small "add need," they would execute a Customer RP, or customer Repo. Customer operations were generally between $1 billion and $3 billion. When the Fed announced a Customer RP, the market knew it was a small operation. In addition, a Customer RP operation was never used to signal a change in monetary policy. The Fed ended Customer RP operations in January 1997.

When the Fed wanted to drain liquidity, they turned to Matched Sales. Here, the Fed added securities to the market, taking liquidity out. It had the effect of pushing overnight rates higher. Matched Sales were first used during the summer of 1966 and ended in December 2002. These operations were technically different from Reverse-Repo operations. The Fed actually sold the securities to Primary Dealers and bought them back at a later date. Back then, Fed lawyers were concerned with a transaction where the Fed was technically borrowing money. They felt it might be inappropriate – or even illegal. That meant the Fed drained reserves via buy-sellbacks for 36 years. By 2002, the Fed's lawyers were more comfortable with the transaction to be booked as Reverse-Repo.

Let's say the FOMC decided to ease the fed funds target rate from 5.50% to 5.25% and the actual fed funds rate was trading at 5.375%. Because the funds rate was already .125% below target, the market would have expected the Fed to drain reserves. The market expected Matched Sales as the Fed attempted to move fed funds back to 5.50%. Instead, the Fed executed a System RP, which implied a new target rate of 5.25%. In fact, on the days immediately following an FOMC meeting, the fed funds market would often place the funds rate right between the old target rate and the expected new target rate, making it easy for the Fed to telegraph its policy decision. It forced the Fed to show its hand. However, it was still up to the market to interpret the Fed's actions. A lot of time was spent analyzing whether the Fed tightened or eased. Most of the time it was clear, but there were plenty of times when we didn't know. Or we were probably sure, but not completely sure. Sometimes we had to wait until the next day to see if they added or drained liquidity to be sure.

Using Open Market Operations to signify changes in monetary policy was the communications methodology that the Greenspan Fed inherited from the Volcker Fed. The FOMC didn't announce what they were thinking. They didn't say if an FOMC member objected or where they expected rates to be in the future. Back then, the theme was "trust in the Fed." They had all of the economic information and access to information that we didn't.

With Bill Clinton's arrival at the White House in 1993, there were more Democrats appointed to the FOMC board, including Alan Blinder in 1994. Chairman Greenspan came under political pressure to make Fed policy communications more open. When policy is decided behind closed doors, it's difficult to criticize. When it's tough to criticize, it's hard to influence. Chairman Greenspan started feeling the influence of politics.

The first step in Greenspan's public relations program was called "the bias." It was an acknowledgement as to what the Fed's next move was – the most likely direction of interest rates. The first bias statement was issued after the May 1993 FOMC meeting. In order for the FOMC to let Greenspan include a tightening bias, he also had to promise not to take action in between meetings.

As the February 3-4, 1994, FOMC meeting ended, the Fed failed to signal clear policy direction through normal Repo operations. We waited through Fed time and nothing happened. The market was somewhat confused. The next day, the Fed actually announced what they were doing: "The Federal Open Market Committee decided to increase slightly the degree of pressure on reserve positions," which meant an increase of 25 basis points in Fed-speak. This new FOMC statement policy continued for the next few meetings, and when it was time to tighten by 50 basis points, the tightening came along with a Discount Rate hike on August 16, 1994: "The Federal Open Market Committee agreed that this increase would be allowed to show through completely into interest rates in reserve markets." The use of Repo operation to signal changes in Fed policy ended in 1994.

During this pivotal 1994 period, a couple of other procedures changed too. First, the time of the announcement moved to around 2:15 PM on the last day of the FOMC meeting - Fed policy changes were no longer telegraphed at Fed time. Then, in April, FOMC members took away Greenspan's power to move rates in between meetings altogether, a power Fed Chairmen had enjoyed for many years. Now, the market entered a period when rate moves were only expected at FOMC meetings. The new openness was actually good for the markets. If the market was pricing an ease or tightening, we knew the expected date. It made it easier to price short-term interest rates.

More communication tools were added to the FOMC's tool box over the next few years. The Balance of Risks Assessment, or BORA, was added at the beginning of 2000. Then, Forward Guidance was first used in 2004 by Chairman Greenspan. He said that rates would rise "at a pace that is likely to be measured." We didn't know it at the time, but that would come to mean 25 basis point increments. Going forward, the gradual 25 basis point eases and tightenings became a characteristic of the Greenspan Fed.

Not much more changed with Fed communications policy until after the Financial Crisis in 2008. Eventually FOMC policy statements were released at 12:30 PM, after the FOMC meeting adjourned. Now they are released at 2:00 PM, with a press conference that follows. The FOMC minutes are released just weeks after the meetings. Looking back, better communication was a good thing for the markets. However, more transparency *did* open the Fed to more political interference.

# The Treasury Market

Treasury securities play a vital role in the financial markets. The Treasury market is massive with a total of $31.5 trillion outstanding and it's still growing! You *could* argue that the Federal Reserve owns roughly $8 trillion of the government's debt, so ballpark, there's only about $23.5 trillion in U.S. Treasurys floating around the market. Still, that's not too shabby!

Treasury securities include Bills, Notes, Bonds, STRIPS, Floating-Rate Notes (FRNs), and Treasury Inflation-Protected Securities (TIPS). The market is huge (Did I already mention that?). It's the most liquid and actively traded market in the world. It's larger than the stock market, foreign exchange, and all other bond markets. It's importance, however, is bigger than that. Treasury securities are *the* risk-free yield curve for all of the financial markets. That's right, the yields of Treasury Bills, Notes, and Bonds from overnight to 30 years make up a yield curve that is used to price all other fixed-income securities. The Treasury market is *the* reference rate for interest rates. Treasurys are a tool for pricing corporate bonds, municipal bonds, emerging market bonds, federal agencies, mortgage-backed securities, and other dollar assets. On top of that, they're also a tool for speculation and hedging risk.

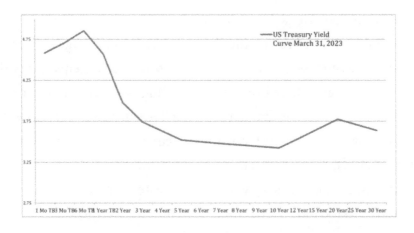

Let's say a major corporation issues a new bond. The yield of that bond will be priced off of the U.S. Treasury yield curve. If IBM issues a 10 year security, their underwriter will price the yield as a spread to the 10 Year U.S. Treasury. The yield might be quoted to yield 25 basis points above the equivalent U.S. Treasury. And when those bonds are traded in the secondary market, they're still quoted as a spread to Treasurys.

Treasury Bills are the shortest securities, and they're discount securities[8]. The Treasury regularly issues 1 Month, 2 Month, 3 Month, 6 Month, and Year Bills. Treasury Notes are securities that were originally issued with maturities between 2 years and 10 years. Currently, the Treasury issues 2 Year Notes, 3 Year Notes, 5 Year Notes, 7 Year Notes, and 10 Year Notes. In the past, there was a 4 Year Note, but it was discontinued. Treasury Bonds[9] are securities originally issued with maturities of either 20 or 30 years.

---

[8] Treasury Bills don't pay a coupon. They are issued at a discount and accrue to par.

[9] It's important to describe the Treasury securities correctly. Don't' refer to the "Ten Year bond," because you'll lose creditability among fixed income people! Yes, it is a "Bond," but technically it's a Treasury Note.

Treasury securities are issued on a very regular schedule. Auction schedules are announced by the Treasury and don't change very often. Keeping Treasury securities regular and predictable helps keeps the market liquid, and therefore reduces funding costs, in theory, for the government. On top of that, large liquid Treasury issues are good for the financial markets. Just remember, large and liquid is certainly better than small and illiquid! Small issues can experience price distortions, so the Treasury will make adjustments in their debt sales to keep the market liquid, running smoothly and predictably.

The exact auction schedules have been jiggled around over the years. The 3 Year Note was cancelled and reappeared many times. It was cancelled in May 1998, when the Treasury was paying down debt. Yes! The U.S. government was actually once running a surplus! The 3 Year Note reemerged in May 2003 and lasted until May 2007, only to reappear again in November 2008. The 5 Year Note auction cycle was moved around a lot, too. In the 1990s, 5 Year Notes were auctioned every three months. In the early 2000s, they were regularly reopened. Now they're on a monthly auction schedule. At one point, 30 Year Bonds were issued every six months. Then, there were no Bonds at all. New Bond issues were temporarily discontinued between February 2001 and February 2006, making the 5.375% 2/15/2031 the current 30 Year Bond for five years! The Treasury began issuing the 30 Year Bond again in February 2006. The 20 Year Bond disappeared in the 1980s, and then reappeared just a few years ago in June 2020. I'm sure I missed some changes, but you get the point. Treasury auction schedules can change.

The 1 Month, 2 Month, 3 Month and 6 Month Bills are issued on a weekly basis. There's a Year Bill issued each month. The Treasury issues 2 Year Notes, 5 Year Notes, and 7 Year Notes monthly. The 20 Year Bond is issued once every three months and reopened two months after it's first auctioned. During what is known as the quarterly refunding, the Treasury auctions 3 Year Notes, 10 Year Notes, and 30 Year Bonds. Quarterly refundings occur in February, May, August, and November. Though 10 Year Notes and 30 Year Bonds are auctioned every quarter, they are reopened a month after their first auction, and then reopened again a month after that. A current 10 Year Note that originally settled in August would be reopened a first time in September and then again in October. After an issue is reopened once, it's called a double issue, and once it's reopened the second time, it's a triple issue. Auction schedules like this will often produce distorted Repo trading dynamics.

The life of a new Treasury security begins with its announcement. After it's announced, there's a period of several days when the new issue trades as a WI, or When Issued. As a WI, the securities are traded based on yield and not price.[10] On the auction day, market participants submit bids to the Federal Reserve Bank of New York. After all of the bids are in, the Fed calculates the best bids and awards the new securities to the best bidders. As the Fed allocates the new securities, the highest yield they accept is called the stop-out rate.

During the WI trading period, bond dealers will often short-sell the new issue to customers who are looking to buy. Wall Street firms will sell their existing securities holdings to make room for new securities that they expect to purchase at the upcoming auction. This has a two-fold benefit for the bond dealer. It makes room on their balance sheet to buy the new securities, and if there's enough selling in

---

[10] That's because there's no coupon until it's set at the auction.

front of the auction, it depresses prices, allowing them to buy back their shorts at lower prices. In fact, there's occasionally so much selling of the WI issue that the size of the shorts is greater than the amount sold at the auction!

Overall, the success of a Treasury auction depends on investor demand. Institutional investors such as insurance companies, foreign central banks, hedge funds, money funds, states, municipalities, Savings and Loans, credit unions, pension funds, and small local banks are all major participants. Depending on who buys a certain Treasury determines how much supply is available in the Repo market. For example, if a large amount of the auction is purchased by securities dealers and hedge funds, there's plenty of supply around the Repo market. Dealers and hedge funds are leveraged players who loan their securities into the Repo market to finance their purchases. That keeps those securities readily available in the market. If, on the other hand, a large amount is purchased by end-user portfolios, such as investors who are more retail and less sophisticated, then there's less supply available in the Repo market.

When someone refers to *the* 2 Year Note, it means something. It's the current U.S. Treasury 2 Year Note, the 2 Year Note that was most recently auctioned. There's a big difference between a 2 Year Treasury and *the* 2 Year Note. It's also referred to as the on-the-run 2 Year Note. Some traders even get cryptic and call it the CT2. The 2 Year Note that was issued last month is a little different; it's called the Old 2 Year Note, and the one that was issued before that is the Double-Old 2 Year Note. Taking it one step further, the Two Year note that was issued before the Double-Old is the Triple-Old 2 Year Note.

The "current" is the most important issue on the yield curve in its maturity sector. It's the one most traded and therefore the most liquid. Being the most liquid means it has the tightest bid/offer spread; it's the cheapest issue to buy, sell, and trade back-and-forth. It's also the issue with the most volume traded every day. However, nothing comes for free. There's a price to be paid for liquidity and it's reflected in the security's yield. The yield of the current issue is always a little bit lower than other Treasury issues with similar maturities. That's what's called the liquidity premium. When investors buy the current issue, they are giving up a little yield in order own the current, which they can buy and sell with smaller bid/offer spreads, and there's plenty of liquidity to move large sizes. However, this liquidity premium fades over time. It begins to fade when a next issue is announced, auctioned, and settles. Basically, when liquidity is moving into the new issue.

In theory, the liquidity premium is reflected in the Repo rate. If the current 2 Year Note has a yield of 1.00% and the off-the-run (older) issues of the same maturity have a yield of 1.02%, it means the current issue has a two basis point premium. That's a 0.02% lower yield than other equivalent maturity Treasurys. Of course, now you're asking, "Why not just short sell the current 2 Year Note, buy an older issue with the same maturity, and pocket the liquidity premium when the next current issue is announced?" Yes, that's possible, but that liquidity premium is also reflected in the Repo rate. The Repo rate to borrow the current issue will be lower than the Repo rate to loan the other, older issues. Basically, the difference between the Repo rates for the current 2 Year Note and the off-the-run issues will generally equal the liquidity premium. That's part of the math in the Treasury market. It usually works that way, but not always.

Let's say a customer calls a securities dealer and asks for an offer on *the* 5 Year Note. They want to buy the on-the-run 5 Year Note, which is on a monthly auction schedule just like the 2 Year Note. During that month, Treasury securities get "seasoned," which is another word for being distributed to end-user buyers. Every time a retail or institutional customer buys a current issue, the more that issue is sold to end-user portfolios and there's less supply available in the market. The longer an issue exists as a current, there's more supply that leaves the market. As supply declines in the market, the security develops a larger and larger liquidity premium. As the liquidity premium grows, the issue attracts more short sellers. When there are more shorts, there's more demand in the Repo market and Repo rates trade lower.

In general, longer auction cycles mean a security will trade Special[11] over a longer period of time. Think of a security that's seasoned for three months instead of just one month. A three-month distribution period will take more supply out of the market. Imagine when some securities had six-month auction cycles! They were very well seasoned – to put it one way – and traded very Special in the Repo market.

On-the-run Treasury issues have unique trading patterns in the Repo market. There are different buyers of different sectors of the yield curve and different parts of the curve attract more short sellers than others. This makes the auction cycle very important for the on-the-runs. Perhaps it's the most important driver of Special Repo rates. It affects when shorts enter and leave, and when supply leaves and then comes back in. The auction cycle drives the liquidity premium,

---

[11] "Special" means short-sellers must pay a premium, or lower Repo rate, to borrow a specific security.

seasoning, short positions, long positions – all important factors that determine fundamental supply and demand.

Treasury issues can be reopened. Most reopenings are a part of the regular auction cycle, but there are times when issues are reopened due to market stress. Regular reopenings occur in the Bill market, the 10 Year Note and 30 Year Bond. There are also occasional reopenings when a new issue ends up with the same coupon and maturity date as an existing, older Treasury issue.

When an issue is reopened, there is both an outstanding and a WI issue. If you buy or sell the outstanding issue, it settles the next day. If you buy or sell the WI issue, it will settle on the 15th of the month or last day of the month, depending on the security. One issue settles immediately and the same security settles at a date in the future. Suppose you bought the outstanding and sold the WI? You'd own the security beginning tomorrow, but you would have sold it at a forward date. The price differential between the outstanding issue and the WI issue will be the cost of carry for financing the issue between the two settlement dates. Basically, the cost of the Repo financing.

10 Year Notes and 30 Year Bonds are not the only securities regularly reopened. In the Treasury Bill market, every time a new 3 Month Bill is auctioned, it's a reopening of an outstanding 6 Month Bill. Once again, the difference in price between the 6 Month Bill that's three months old and the new 3 Month Bill is the cost of carry in the Repo market.

With the 2 Year Note[12] on a monthly auction schedule, the new issue is announced during the third week of the month, the auction is

---

[12] I chose to only detail the 2 Year Note, 5 Year Note, and 10 Year Note. Though every Treasury issue has a typical Repo trading pattern, these three issues cover the general concept.

during the last week, and the new issue settles on the last day of the month. Below is a typical 2 Year Note trading pattern in the Repo market. The graph shows the overnight open, high, low, and close Repo rates for the current 2 Year Note in January 2022.

Stage 1 - Early in the issue's life as a current, it trades near General Collateral. There are few shorts and it rarely trades Special.

Stage 2 - Shorts are beginning to build and supply is leaving the market as institutional customers are buying. There's some overnight rate volatility, but not much.

Stage 3 – This stage usually begins near the announcement of the new WI issue. There's increased overnight rate volatility, and Repo rates generally decline in front of the auction.

Stage 4 – The issue loosens up (trades less Special) as shorts roll out of the outstanding issue and into the WI. Traders who are short like to avoid paying the Special Repo rates, and move their shorts into the new current issue.

In general, outside of the auction cycle, 2 Year Notes accumulate the most shorts when the market expects the Fed to raise rates or there are a lot of yield curve flattening trades. "Flatteners" mean the Street is expecting short-term rates to rise relative to long-term rates. Proprietary trading groups will short-sell the 2 Year Note and buy the 10 Year Note against it. Given that the duration of the 10 Year Note is about five times greater than the 2 Year Note, it means that they are short-selling about five times as many 2 Year Notes as 10 Year Notes to be correctly risk weighted. When big hedge funds are in this trade, the 2 Year Note can get extremely Special.

5 Year Notes will usually trade more Special than 2 Year Notes. They're both monthly issues, but the 5 Year Note generally has more short-sellers from hedging corporate bonds, municipal bonds, and MBS than 2 Year Notes. Here's a typical Repo trading pattern for a 5 Year Note.

*0.50% 2/28/26 – The current Five Year Note in March 2021*

Here's where it gets more interesting. Because a new 10 Year Note is auctioned every quarter and reopened twice, the schedule will occasionally generate Repo rate distortions. The 10 Year Note Repo trading pattern is much different than a 2 Year or 5 Year. Typically, after the new 10 Year settles, the market is quiet for about two weeks. The issue is easy to borrow and it trades near General Collateral. When the reopening is announced and it's auctioned, shorts begin to accumulate and Repo rates decline. Once the reopening supply settles and the 10 Year is a double issue, there's usually plenty of supply to cover all of the shorts.

When the 10 Year Note [below] was a single issue, overnight Repo rates declined to a low of -0.50%. Once the reopening supply settled and it became a double-issue, Repo rates moved back to near General Collateral. Once a 10 Year is a double- and triple-issue, it rarely trades Special.

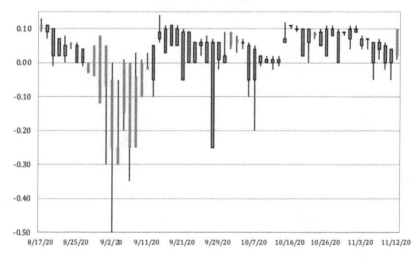

**10 Year: Overnight Rates**

*A typical 10 Year Note in the Repo market. The 0.625% 8/15/2030,*
*which was the current 10 Year Note from August 2020 to November 2020*

However, 10 Year Notes can get extremely special. When the new 10 Year Note settles, it's replacing an old outstanding 10 Year Note that's a triple issue, the previous 10 Year that was already reopened twice. There's plenty of supply of Old 10 Year Notes around in the Repo market to cover all of the shorts in the 10 year sector. However, traders want to move their short positions forward into the current issue. Liquidity is important! At the same time, a single-issue current 10 Year Note can get very Special, and no one likes to pay the Special Repo rates. Thus, the dilemma. Traders want to be short the current issue and buy it back at the reopening auction. However, if too many shorts roll into the current issue, it will trade extremely Special. It's a game of cat and mouse. "Did the shorts roll forward?"

When all the stars are aligned, there's a deep short base in the 10 year sector, and a majority of the shorts roll into the new issue. That's when a severe shortage occurs. Most 10 Year Notes won't trade extremely Special, but when one does, it can be big! The graph below illustrates the 1.125% 2/15/2031 as a current 10 Year Note. During the week before the first reopening settled, it averaged below -3.00%, and even traded as low as -4.25% one day.

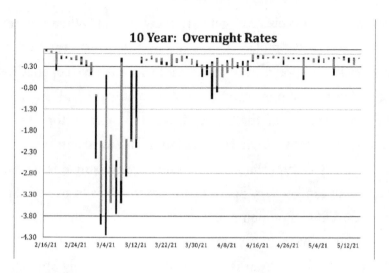

*The 1.125% 2/15/2031 was a 10 Year Note that became extremely Special. It was the current 10 Year Note from February 2021 to May 2021*

The graph below shows the average daily Repo rates for 10 Year Notes issued in 2020 and 2021 during their first month outstanding before the reopening supply settles. Most 10 Year Notes issued in 2020 and 2021 did not trade extremely special. Only one did.

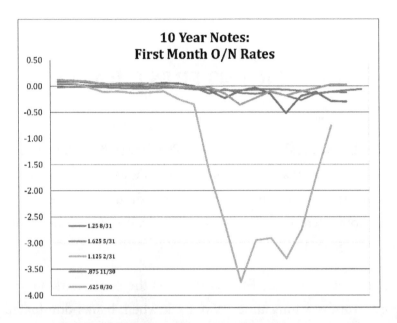

These severe shortages don't occur often, maybe once every eight issues (about once or twice every two years). Because of the possibility of such a severe shortage, this is why traders will often pay a premium in the term Repo market to avoid getting squeezed.

# OTHER INTEREST RATES

It's not called Federal Reserve Funds. The money doesn't belong to the Federal Reserve. It's never called "Fed Funds" with capital "F's." Officially, the market is called "federal funds," though it's often referred to as "fed funds," and sometimes called just "funds." But the "f" is never capitalized.

The overnight federal funds rate was the benchmark short-term interest rate for a long time. Way back when, banks dominated the financial system, the overnight inter-bank rate anchored short-term interest rates. Market participants, like federally-chartered banks; state-chartered banks; the GSEs like Fannie Mae, Freddie Mac, Ginnie Mae, and the Federal Home Loan Banks; and foreign banks all had a place to go when they were long or short cash. The first fed funds trade occurred a long time ago, in 1921, and the market has changed little since then. Well, until the Financial Crisis.

An important event occurred at that time. The Fed began paying interest to banks on their required reserves. All of the cash that banks were required to leave at the Fed could earn interest. The new rate was called Interest On Reserves (IOR) and the change made a lot of sense. Had it ended there, this would be a much different chapter. However, the Fed went one step further and offered to pay interest on any excess reserves that banks deposited at the Fed. That became known as the Interest On Excess Reserves (IOER) and it was effectively the final nail in the coffin of the fed funds market.

For banks with excess cash, depositing at the Fed was a no-brainer. Why give your cash to another bank when you can give it to the risk-free Federal Reserve? And, on top of that, the Fed paid higher than market rates. A layup. So, it's no surprise that cash began to move out of the fed funds market. Pre-Financial Crisis, in 2007, the size of the funds market was around $200 billion, and it peaked at $400 billion in 2009 during the crisis. Since then, it's declined just about every year since. Currently, somewhere between $70 billion and $100 billion trades each day.

Of course, there were other reasons why the fed funds market declined in importance. Banks are no longer the center of financial intermediation anymore. Much of that intermediation emigrated to the Repo market – that whole part about shadow banking and all. The idea was even bounced around at an FOMC meeting in 2013 of "the possibility the federal funds rate might not, in the future, be the best indicator of the general level of short-term interest rates." The fed funds market became like the singer in a rock band who only sings, when it's the guitar player[13] who writes and plays all the music.

The fed funds market is not dead, however, mainly because all of its market participants don't have access to the IOER. Due to the legal structure of the Federal Home Loan Banks (FHLBs), they can't loan cash to the Fed. That makes them the largest lender of fed funds out there, supplying about 75% of the cash in the market each day. To add insult to injury, foreign banks are often the cash borrowers, relending

---

[13] The guitarist is the Repo market of course!

the funds back to the Fed and taking advantage of the spread between fed funds and IOER. Yes, effectively arbitraging the U.S. government.[14]

Whereas the fed funds market itself declined in importance, the actual fed funds rate still carries weight. It's still the target rate for monetary policy and the "fed funds effective rate" – which is published daily by the Federal Reserve – is used in many financial contracts, like fed funds futures and OIS swaps. This means the relationship between fed funds and Repo is still important. Both markets are very similar. They're both overnight funding markets and both structured similarly. There's no exchange or central marketplace; buyers and sellers meet through the inter-dealer brokers (IDB). Firms include Brokertec, ICAP, Tullet, Tradition, Cantor, etc. The fed funds market, however, is limited to bank participants, whereas the Repo market is generally open to all comers.

There's a subtle difference between an overnight Repo investment and an overnight fed funds investment. Repo General Collateral is collateralized with securities, whereas fed funds are uncollateralized. A fed funds cash investor doesn't hold any collateral; they rely on the credit of their counterparty – another bank. Now, given the collateralization of Repo transactions, you would assume that Repo rates will always trade below fed funds. Sometimes, but not always. Over the years, Repo GC[15] has traded anywhere from 25 basis points above fed funds to 500 basis points below. That's a huge range and just partly driven by the collateralization.

---

[14] In 2012, it was estimated that foreign banks were borrowing about $30 billion a day in fed funds and investing in other markets, arbitraging the U.S. government.

[15] GC is short for General Collateral.

The GC/fed funds trading range is limited on the upside, but seemingly unlimited on the downside. That's because there's an arbitrage possible between the two markets, but it only works in one direction. If Repo GC rates are higher than fed funds, fed funds traders will invest their cash in Repo instead of lending it to other banks. That means when GC rates are high, cash moves from the funds market into the Repo market.[16] The arbitrage will push relatively high Repo rates lower and fed funds rates higher - narrowing the spread until the arbitrage is gone. However, the arbitrage doesn't work the other way around. If GC rates are below fed funds, there's really nothing that can be done. If a cash investor needs to invest in U.S. Treasury collateral, you can't substitute uncollateralized fed funds.

Given all of this, the spread between Repo GC and fed funds still remains pretty constant, but trends in one direction over time. In a simple world, the spread between GC and fed funds would be a direct function of the number of Treasurys outstanding, and would move higher or lower based on the number of new Treasury supply entering or leaving the market. However, the market has many moving parts, which makes it more complicated. When GC is above fed funds, it usually means there's an abundance of Treasury securities in the market. When GC is trading below fed funds, there's often increased demand for Treasury collateral.

In general, things like Flights-To-Quality and customer demand for Treasurys are factors which move Repo rates around, but not fed funds. It usually takes a crisis to move GC well below fed funds. We've seen strong demand for Treasury collateral when there are terrorist

---

[16] We will see a lot of this between 2017 and 2020.

attacks, banking crises, liquidity crises, or the collapse of a hedge fund, bank, and/or an insurance company.

The spread between GC and fed funds also tells a lot about the health of the financial markets. The spread is a gauge of the market's perception of risk. When the GC/fed funds spread is distorted, there are often problems brewing in the market. The spread is an especially good indicator of what's going on behind the scenes, especially when it moves significantly on a quarter-end or a year-end; when bank balance sheets are tight.

Back in the 1980s, GC generally traded between 25 and 30 basis points below fed funds. If you're investing cash, you prefer to hold a U.S. Treasury as collateral over the credit of a bank, especially a small bank. Even back then, cash investors knew Repo was a collateralized loan, even if their Repo investments were often under-collateralized in their hold-in-custody accounts.

During the Savings and Loan Crisis in the early 1990s, the GC/fed funds[17] relationship reversed. Repo GC traded between 20 and 25 basis points above fed funds. Due to the crisis, banks could not arbitrage the two markets to bring them back in-line. By the end of the 1990s, that spread reversed again. At the time, the U.S. government was running a budget surplus and paying down debt. The size of the Treasury market was shrinking, and fewer U.S. Treasurys meant Treasury collateral traded at a greater premium to fed funds.

---

[17] Theoretically, secured financing rates (Repo) should never trade above unsecure (fed funds) rates.

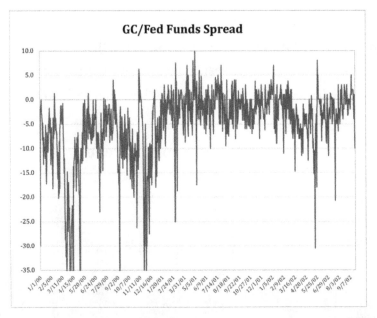

*GC/Fed Funds Spread 2000-2003*

Beginning in 2001, there was another shift in the Repo market. The CFTC changed their margin investment rules, allowing for FCMs (Futures Commission Merchants) to invest their cash in federal agencies, municipal bonds, and corporate bonds, instead of just Treasurys. The premium that U.S. Treasury collateral enjoyed narrowed. Before the rule change in 2000, GC was averaging around 7 basis points below fed funds. Beginning in 2001, GC was averaging almost flat to fed funds. When there's less demand for Treasurys, there's a smaller premium.

The Financial Crisis saw the largest distortions in the Repo market *ever*. Leading up to the Financial Crisis, there were severe liquidity problems on every quarter-end and year-end. The funding stress was a clear sign of the fragility of the financial markets. The Liquidity Crisis of August 2007 – which occurred 13 months before the Financial Crisis - was clearly a prelude. Looking back, there was so much foreshadowing before the crisis, but, of course, hindsight is always 20/20. During the Financial Crisis itself, there was a Flight-To-Quality like no one has ever seen! The demand for Treasury securities was unprecedented, with GC trading 500 basis points below fed funds.

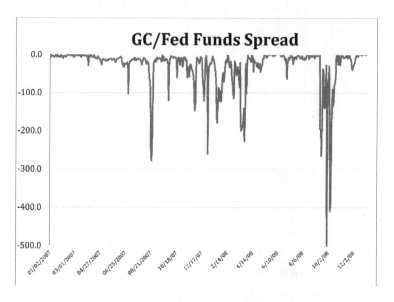

*GC/Fed Funds Spread During the Financial Crisis 2007-2008*

Once the market moved past the crisis and it was time to clean up, Treasury issuance and Fed QE purchases became the main drivers of the spread between GC and fed funds. When Treasury issuance is high, Repo GC rates increase relative to fed funds. When the Fed launches a QE program, Repo GC rates tend to move lower. Think of it as pure supply and demand. When the Treasury issues more Treasurys, there's more supply in the market and Repo rates move higher. When the Fed is buying, it decreases the number of Treasurys in the market and Repo rates decline.

Looking at the graph below, during QE2, which ran from November 2010 to June 2011, GC rates moved lower relative to fed funds. When the QE buying stopped, GC started to rise relative to fed funds. The Fed started QE3 at the end of 2012 and ended it in 2013. Once the buying ended, GC rates began to drift higher again.

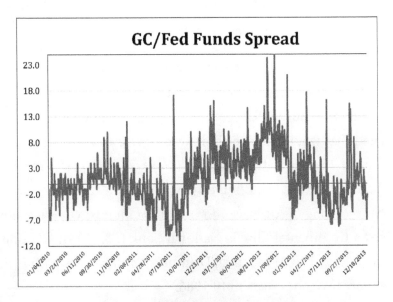

*GC/Fed Funds Spread Post-Financial Crisis 2010-2013*

The London Inter-Bank Offered Rate (LIBOR) may seem pretty similar to fed funds, but they're very different. LIBOR came about when banks began looking for an interest rate as a gauge of their funding costs. The fed funds rate is useful, but it's where banks borrow from other banks. It doesn't represent where banks issue CDs (where they borrowed from institutional investors).

LIBOR slowly grew through the 1970s, but got its big break when the Chicago Mercantile Exchange (CME) devised two new futures contracts to represent bank funding costs. The CME launched the CD futures and the Eurodollar futures contracts in 1981. CD futures were based on a basket of 10 actual bank CDs, with any of them deliverable at the end of the contract period. The Eurodollar futures contract was unique. It was the first futures contract to settle for "cash," and was based on a daily survey of bank funding rates. Twelve different banks were surveyed twice a day, with four of the bank funding rates discarded. No one would know which bank rate was used on which day; the market only knew the average.

Initially, the CD futures contract was the most popular. In fact, for the first four years, it had twice the open interest and trading volume as the Eurodollar futures contract. However, something happened that would change short-term interest rate futures forever. Continental Illinois National Bank, the seventh largest bank in the U.S., began suffering from liquidity problems. In the futures market, anyone receiving a delivery on the CD futures contract *always* received a Continental Illinois National Bank CD. When Continental Illinois collapsed in 1984, the CD futures contract was all but dead, lasting only two more years until 1986.

What was bad news for the CD futures contract was good news for its sister contract, Eurodollar futures. The Eurodollar contract proved to be resilient during that banking crisis. Banks could still estimate their borrowing costs, and the survey method allowed banks to patch the holes in their yield curve when there was no actual CD issuance. The Eurodollar futures contract went on to become one of most successful futures contracts ever.

The first cracks in LIBOR appeared during the Liquidity Crisis of August 2007. At the time, cash investors were unsure which banks were holding subprime debt and CDOs linked to subprime, so they stopped buying bank CDs altogether. Between August and September 2007, no bank could issue CDs with a maturity greater than one month. So, what do you do as a LIBOR submitter when you're called at 11:00 AM and asked where you are issuing CDs? Ironically, banks did what they were supposed to do: they estimated. Of course, those estimates ended up being extremely low.

The Liquidity Crisis of 2007 showed that the LIBOR survey method could break down during a major crisis. Word eventually leaked out that banks had underestimated LIBOR in August and September 2007. Those rumors led to studies and newspaper articles, which then led to regulators investigating the LIBOR market. They didn't like what they found. Further examination found an active LIBOR fixing ring,[18] led by two large global banks and their inter-dealer brokers.[19]

With no way to replace the survey method without the chance of rigging reoccurring, global regulators agreed to scrap LIBOR altogether. The problem was finding a replacement. It's important to understand what LIBOR actually represents. Yes, it represents bank funding costs, but what does that mean? Theoretically, there are two interest rate components that make up LIBOR. The general level of risk-free interest rates and a credit spread. The risk-free interest rate is the equivalent of the U.S. Treasury yield with the same maturity date. The credit spread component represents something like the probability that the bank might default before the maturity date. Remember, CDs are uncollateralized cash, so they're deposits at a bank. For most banks, the probability of a default is extremely low. But it's not zero. Let's say a 3 month U.S. Treasury trades at a yield of 1.15% and a three month bank CD trades at 1.25%. The risk-free rate

---

[18] For the inside story on the LIBOR rigging scandal, read my book *Rogue Traders*.
[19] To be fair, it was rumored that central banks were encouraging their own domestic banks to underestimate the borrowing costs.

is 1.15% for three months and the credit component equals 10 basis points. The LIBOR replacement needed to be able to capture the general level of interest rates and the credit spread. It needed to be observable and traded in a market to generate a reliable reference rate. Of course, any kind of survey method was out.

Initially, the Fed looked at "the possibilities for changing the calculation of the effective federal funds rate in order to obtain a more robust measure of overnight bank funding rates." They wanted to take a wider range of loans between banks: fed funds (domestic), LIBOR (foreign), and Repo (technically a different kind of market, but with bank participants). There were problems here. The idea combined a weighted average with a survey. Also, how could the Fed use LIBOR in the replacement for LIBOR right after LIBOR had been shown to be manipulated? On top of that, could the Fed have a foreign interest rate component (LIBOR) as a part of its reference rate for U.S. bank funding? The idea never went anywhere.

Next, Repo rates appeared to be in the running. It looked like it was finally time for the Repo market to shine! However, there were problems with Repo rates. They trade reasonably actively for overnight, one week, one month, and three months, but not very active for four months through twelve months. Yes, Repo rates are observable, liquid, and can be published. However, they are a risk-free rate which doesn't capture the credit spread. Repo rates could never fully represent bank funding costs. During the time a Repo rate replacement was being discussed, it was discussed at an FOMC meeting and once the FOMC minutes were published, it was clear Repo was not in the running.

The hunt for the LIBOR replacement continued through 2018, when the Fed's Alternative Reference Rates Committee finally announced their new rate. The new rate was called the Secured Overnight Funding Rate, or SOFR for short. With a LIBOR replacement in hand, over the next few years, LIBOR would be slowly strangled by regulators. Its use as a reference rate was ended on December 31, 2021, and it is scheduled to be completely terminated from all use in the financial markets on June 30, 2023. Though LIBOR was officially replaced by SOFR, a benchmark interest rate to gauge bank funding costs was never created.

SOFR is a combination of three Repo rates: deliverable GC, GCF, and Tri-Party. The deliverable GC component is an average of all inter-dealer U.S. Treasury General Collateral trades that settle in FICC (Fixed Income Clearing Corp.). GCF is short for General Collateral Finance, and it's basically inter-dealer Tri-Party trades that settle within FICC. The last component is the Tri-Party rate, and this rate is very important for understanding SOFR. Tri-Party is the average rate for Tri-Party trades that settle at the Bank of New York (BONY). Whereas GC and GCF are dealer-to-dealer rates, Tri-Party is a dealer-to-customer rate. What does that mean? It's where the Street borrows money from customers, not from each other. Dealer-to-customer means the rate is on the offered side of the market, or lower if the dealer marks up the rate, which we commonly do. The Tri-Party rate is always lower than the inter-dealer rate. And it means that SOFR should always trade below Repo GC.

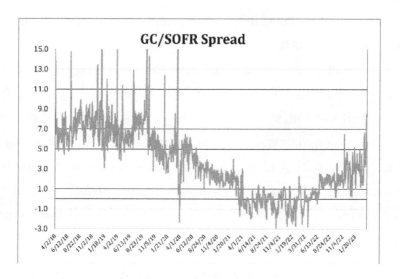

Looking at the graph above, SOFR averaged between 6 and 8 basis points below Repo GC when it was first launched. That's a pretty large spread, and it's a good indication of how spreads widen in the Repo market when nominal Repo rates are high. As the Fed cut rates from 2019 through 2020, that spread narrowed. When nominal interest rates are lower, spreads in the market are narrower too.

Once Repo rates dropped down to zero, there was an exception to the GC/SOFR relationship. For most of 2021 and some of 2022, the Fed had set the RRP rate at .05%. Banks knew that if they offered their customers Tri-Party rates below .05%, their customers would take their cash to the Fed's RRP facility. As a result, SOFR rates stood like a rock at .05% from June 2021 through March 2022. The Street had to give up its markup on most Tri-Party customers for that time period.

Where does the market expect SOFR to trade relative to fed funds in the future? It's easy to see because there are monthly futures contracts for both rates. The fed funds and SOFR futures contracts imply the expected interest rate for each month going forward. In the graph below, I combined the single months together to generate a yield curve for each contract, called a "strip." In March 2022, the SOFR and fed funds yield curves indicated the market expected SOFR to continue to trade just below fed funds for the foreseeable future.

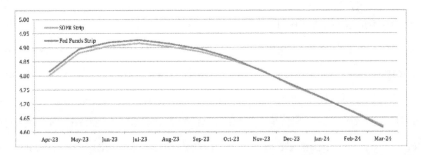

*Fed funds futures strip Vs. SOFR futures strip March 2023*

SOFR has been dogged with complaints since the Fed anointed it the new benchmark. SOFR, as we know, is calculated using Repo transactions, which are all fully collateralized. SOFR really can't be used as a proxy for bank funding costs. It doesn't have the credit spread component. The result is that SOFR can never be used as a replacement for LIBOR. It just won't happen. However, SOFR still has a role to play. Though it was badly constructed, it's still better than fed funds for hedging the multi-trillion-dollar Repo market.

# Settlement & Clearing

Back in the late 1990s, I had a client who wanted to finance physical Treasury STRIPS (Separate Trading of Registered Interest and Principal of Securities). These were not the TIGRS (Treasury Investment Growth Receipts) created by Merrill Lynch in the early 1980s, nor the CATS (Certificates of Accrual on Treasury Securities) created by Salomon Brothers, nor the LIONS (Lehman Investment Opportunity Notes) created by Lehman Brothers. But regular U.S. Treasurys that were stripped into two components by the Federal Reserve: a series of coupon payments and the principal payment at the maturity date. When you think about it, that's really what a bond is in the first place. It's a series of coupon payments and a principal payment at the maturity date. With this customer, I borrowed the STRIPS[20] and loaned them to a bank customer. Sounds like a pretty simple trade, except these STRIPS were a little different. They were in physical form. Physical certificates.

The Treasury stopped issuing physical certificates, a.k.a. registered debt, in 1986, and all Treasury securities thereafter were issued in book-entry form, which means they settle on the Fedwire system. But for years there were physical Treasury certificates still floating around the market. Because these securities could trade anonymously, there was a big secondary market for them, primarily because it was hard for the IRS to know exactly who owned them. As a

---

[20] I can't remember if they were coupon or principal.

physical certificate, the coupons were actually attached. Each coupon was a small rectangular portion attached to the certificate. The amount of the coupon was stated on each square, along with its payment date. When the coupon payment date arrived, the owner literally clipped the coupon off of the certificate and brought it to a bank for payment.

Financing these STRIPS was a great trade. The physical certificate and fact that they were STRIPS meant I could charge a large spread. Since the securities didn't settle on the Fedwire, they had to be physically delivered to our clearing bank, the Bank of New York. This may seem pretty crazy today, but a messenger had to pick up the certificate at the customer's clearing bank and deliver it to our clearing bank. The settlement instructions were the bank's physical address and the floor number, which I cannot specifically remember today. The part I do remember vividly was the specific instruction "Window B."

While we were waiting to receive the delivery, I pictured a messenger arriving with a sheet of coupon payments at "Window A" by mistake, and the clerk then saying, "I don't know this delivery." The clerk might "DK" the settlement and send the STRIPS back to where they came from. Had the messenger only gone to Window B and the securities would have settled! Of course, everything settled fine, but the basics of the old settlement system are about the same today, except now they're computerized.

These days, there are no more physical Treasury certificates. They all matured. All U.S. Treasury securities settle on the Fedwire. This is an electronic payment system maintained by the Federal Reserve. All government debt is issued in electronic form and held at a bank that has an account at the Fed. Banks who are members of the Fedwire system are called clearing banks. Every major broker-dealer, Money Market Fund, or bank has an account at a clearing bank. The clearing banks maintain trade processing systems that allow their customers to send and receive securities. The largest clearing banks are The Bank of New York, Bank of Montreal, JP Morgan Chase, Citibank, State Street, U.S. Bank, and Bank of America. If you've ever sent a money wire from one bank to another, it goes through the Fedwire. Have you ever been asked for an ABA number? That's the receiving bank's code on the Fedwire system.

Every securities dealer has a specific address at their clearing bank. This address is similar to an internet address. It has the name of the clearing bank and the sub-account of the securities dealer. An example might be BK OF NYC/American Securities. When securities are delivered or received, they are transferred Delivery Versus Payment (DVP) or Receive Versus Payment (RVP). That means the securities and cash are exchanged simultaneously. When securities arrive at the clearing bank, the cash amount is automatically debited. Imagine the risk issues if securities were transferred for free and the cash delivered after the securities had settled.

Throughout the course of a day, securities dealers have thousands of securities to receive and deliver. The Fedwire opens at 8:30 AM and closes at 3:00 PM. Well, officially at 3:00:59. Those extra 59 seconds can mean a lot where there are big deliveries settling at the end of the day! Between 3:00 PM and 3:15 PM is officially "customer time," when dealers can deliver to customers, but customer time isn't really followed anymore. Trades must settle with the exact details expected by both parties. The exact par amount, price, principal amount, and exact counterparty settlement address must match. The smallest error prevents a security from settling, and thus being DK'd. However, at 3:30:59 the Fedwire is permanently shut for the day and securities cannot be sent through it anymore.

Remember the part about physical bond certificates? Picture the back office of a broker-dealer years ago, with piles and piles of certificates before the days of book entry. Securities dealers kept the certificates for each customer in a box. Yes, imagine something like a cardboard box, but it was probably metal. And that term is still around today. When a securities dealer or bank describes securities in their account at their clearing bank, the account is referred to as their "box." Keep in mind, some of these terms might seem meaningless now, but they'll be important later.

After the fall of Drysdale, Lombard Wall, and the slew of small broker-dealers in the mid-1980s, the Fed and SEC were worried about the possibility of the collapse of a major securities dealer. There was a large push to regulate the previously unregulated government securities market, which resulted in the passage of the Government Securities Act of 1986. It allowed for the regulation of government securities broker-dealers, though not government securities themselves. Shortly thereafter, the National Securities Clearing Corporation (NSCC) established what was then called Government Securities Clearing Corp. (GSCC), though it's now known as Fixed Income Clearing Corp. (FICC). The new subsidiary was specifically designed to be the Central Clearing Counterparty (CCP) for the bond market.

Though CCPs began to emerge several years ago, they are not new. In fact, they were very popular during the so-called National

Banking Era of the 19th century. At that time, there was no central bank. There was no government regulator that provided supervision, nor one that provided liquidity during an emergency. Back then, as a depositor, you were basically on your own. Clearinghouses were developed to fill the void of support now provided by the Fed and the government.

The first bank clearinghouse was established in 1853 as an organization to clear checks. Back then, there was no email, electronic commerce, fax machines, or phones. Banks received checks written from other banks all day long. During the day, they sent messengers to settle their net cash balances. The system was inherently inefficient. Imagine messengers crisscrossing all over the city all day long. You can picture how one messenger had an epiphany one day: "Ezekiel, didn't I see you delivering to my bank four times this morning? I just came from a drop-off at your bank. Tomorrow, let's just meet halfway and save all of the trips back and forth." Then, maybe all of the messengers got together to meet at a central location a few times a day. When the whole process was formalized, everyone met at the same location to exchange bank drafts. The central location became organized as the clearinghouse.

The idea spread across the country. Banks organized clearinghouses everywhere. Each region, like New York City, Chicago, and Philadelphia, had its own clearinghouse. The New York Clearinghouse Association (NYCHA) was the largest, and represented over $1 billion in deposits, which was a *lot* of money back then!

The clearinghouse served as support for its members during times of crisis. Bank panics were pretty common in the 19th century. When a bank went bust, a depositor could lose everything. There was no FDIC insurance, no Federal Reserve, and no government bailouts! During a panic, the public never really knew which banks were at risk, so depositors often withdrew all of their deposits at any sign of trouble.

A banking system is by definition illiquid. The assets are long-term and the deposits are short term. On top of that, the deposits are available upon demand. The loans, on the other hand, can't be recalled or quickly sold. When deposits are withdrawn from the banking system on a massive scale, the whole banking system becomes technically insolvent. These days, we have the Fed. In the past, the clearinghouses assumed that role. During a crisis, all members of the clearinghouse jointly suspended the withdrawal of deposits. Next, the clearinghouses ceased publication of the members' financial information. That way, the public did not know which banks were in trouble.

Most important, the clearinghouses issued bank notes called clearinghouse loan certificates to the public in small denominations. The loan certificates were effectively money that was the joint obligation of all of the members of the clearinghouse. Instead of depositors withdrawing their cash from a bank member, they were given the certificates. These loan certificates acted as a currency that was used in the local economy, and further liquidity wasn't withdrawn from the banking system. The clearinghouse association effectively became the lender of last resort by mutualizing the risks among all members. Not such a bad system.

Clearinghouse loan certificates have been called the most important development in American banking during the 19th century. They created liquidity during times of crisis. They prevented panic from spreading to healthy banks. Not surprisingly, the clearinghouse was the model and framework for the Federal Reserve when it was created in 1913. Look at the initial set up of the Federal Reserve. There were 12 regional banks, including New York, Chicago, and Philadelphia. The Fed performed bank supervision and provided liquidity in times of crisis. One hundred years later, the basics are not too different.

After the Fed granted FICC registration as a clearing agency, it began operations on August 26, 1988. It's important to remember that FICC is a central clearing counterparty. They're not a clearing facility like the Fedwire or DTC. Nor are they an exchange like the Chicago Mercantile Exchange. Securities don't clear through FICC; they compare and net. Instead of moving securities back and forth between securities dealers and banks, members submit their trades to FICC. Basically, everyone meets at the same place to net their receives and deliveries. Not too different from the clearinghouses of yesteryear! FICC uses a clearing bank just like everyone else. Securities positions that don't net in FICC are settled over the Fedwire.

However, unlike the clearinghouses of the past, the central feature of FICC is the Default Fund. If a member defaults, goes bankrupt, or just can't pay its debts, the Default Fund assumes and liquidates their securities positions. FICC collects margin on every transaction between its members. The more trades that go through FICC, the more margin they collect. They look at each member's trades as a portfolio. They calculate a VaR (Value at Risk) number for each member and then collect margin based on the VaR twice a day. FICC updates its VaR calculation to keep up with the changing market, but they never publish the formula.

Repo comparison began in 1995 and netting the following year. This was a great leap forward for the Repo market. However, at the time, FICC was not the only game in town. By the late 1990s, there were two rival clearinghouses: Delta Clearing Corp. and FICC. They fought for control of the Repo market between 1997 and 1999. Back then, when you traded through the inter-dealer brokers, you had three options: Give-Up, FICC, or Delta. By 1999, all securities dealers and liquidity had migrated to FICC. The Delta Clearing and Give-Up markets were forever gone. Today, anyone trading through the inter-dealer broker must be a member of FICC.

Trade comparison and netting were big boosts to market efficiency. As the central counterparty, FICC is the counterparty on all of the trades between its members. All members submit their trades to FICC just seconds after they're executed. FICC automatically compares the trades and makes sure all of the details match. If a detail doesn't match, the trade is rejected. Before FICC, sometimes you didn't know about a trade discrepancy until the next day, when the trade settled and it was DK'd by the counterparty!

When it comes time to settle transactions, there's only one net settlement between the member and FICC. Suppose one member bought the same security five times and sold that same security three times. The next day, all of the buys and sells are netted together and there's one settlement with FICC. The netting facility reduces settlements, which is a big cost savings for the Street, but not so good for the clearing banks.

FICC members can also net their balance sheets. Before Repo was eligible in FICC, dealers grossed their assets with multiple Repo trades spread across the entire inter-dealer market. Members net their trades under an accounting rule called FASB Interpretation No. 41. The rule permits offsetting Repo and Reverse-Repo transactions as long as they're the same type of securities, the counterparty is the same, and the Repo end-dates are the same. For example, if Bank A borrows a security from Bank B, who borrows it from Bank C, the transactions were previously on the balance sheets of all three banks. Once FICC began netting Repo trades, there's only one Reverse-Repo transaction with FICC and one Repo transaction with FICC. Initially, it was originally estimated that the Street was able to net their balance sheets by about 50%. These days, FICC estimates the number to be closer to 75%.

Back in 1994, the Federal Reserve realized the clearing banks (like Bank of New York and Chase Manhattan) were extending massive amounts of intra-day credit to their clients. Billions of dollars of securities arrived at each clearing bank when the Fedwire opened at 8:30 AM. Those securities would sit in the clearing bank's accounts for hours before they were delivered. The Fed realized, at time, they were extending the same hundreds of billions of dollars of intra-day credit to the clearing banks. That led them to institute the Daylight Overdraft (DOD) charge in 1994. They began charging the clearing banks a basis point fee for every minute they were overdrawn. The idea was that the clearing banks would pass on the charge to their clients. And they did! The charge evolved over the years and increased several times. There's even an additional surcharge for overdrafts in excess of $500 million.

When adding up the DOD charges, there's a huge incentive for securities dealers to get all of their securities out of their box as soon as the Fedwire opens. For securities that are going to be Repo'd that day, there's little reason to hold on past 8:30 AM. I've done the calculation myself. The few possible basis points you might earn if Repo rates decline as the morning moves on are not worth the DOD charges. The move by the Fed back in 1994 effectively created a "cost of carry" in the Repo market.

*     *     *

As the Tri-Party Repo market continued to grow in the 1990s, FICC decided to add a Tri-Party facility of their own. GCF stands for General Collateral Finance, and it was first introduced in 1998. Naturally, only FICC members can participate, but not all FICC members are a part of GCF. The GCF Repo markets are technically a different type of trade, so they are quoted separately in the inter-dealer broker markets. Regular General Collateral Repo trades are often called "deliverable GC," and GCF trades are simply called GCF. They are two parallel markets. Most of the time the rates are the same, but sometimes the rates diverge based on the supply and demand of cash and securities in each separate market.

FICC now has 209 members, though many members are subsidiaries of the same financial institution, like both the bank and broker-dealer. When accounting for the multiple subsidiaries, there are about 100 separate financial institutions that are dealers in the Repo market.

# FAILS

I believe a good analogy is in order! Suppose someone wants to buy a book online. Let's just pick a book at random, maybe something like More Rogue Traders (available on Amazon) by an established financial author. The buyer clicks to buy the book and Amazon puts the book in the shopping cart. Let's say the buyer chooses standard shipping of 3 to 5 business days, which is kind of like the settlement date. The book is listed as "in stock," so no delivery problems are expected. The individual goes to the online checkout and pays for it. Once the buyer inputs their credit card information, they agreed to exchange money for the book, kind of like a delivery-versus-payment (DVP).

Let's say More Rogue Traders became a hot book and lots of people are trying to buy it. Amazon runs out of inventory and has to order more. After five business days, the buyer realizes they still haven't received the book. Unbeknownst to the buyer, Amazon is waiting for books from the publisher. The publisher is waiting for books from the printer. Amazon "failed-to-deliver" the book on time. The book buyer is pretty unhappy with the delay, since the book was listed as "in stock." Of course, Amazon didn't know there would be so much demand. Luckily in the book world, just like in the securities world, Amazon is able to go to the publisher and order more books to clean up the failed deliveries. It's just like how the Federal Reserve can loan securities into the market and clean up fails. Eventually, the market gets all of the More Rogue Traders books that it wants, even though the deliveries failed for a few days.

"Fails" are pretty common in the securities markets. They're driven by limited securities supply and increased demand. Pretty simple, right? Each Treasury security has a fixed amount outstanding, but not all of that is available in the Repo market. A large percentage of every Treasury is packed away in investor portfolios. When there's not enough supply, Repo rates decline and fails increase.

That means there's a connection between settlements, fails, and Repo rates. In a way, the settlement system is an early warning mechanism for securities shortages. Securities that settle quickly after the Fedwire opens at 8:30 AM are readily available. When it takes all day for a security to settle, it's an indication that there's fewer around in the market. If there are fails at the end of the day, it's a sign a shortage is brewing.

Some fails are a normal part of the business. They're officially called "frictional fails," though no one really uses that term. They're caused by errors and mistakes. They can happen at any time and are a regular occurrence. Chalk it up to human error. They can also be related to mismatched settlements. Let's say someone bought a security in three pieces of $10 million and sold the security as one piece of $30 million. Normally that's not a problem. There are three receives of $10 million each to make one delivery of $30 million. However, what if one of those $10 million pieces is not received, maybe due to an error or mistake? The bank has $20 million of the security in their box to make a delivery of $30 million. At the end of the day, it's a fail. The bank failed to deliver the $30 million. Most of the time, these fails are one day events.

"Cascading fails" are more serious. Once again, no one really uses that term, but it's in the dictionary. They occur when there's a lot of demand to borrow a security and there is little availability. In a broader sense, it also occurs when the financial system is locked-up. Buyers are unable to receive securities from sellers because the sellers haven't received them either. Repo desks keep borrowing and lending the security and the fails increase each day. There's a web of fails between everyone in the market. This situation is referred to as a "dead fail." It happened after September 11, with the 3.625% 5/13, during the Financial Crisis, and with many 10 Year Notes.

Economically, there are good fails and bad fails. A "positive fail" is when you make money from someone failing to you. A "negative fail" is when you lose money because you failed to deliver to someone else. Let me explain. A fail-to-receive is when you bought or borrowed a security and you didn't receive it. Since the securities were never delivered to your clearing bank, you didn't pay for them. When someone buys a U.S. Treasury, they're investing cash and interest begins accruing on the settlement date. The key point here is that the buyer receives the interest whether the securities are delivered or not. Now, because the seller failed-to-deliver, the buyer didn't have to pay for the securities. Not only does the buyer receive the interest on their original investment, but they didn't have to pay for the securities. They were left with their cash and they were able to invest it. It's like earning double interest, at least until the securities arrive and are paid for.

Think of a negative fail as the opposite of a positive fail. A security was sold, but not actually delivered. The seller does not receive any interest for the day, but since the security was never delivered, they have to borrow money to finance the security. Fails are a big part of the Repo market. Traders are constantly trying to "pick up positive fails" and avoid negative fails.

After the September 11 attacks, a massive number of fails swept through the financial system. As the power shut down in Lower Manhattan, financial firms lost power and no one down there was able to process their trades. Their lights were literally out. As companies migrated to their back-up sites, a major problem was discovered. The Bank of New York (BONY), which is the largest clearing bank, was completely dead in the water. As it turned out, their back-up site was located just blocks away from their main office. The largest clearing bank in the world was completely frozen.

Over the next few days, the Fedwire system was still technically up and running, but anything delivered to BONY never came back. Nothing moved for days, and once BONY was back online, there were still some fails for up to two months later. Fails reached a record of $1.48 trillion during the depth of the crisis.

The fail problem came back just two years later. No security ever failed as long as the 3.625% 5/15/2013, and that's even counting the Salomon Two Year Note squeeze. The 3.625% 5/13 was the 10 Year Note issued in May 2003. At the time, the market was expecting a 50 basis point ease at the June FOMC meeting. The fed funds target rate was 1.00%, and the market was expecting a new target rate of .50%, or at least .75%. The ease never happened, and the market took that as the turn in the easing cycle. It was. The 10 Year Note yield, which was trading at 3.15% in mid-June, backed up to 3.50% by the end of June, and eventually hit 4.50% by mid-August.

Many investor portfolios had purchased the 3.625% 5/13 as long-term investments. An abnormally large percentage of the issue was in hold-to-maturity portfolios. And, by the middle of June, those positions were underwater. That meant investors could not sell the securities or loan them into the Repo market without creating a tax event. Then, as the market sold off further, MBS trading desks kept short-selling the issue to hedge their long MBS positions. It left very little supply in the market and a lot of short-demand.

The 3.625% 5/13 failed from June 2003 through November 2003. It briefly cleaned up in December, and then failed again in January and February 2004. Remember, this was back in 2003 before the "fail charge," so the cost of a fail was the equivalent of a zero percent Repo rate. If you couldn't borrow the securities with a Repo rate above zero, you had the option of just failing. Economically, you earned no Repo interest either way. At one point, the web of fails reached as high as $1.62 trillion. This security forever changed the landscape of fails and the Repo market.

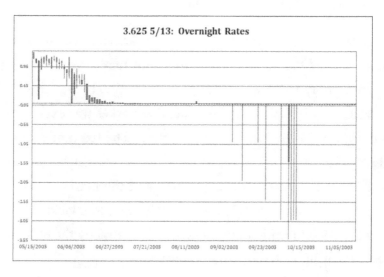

The 3.625% 5/13 showed the market the true cost of fails. After it had failed for weeks, dealers noticed their regulatory capital charges increased. Then, the fails were counted assets to their balance sheet. Pretty soon, good clients were getting annoyed. They wanted to know why their bonds weren't delivered. The risk management groups started to realize there was increased credit exposure. Because you couldn't call margin on a fail, there was no way to eliminate the exposure to a counterparty on your fails-to-deliver. Fails-to-receive were not a problem because there was positive counterparty exposure on them, but the fails-to-deliver were a big problem because the price of the 10 Year Note had declined so much. If you had to sell the security to another counterparty in a liquidation, the price would be much lower than the original trade[21]

By September, the market needed a mechanism to price the value of a good delivery. Dealers were desperate to get small pieces of the security to help clean up their fails. Traders were happy to pay extra just to receive the securities. When someone received a delivery of the 3.625% 5/13, they knew they had something of value. The Repo market developed the guaranteed delivery (GD) Repo trade. This was the first official negative rate trading in the Repo market. Yes, negative rates in the Repo market were born from the 3.625% 5/13![22] Here's how it worked. Anyone lending the issue had to guarantee the delivery. They had to confirm they had the securities in their box. This allowed traders with a need to clean up a fail a mechanism to pay extra in order to do so.

---

[21] More on this in the "Risk Management" chapter.

[22] That's why there were no negative rates before September 2003. See the overnight Repo rate graph

Theoretically, there's supposed to be a natural market mechanism to eliminates fails. Markets tend to work in efficient ways. Where there is a problem, the market usually finds a way to correct itself. In theory, if there's a shortage of supply, the market adjusts. As short-demand for an issue increases and Repo rates decline, there are more securities available at lower rates and more securities come back into the market. Customers who are outright long will swap their rich Treasury issue for a similar issue with a higher yield. Also, when traders know of fail problems, there are fewer new short-sellers. Traders with short positions will eventually throw in the towel and cover their shorts back. But when the market can't self-correct, the Fed and the Treasury step in.

During periods of severe securities shortages, the Treasury can reopen a failing issue. Instead of issuing a new security at an upcoming regular auction, the Treasury can reopen an outstanding issue. Though this is common in other sovereign bond markets, it's not common in the Treasury market. The Treasury first used a "snap reopening" after September 11. In a surprise move in October, they announced an auction of more supply of a failing issue in an unscheduled auction. Though the Treasury maintained that the snap reopening would not be a regular tool for addressing fails, they used it again in October 2008 to reopen the current 10 Year Note.

Is there anything inherently wrong with fails? Before 2003, fails were not considered such a big problem in the Treasury market. Even during times of large fails, the overall market continued to function. When a Treasury was hard to borrow and/or was failing, the Repo rate dropped to 0.0% and no one covered their shorts. In most cases, zero percent rates for a few days were not a problem. Yes, some traders lost money, but that's life in the big city! The 3.625% 5/15/13 magnified the problems with prolonged fails: added assets, increased regulatory capital charges, unhappy customers, distortions in the market, and most of all, unwanted counterparty risk. From the market's perspective, counterparty credit risk was the big issue. Fails were a loophole in counterparty credit exposure. There was a crack in the system and the dealer community needed a way to correct it.

Here's the good news: a financial crisis doesn't always mean there are fail problems. During the Liquidity Crisis of August 2007, there were no fail issues, mostly because that crisis occurred outside of the Treasury market. It was a crisis in bank CDs, commercial paper, collateralized debt obligations (CDOs), subprime debt, and LIBOR. During August 2007, fails peaked at only $124 billion. Nothing big.

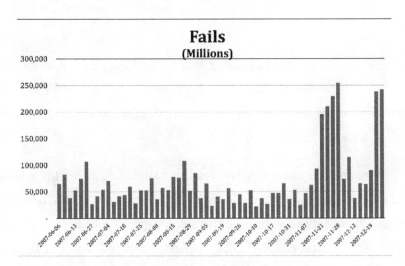

However, when the Financial Crisis kicked in a year later, fails *were* a problem. A massive problem. After September 15, 2008, customers stopped lending their securities into the Repo market. They were worried they wouldn't get the securities back if their counterparty went bust. Of course, it was a self-fulfilling problem. With fewer Treasury securities available in the Repo market, it was nearly impossible to cover shorts and fails increased. Fails hit an all-time high of $5.06 trillion[23] on October 15, 2008. If there ever was systemic risk in the bond market, this was it!

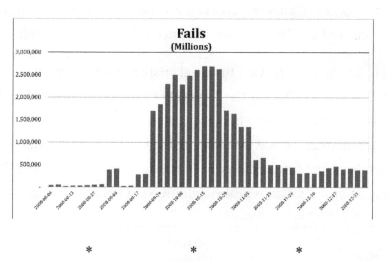

          \*                   \*                  \*

The Financial Crisis made it clear that something needed to be done about the fail problem. The Fed put pressure on the bond market to figure out a solution and the Treasury Market Practices Group (TMPG) took up the cause.

Before the fail charge, many traders just didn't cover their shorts when rates hit zero. When daily overnight rates were 5.00%, or 4.00%, or even 3.00%, failing with an equivalent Repo rate of zero *was* a stiff penalty. In December 2008, the Fed dropped the fed funds target range to 0.0% to .25%. Effectively zero. Given that rates were so close to zero, there was little incentive to cover shorts once rates got close to zero. Just as the Financial Crisis was winding down, the fail problem

---

[23] The $5.06 trillion is the combined Fails-To-Receive and Fails-To-Deliver

came back. Some might call it an unintended consequence of the ZIRP (Zero Interest Rate Policy).

In January 2009, the TMPG announced plans to institute a steep penalty for fails: a 300 basis point charge. Once FICC was onboard, the whole market adopted it. The new rule would also allow for margin calls on fails. The SEC took comments on the fail charge in April 2009, and the charge became effective on May 1, 2009.

When the TPMG fail charge dropped the cost to fail from 0.0% to -3.00%, it gave the market a big incentive to cover shorts. In fact, it ushered in an era of negative interest rates that wasn't previously possible. The playing field in the Repo market was extended 300 basis points lower.

The fail charge was a very successful update to the Repo market. It provided a mechanism to price failing securities and securities in *very* high demand. Once the fail charge began, there were no periods of protracted fails. Yes, a 10 Year Note traded very Special every once in a while, but nothing systemic.

Just how zero percent was the barrier in the Repo market before the fail charge, you would think -3.00% was the new barrier. That's not the case. Why would someone pay a rate below -3.00%? Why not just fail and take the equivalent of the -3.00% rate? In recent years, a 10 Year Note even traded as low as -5.50%. Here are some reasons why:

1. Internal Rules. The Repo desk at the bank or Prime Broker is required to cover all shorts. Those are the internal runs and you don't want to break the rules!

2. Bureaucracy. The Repo trader doesn't want to write memos and have meetings with the risk/credit people or their boss about why a short wasn't covered. Yes, this actually happens!

3. They need to cover their shorts to make a delivery to a good customer.

4. Regulatory capital charges for aged fails.

# Supply and Demand

Remember the part of about supply and demand in the first chapter? There's a lot of it here. Bear with me; it's hard to keep this topic interesting. I'll try to make it as painless as possible! This chapter is about the "why." Why are there more or less securities in the market? Why does the supply and demand for cash and securities affect the Repo market? These are the factors that put Treasurys in the market or removes them. Factors that put cash in the market or removes it. Basically, circumstances that affect supply and demand.

The Repo market is an interesting market from an economics perspective. Unlike traditional markets where there's a supply and demand curve, in the Repo market there are two supply and two demand curves.[24] In the Repo market, there's the supply and demand for securities and the supply and demand for cash, with both intersecting in the same market.

Let's start with the basics. When there are fewer securities, Repo rates move lower. When there are more securities, rates move higher. When there's more cash, rates move lower. When there's less cash, rates move higher. The rest is just variations on these basic principles.

---

[24] I promise this won't be an economics lecture!

## Changes In Securities

U.S. Treasury issuance is, by far, the largest factor that affects Repo rates. It's the Treasury market after all! When the U.S. government is running a budget deficit – like it normally does – the supply of Treasurys is increasing. There are typically more new Treasury securities coming into the market than maturing securities. That's called net new issuance.

The size of each new U.S. Treasury issue varies based on the government's funding needs. The Treasury has larger issue sizes when they need to borrow more and smaller issue sizes when they need to borrow less. A large size on-the-run Treasury note is less likely to trade Special than a small issue. When issues sizes are smaller, there's a greater chance of a shortage.

On days when there are large new Treasury issues settling – like the 15th of the month or the last day of the month – it puts upward pressure on Repo rates. Luckily, the market is usually able to absorb new supply over the course of a day or two. Conversely, when the Treasury was paying down debt between 1997 and 2001, securities were leaving the market each month. Supply in the Repo market was slowly declining. Back then, I remember traders declaring how the Treasury Repo market was going to disappear once the budget surpluses had paid off all the outstanding Treasury debt. That didn't happen!

Treasury coupon issuance (notes and bonds) has a different impact on the Repo market than bill issuance. Yes, they're all Treasury securities and they all increase the supply of collateral, but there's a subtle difference between bills and coupons. Bills compete with Repo as a cash investment. An increase or decrease in the bill supply has a much greater impact on the Repo rates than changes in coupon supply.

After the U.S. Treasury, the Federal Reserve has the next largest impact on the Repo market. Federal Reserve operations are specifically designed to add and drain liquidity from the market. But recently, the Fed acquired a new tool: expanding or contracting the balance sheet. Also known as Quantitative Easing, or QE for short. When the Fed is buying for the SOMA portfolio (System Open Market Account), they're regularly taking supply out of the market. GC Repo rates trend lower during QE. When the QE programs end and the Fed is no longer buying, like during Balance Sheet Runoff, or when they're actually selling securities like in Quantitative Tightening (QT),[25] securities are coming back into the market and it pushes GC rates higher. Makes sense? When supply leaves the market, rates go down. When supply comes back into the market, rates go up.

Is the market long or short? Primary Dealer long and short positions are published by the Federal Reserve each week, and they're a good indication of how banks are positioned in the market. Remember, Primary Dealers are leverage market participants, just like the hedge funds, though they're not as leveraged as the hedge funds! When banks are long or short, their positions show up in the Fed data. Bank and hedge fund positions all show up through their Repo positions.

Another window into market positioning is through TED spreads (Treasurys over Eurodollars[26]). That's the difference between the U.S.

---

[25] There's plenty more on this later!

[26] Assume Eurodollar futures contracts and LIBOR are the same thing.

Treasury rates and LIBOR rates (Eurodollar futures contacts). If Treasurys are cheap relative to futures, traders buy Treasurys and hedge them with futures. That's when traders say "the market is long." Conversely, if the Treasury curve trades below the Eurodollar curve, Treasurys are rich to futures. Traders short Treasurys against being long futures. When the Fed is running a QE program, they will often push the Treasury yield curve below the Eurodollar curve. However, left on its own, constant Treasury issuance can even push Treasury rates above Eurodollar rates.

How well a new Treasury is received at the auction can impact how it trades in the Repo market. When there's strong interest from institutional portfolios, there will be less of that new issue floating around in the secondary market, and thus less in the Repo market. The opposite is also true. If a Treasury auction doesn't go well, the Street gets stuck owning a large percentage of it. When the Street is long, those securities are generally readily available in the Repo market.

Some institutional investors are more Repo friendly than others. Some investors just don't loan their securities into the Repo market, but most will. Sometimes bonds that were bought by hold-to-maturity portfolios don't come back into the Repo market, like the 3.625% 5/13. Or even foreign accounts, like that ever-elusive "Japanese insurance company." There are always rumors about a Japanese insurance company who owns a lot of a U.S. Treasury, but doesn't lend it. Individual investors, too. Whatever percentage is bought by individual investors can be considered permanently gone from the market.

There are times when there are more shorts in the Treasury market and times when there are less. The overall short-base of the market affects General Collateral Repo rates. When there are more shorts in the market, it means there are fewer securities in the market overall. Those securities that were previously being used as General Collateral are now being used to cover shorts. During times with a large market short-base, there's downward pressure on GC rates. Less collateral supply means lower rates.

STRIPS again! The Federal Reserve allows Primary Dealers to separate the principal payment and coupon payments of a bond. When a Treasury issue is stripped, there's less supply in the market. Yes, I specifically said bond. Due to buyer preferences, Treasury bonds are the most often stripped - Treasury securities originally issued as a 20 Year or 30 Year Bond. The point here is that when there are a lot of STRIPS, it can create a shortage of the bond in the Repo market.

No one likes a fail, unless you're trying to pick up a positive fail. When fails increase, both the Street and investor portfolios stop lending securities into the Repo market. If you might not get your security back the next day, why lend it? This, in turn, compounds existing fail problems.

During a Flight-To-Quality, there's a flurry of buying by panicked investors. Securities are purchased by end-user cash investors and packed away in their portfolios. These securities are usually not loaned back into the Repo market.

# Changes In Cash

When talking about "cash," it's not about the cash in the financial markets overall, just cash in the Repo market. Here are some factors that affect Repo rates.

When cash moves in and out of money market funds (MMF), it affects Repo rates. Yes, these funds invest a majority of their funds in bank CDs, commercial paper, U.S. Treasurys, corporate bonds, and discount notes, but their uninvested cash goes directly into the Repo market. Large funds like Fidelity, Vanguard, Federated, PIMCO, and Blackrock invest hundreds of billions of dollars in the Repo market each day. When individual inventors put money in these funds, a percentage of that cash filters into the Repo market. When individual investors redeem investments in those funds, cash leaves the Repo market.

Investor portfolio allocations are similar, too. Many investors position themselves with a balance of fixed income, equities, and cash. Think of times when "cash is sitting on the sidelines." If market participants don't like the bond market and don't like the stock market, their money will be "in cash." Maybe they're waiting for an event like a Fed ease or tightening. Maybe they're afraid to invest due to a panic. Maybe they're waiting for a new opportunity. Whatever the reason, it brings cash into the Repo market, generally through the MMFs. I remember back in May 2000 when no one was sure if the Fed would tighten at the upcoming May FOMC meeting. A lot of cash flowed into the Repo market. The same thing reoccurred just six years later in May 2006. The result was a lot of cash sitting in the Repo market for a few weeks waiting to be allocated to new investments.

Remember what I said before: The Repo market is all about supply and demand.

When one thinks about a central bank, they usually imagine the nation's top economists dedicated to optimizing the country's monetary policy. However, central banks participate in the market in very different ways. Many central banks don't lend the securities they own in their portfolios, though some do. In the past, there were many times when securities have traded Special because a large amount was purchased by foreign central banks. Some central banks are large cash investors. Some are more like hedge funds, running leveraged speculative trading portfolios.

States, cities, and municipalities are big buyers of Treasurys. State operating funds, pension funds, surplus cash funds, reserve funds, and retirement funds all buy Treasurys, and invest their extra cash in Repo. If a state or municipality runs a defeasance program, they remove U.S. Treasurys from the market. When interest rates decline, local governments will often refinance their debt, just as an individual might refinance their home mortgage. The municipality will issue new municipal bonds at lower interest rates. At the same time, they buy Treasurys and place them in a trust to pay the outstanding bond issue. The municipality matches the cash flows of the outstanding municipal bond issue with cash flows of the Treasurys.

Storms and hurricanes affect the Repo market too. I promise you I'm not crazy! But, yes, the weather affects Repo rates. It's called "float." When there are severe storms or hurricanes, payments are slowed in the mail. Weather has less impact on the Repo market these days because payments are more frequently made electronically. But when the weather does slow payments, it usually means Repo market funding pressure, but not always.

# Calendar Events

There are seasonal factors that affect Repo rates. Who would have thought? Tax dates, quarter-ends, year-end, and mortgage loan payments can all impact the market.

At the beginning of every month, homeowners send mortgage payments to their bank or mortgage servicing agent. Many of these mortgage payments are either securitized or guaranteed by Fannie Mae, Ginnie Mae, or Freddie Mac – the GSEs, or Government Sponsored Enterprises. That means billions of dollars of mortgage principal and interest payments are being collected by the GSEs at the beginning of the month and paid to bondholders later in the month. During the period of the time between payments, the GSEs invest a substantial amount of cash straight into the Repo market.

Typically, GSE cash begins to flow into the Repo market on the 19th of the month and leaves on the 25th. Depending on some other factors, GSE cash can have a major or minor impact on Repo rates. At times, the GSE cash will push rates much lower. Sometimes barely at all.

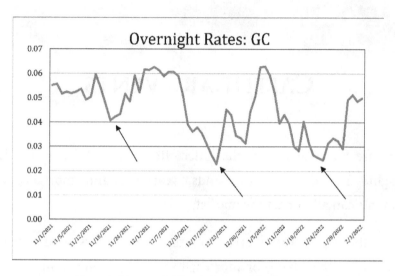

*The typical impact of GSE cash. Rates are a few basis points lower*

Corporations pay taxes quarterly on March 15, June 15, September 15, and December 15. The market calls them "corporate tax dates." On the days when corporations send tax payments to the Treasury, there's a little less cash in the market. The Repo Market Panic of September 2019 was initially blamed on the September 15 tax date, but after further review, it was clear the tax date played only a minor role, if any.

April 15 is the big tax date for individuals. People transfer cash out of their bank account to pay their federal and state taxes. This large transfer of cash affects the market, but not in the way you'd expect. As it turns out, Repo rates generally decline after the April 15 tax date. This is known as the "April Collateral Shortage," or "Seasonal April Collateral Shortage," or anything similar.

Traders first started noticing this collateral shortage in April 1997, which happened to be the first year the U.S. government ran a budget surplus. For the last two weeks of April 1997, General

Collateral rates averaged 12.8 basis points below fed funds. This was a large enough move for traders to take notice each April thereafter.

Here's how the story goes: In anticipation of the tax revenue arriving on April 15, the Treasury increases the size of its bill auctions, both CMBs and regular bills, beginning in February and March. The large bill issues guarantee there's plenty of funding for the government through April 15. Once the tax payments arrive, the government has plenty of cash. However, when all the bills mature, there is a steep decline in the amount of collateral in the market. That leaves cash uninvested that goes straight into the Repo market. There isn't a collateral shortage every April, but it's an occasional occurrence.

Many financial institutions "clean up" their financial statements at the end of each quarter. It's called "window dressing." Naturally, window dressing is not really supposed to happen, but in reality, there are plenty of financial institutions that say, "Let's get our balance sheet down for quarter-end." That way, they appear less leveraged and avoid regulatory capital charges. It's a little like driving 35 MPH in a 25 MPH zone. Yes, it's over the limit, but no one is getting a ticket.

Window dressing doesn't distort the market as much as it did years ago due to recent changes in the Repo market. Investors (mostly MMFs) can take their cash to the Fed's RRP facility when the banks turn them away. When customers have an alternative place to invest, closing down trades with the bank on quarter-end is much easier to accept. FICC Sponsored Membership is a big help, too. It allows hedge funds and MMFs direct access to FICC, thus avoiding the bank balance sheets. It's kind of a win-win for the market. The banks get assets off of their balance sheets and customers still have access to the Repo market.

Though these developments mitigate the effects of window dressing, there are still distortions because many financial institutions still pull their securities or cash from the market on quarter-end, year-end, and sometimes even month-end.

Quarter-end affects the Repo market in a number of ways. There could either be funding pressure or soft funding. There could be more Specials or relatively few. One thing that is for sure, though, is that there's always more volatility. Here's what typically happens on quarter-end:

1. GC rates can go in any direction. If everyone is expecting overnight rates to go lower, they invariably go higher, and vice-versa. In a way, it makes sense. When the Street is long and banking on lower rates, the market often has too much collateral in the afternoon, pushing rates higher. It's just what happens.

2. Specials become more Special. On-the-runs, Cheapest-To-Deliver issues (CTDs), and off-the-runs can all trade with a larger premium. Bills especially. Many investor portfolios that were loaning their securities into the market pull those securities back. As customers close out positions, dealers have more shorts exposed. Since Primary Dealers generally have balance sheet constraints,[27] they're less willing to go to the Fed's SOMA Securities Lending facility to cover shorts. Anything that's

---

[27] When they're a subsidiary of a bank.

even a little Special before quarter-end can trade much more Special. Securities can even "disappear" from the market completely.

3.  GC/fed funds spread. The Spread between GC and fed funds widens. It could be a larger positive spread or a larger negative spread. It all depends on the state of the market.

4.  There can be rate differences between the different types of Treasury collateral. Bill collateral is the preferred collateral on quarter-end. TIPS and STRIPS are the least desirable. There can even be spreads between two and three basis points between the different types of Treasurys.

5.  Lower quality collateral is harder to finance. Spreads will widen considerably for agencies, agency MBS, corporate bonds, emerging markets bonds, CDs, commercial paper, etc. When the cash for these types of securities disappears, it's very hard to replace – especially on quarter-end!

6.  There's always a "wild card" surprise. A specific Treasury issue might trade very Special. Maybe there's a large decline in overnight rates. Maybe there's severe funding pressure. Each quarter-end usually holds a surprise.

7.  Fails Increase. Because there's less liquidity, fewer securities, and often more settlements moving around, there is more congestion in the settlement system, which increases fails.

8. Sometimes quarter-end will tell the story of what's to come. I'm not saying quarter-end has special fortune-telling properties, but the securities and cash that are pulled from the market can show where there's stress or too much leverage. Funding problems at a bank? Lack of cash in the market? Too much collateral? In the years of 2007, 2008, 2018 (year-end), quarter-end distortions foreshadowed future crisis events.

In general, preparations for quarter-end begin at least three days in advance, though most of the securities are pulled from the market on the day of quarter-end. Why would some institutions begin three days ahead of time? Because they don't want fails. If they wait until the last day, a security might fail back to them, and a fail defeats the purpose of the window dressing in the first place! Just as quarter-end begins early, it doesn't fully end until after the new quarter begins. There's often carry-over pressure in the market for a few days.

Japanese year-end (March 31) has the second largest impact on the market, but not as much as years ago. Back then, Japanese banks did not book securities financing trades as a Repo or as securities lending with other Japanese banks. Instead, they booked them as non-collateralized loans. They would deliver securities to their counterparty for free and earn a fee. Keep in mind, lending free securities does not look good on a balance sheet. Japanese banks close their non-collateralized trades for their March 31 year-end.

Overall, the worst quarter-ends are those with the most volatility, with the largest spread between GC and fed funds, with the largest number of fails, with the most Specials, or when less liquid paper is the hardest to finance. Quarter-ends get pretty bad during a market crisis, like September 2007 or March 2008. A few quarter-ends were rough during the European debt crisis in 2011 and 2012. However, the top of the list will always be September 2008. That quarter-end experienced the widest spreads and volatility in the Repo market ever!

December 31 is the most important quarter-end, since it's also year-end. It's often referred to as "The Turn" in the Repo market. Whatever distortions occur on quarter-end are multiplied for year-end. Less cash, fewer securities, more volatility, and less liquidity. Year-end has evolved considerably over the years, mostly because the Fed became more accommodating. It took many years for them to realize that the rate spikes and extreme volatility are not good for the market. Over time, the Fed got better at managing year-end. Here's a brief history of year-end:

## 1980s: The Free Market

Throughout the 1980s, there was constant funding pressure and rate volatility on year-end. The Fed kept a *laissez-faire* approach. They let market forces drive rates. Here are two highlights:

- For 1985 year-end, the effective fed funds rate came in at 13.46%, compared to a fed funds target rate of 7.75%. Granted, there were technical problems with the Fed's money wire system which compounded the year-end pressures. Fed funds traded as high as 40% that day.

- For 1986 year-end, the fed funds effective rate clocked-in at 14.35%, versus a target rate of 6.00%. Fed funds traded as high as 38% before closing at 0.0%. Imagine a 3,800 basis point swing in one day!

## 1990s: Light Intervention

By the 1990s, the Fed had learned to provide more liquidity to the market, but they still didn't telegraph what they were doing very well. Consequently, the market always worried about their commitment. I remember the big rate swings of the 1990s. Rates could move in 100 basis point increments. Just when you were long and thought rates might drop to zero, all of the bids would suddenly disappear!

## Y2K

There was considerable market anxiety as the millennium year-end approached on December 31, 1999, but it was also a big turning point for the Fed. There was mass concern that computers would shut down and turn from 12-31-1999 to 12-31-1900. As the old computer systems shut-down, the world would stop. There were rumors of utilities shutting down, cash machines not working, and even champagne shortages! Yes, that all seems pretty crazy now.

At the time, the Fed was serious about addressing year-end funding pressure. They provided massive liquidity. I mean massive. They pumped more liquidity into the market than they had ever before. They did term operations beginning in November, and the markets took notice. Fed operations were extremely successful. A change took place after the turn of the millennium. The Fed continued to properly address year-end funding pressures and the market developed more confidence in the Fed.

## 2001-2008: Faith In The Fed

From 2001 until 2008, the market finally had faith in the Fed. Each year, the Fed flooded the market with liquidity. GC often traded below fed funds, and there were no year-end rate spikes. During those years, the market experienced some of the mildest year-ends ever. Back then, I often referred to year-end as a "glorified quarter-end."

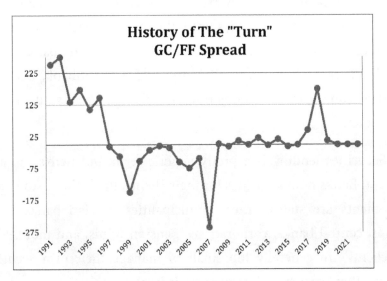

*Average GC rate versus the fed funds effective rate on year-end. Most years experienced a lot of volatility. Big highs and low lows!*

## 2009-Present: Just Right

Since the Financial Crisis, there's a lot less volatility on year-end[28] The Fed continues to be diligent and tends to err on the side of too much liquidity rather than too little. Remember, if overnight rates trade at 0% for the day, it's no big deal. If they trade 40%, it's a news headline!

---

[28] Except for year-end 2018, which we will discuss later.

# SECURITIES LENDING

The securities lending groups around the Street play an important role in the Repo market. They are the gatekeepers for the institutional portfolios that loan securities into the market. Picture all of the securities sitting in investment portfolios. The custody banks, banks like the Bank of New York, JP Morgan Chase, Citibank, and State Street, all run securities lending programs that get those securities into the market.

Securities lending is a pretty generic term, but here's the basic concept: Banks hold securities for their clients; that's the custody part. The clients are states, cities, municipalities, foreign banks, credit unions, central banks, corporations, pension funds, and more. Since the clients are generally too small to manage their own securities lending, they partner with their custody bank.

The securities lending business boils down to one concept: exchanging a security that someone needs for a different security or cash. The business is driven by the need of the dealer community to cover short positions, be it in stocks, Treasurys, agencies, corporate bonds, ADRs, or even ETFs. When a dealer is looking to cover a short position, they first check what are colloquially known as the "sec lenders." The securities lending group will pull the security out of the end-user portfolio and lend it into the Repo market.

When a securities lending group loans a security, they either receive cash or bonds in return. If they receive cash, they reinvest the cash. If they receive a bond, they earn a fee on the spread between where they loan the bond and borrow the other.

In the case of cash, they need to invest it. They need an investment that generates a sufficient return to make the business viable, yet, at the same time, without taking too much risk. The safest and easiest way to invest is in overnight Treasury repo. The problem is that there's very little profit lending a Treasury and reinvesting in a Treasury. In order to enhance returns, the securities lending groups take some risk. It's not necessarily a lot of risk, but increasing returns involves increasing risk. It can be either interest rate risk, credit risk, or liquidity risk. Technically a combination of all three is possible, too, but that's pretty dangerous.

The yield curve is upward sloping most of the time, so investing for a longer period of time generally generates a higher yield. Let's say the overnight rate is 2.00%, the one-month rate is 2.05%, and the three-month rate is at 2.15%. Instead of reinvesting cash overnight, there's an extra 15 basis points for investing for three months. Since the end-investor clients usually hold their bonds to maturity, there's only a small chance they will sell a bond during that three-month period. On top of that, the securities lending groups run multi-billion dollar portfolios, so they can ladder their investments. They can invest a percentage of the cash for a year, some for six months, some for three months, some for one month, and the rest for overnight. Of course, the amount of interest rate risk that they take is a business decision.

The next form of risk is credit risk. That's investing in securities that are not considered risk-free. Theoretically, if there's credit risk, there's a chance the issuer could default. The default risk might be very small, but it still exists. These are investments like agency discount notes, bank CDs, and commercial paper. They have higher yields than U.S. Treasurys, but there's a risk that goes along with them. An investor might look at it this way: What's the chance a single-A rated bank will default in a week? Or a month? Or three-months?[29] Very small.

The third form of risk, liquidity risk, is often overlooked because investors usually don't know they have it. It's the type of risk that's the worst-case scenario in a market panic or crisis. If there's any sign of trouble, these securities are hard to sell. There's no liquidity. No market. All of the bids disappear, and no one wants the securities. The owner might be stuck with the securities until maturity or until the crisis is over. Think of CDOs during the Financial Crisis or bank CDs during the Liquidity Crisis of August 2007. The securities lending groups generally don't buy investments with liquidity risk. Or, if they once did, they no longer do. Those groups are gone.[30]

There's a second form of reinvestment: swapping one bond for another. Historically, this was the original securities lending transaction. Years ago, it was the only way securities dealers covered their shorts. They went to a securities lending group, borrowed a bond, and gave them another bond in return. These transactions were called bonds-borrowed bonds-loaned. Even as recently as 25 years

---

[29] The risk is close to zero, but there's always *some* risk. As we saw during the Liquidity Crisis of August 2007 and the Financial Crisis of September 2008, if investors perceive any chance of default, they stop buying bank CDs.
[30] AIG Securities Lending.

ago, some clients would still only book bonds borrowed/bonds loaned trades. These transactions are a little different now. The securities lending group still loans the securities, but now they receive bonds in a Tri-Party account. The counterparty deposits agencies, municipal bonds, corporate bonds, MBSs, etc. in the Tri-Party account to cover the reinvestment side of the transaction.

Here are some examples of reinvestment collateral, the incremental return over Treasurys, and the haircuts. Naturally, the further you go down the credit curve, the spreads and the haircuts increase. The more credit risk and/or price volatility, the larger the spread and haircut.

- <u>Treasurys or Cash</u> – This is the safest form of reinvestment because it's essentially risk-free, but there's little return. Haircuts can be anywhere from a 0.0% to 2%.

- <u>Agencies and Agency MBSs</u> – Swapping Treasurys for agencies and agency MBSs will increase returns by a few basis points, even though they're both AAA-rated. Generally a 2% haircut.

- <u>Agency CMOs, IOs, POs</u> – Here's where returns really start to increase. Though agency CMOs are AAA-rated, there's a significant amount of price volatility and liquidity risk. It's the pricing volatility of the underlying asset that accounts for the increased return. Spreads can be 15 to 25 basis points above Treasurys. Haircuts can be between 5% and 10%.

- <u>High-Grade Corporate Bonds and Municipal Bonds</u> – These products have some credit risk and some price volatility. The incremental returns can range from 15 to 50 basis points above Treasurys. Haircuts are between 5% and 10%.

- <u>Private Label MBSs, High-Yield Corporates, Emerging Markets Debt, Low-Rated Sovereign Debt</u> - Once securities are below investment grade or are extremely price volatile, there's probably no bid for them during a panic or crisis. In these cases, the credit of the Repo counterparty is the most important part of the trade. As a rule of thumb, when the quality of the collateral is low, the market looks to the credit of the counterparty. Returns on these products can range from 50 basis points to hundreds of basis points above Treasurys. Haircuts can range from 10% to 50%.

## SOMA Securities Lending

Custody banks are not the only ones running a securities lending program. As it turns out, the Federal Reserve has one too. Their purpose isn't to make money, but instead to provide the market with liquidity. The goal is to help ease securities shortages. Just like the Standing Repo Facility (SRF) and Reverse-Repo Program (RRP) are tools to provide liquidity to the market, the Securities Lending Program is a tool to provide securities.

The Fed had a small securities lending program for ages, but it was very limited. The original program allowed Primary Dealers to borrow up to $50 million of any Treasury bill and $10 million of any coupon. Yes, that's pretty laughable today, but given the size of the

Treasury market back then, the sizes were appropriate. By the mid-1990s, however, the program clearly had no impact relieving securities shortages. In April 1997, the PSA (Public Securities Association) made a recommendation to the Fed to expand the Securities Lending Program. The new program was officially proposed in June 1998, approved by the FOMC in February 1999, and the first trade occurred in April 1999.

The new program was officially called the SOMA Securities Lending Program. The Fed pledged to make the securities it owned in its SOMA investment portfolio available to Primary Dealers at a spread of 150 basis points below General Collateral. Each Primary Dealer was allowed to borrow up to $100 million of any Treasury issue, and, during times of severe shortages, the Fed pledged to make more available. The Fed created a good mechanism to automatically put supply into the market when there was a shortage. But the Fed didn't launch the program because they foresaw the severe security shortages that occurred in 2001, 2003, 2007, and 2008. At the time, they were focused on dealer-orchestrated short squeezes.

Here's how the program works: The Federal Reserve Bank of New York holds an auction each day at 12:00 PM. Any Primary Dealer can bid for the securities in the SOMA portfolio with a minimum bid that changes over time. Each dealer is subject to a counterparty limit. If the dealer wins an allotment of a security, they give the Fed General Collateral in exchange. It's the equivalent of a bonds borrowed/bonds loaned transaction. The Primary Dealer effectively swaps a security that they don't need for a security they do need.

The program continued to change over the years. In 1999, the Fed's Securities Lending Program started as a facility to provide temporary relief from unexpected supply shortages. It was always a competitive auction conducted at noon and the securities were always collateralized with U.S. Treasurys. Originally, the Fed only loaned up to 45% of each Treasury issue, dealers were limited to borrowing $100 million of any one issue, and total borrowing was capped at $500 million. The 150 basis point fee was a significantly large enough spread to make sure the Fed's securities only entered the market when there was a significant shortage.

Over the years, the Fed adjusted the minimum spread to reflect changing conditions. The long-held 150 basis point spread was cut to 100 basis points after September 11, 2001, then it was further cut to 75 basis points at the end of the easing cycle in June 2003 with the 3.625% 5/13 shortage. The spread was cut again during the Liquidity Crisis of August 2007, the first installment of the Financial Crisis. The Fed dramatically cut the spread in October 2008 following the collapse of Lehman Brothers to only 1 basis point. At the time, they wanted to pump as much liquidity into the market as possible. The chart below shows the announcement dates of changes in the securities lending spread.

## Spread History

| Date | Basis Point Spread |
|------|--------------------|
| September 7, 1999 | 150 |
| October 18, 2001 | 100 |
| June 25, 2003 | 75 |
| July 1, 2004 | 100 |
| August 21, 2007 | 50 |
| October 27, 2008 | 10 |

| December 18, 2008 | 1 |
|---|---|
| April 7, 2009 | 5 |

Since April 2009, the minimum spread was set at 5 basis points. Under the current rules, the Fed will loan up to 90% of the securities in their portfolio, and no dealer can take more than 25% of any issue. Each dealer is limited to a total borrowing of $5 billion. That's a pretty far cry from the original $100 million limit!

Overall, the size of the Treasury market is much larger and there are a lot more securities in the SOMA portfolio these days, courtesy of the many years of QE programs. The Fed's Securities Lending Program is supposed to provide liquidity and promote the smooth functioning of the Treasury market. Originally, with a 150 basis point spread, it was designed to be punitive and only add securities when there was a severe shortage.

Right now, the market uses the program more like the other securities lending groups, covering their shorts and financing their General Collateral at a cheap spread.

# VOLATILITY AND VELOCITY

The term volatility is often associated with risk. It's true, volatile securities are inherently riskier than less volatile securities. A volatile stock or bond implies large price swings, and that's not different in the Repo market. Pound for pound, the Repo market is one of the most volatile markets around. In a way, the volatility of the Repo market makes it more interesting.

What causes volatility? Another question might be: Why does the market go up or down? The age-old snarky answer is "more buyers than sellers" or "more sellers than buyers." That's true, but markets don't just move in one direction. They move up and down all day long. That's volatility.

One cause of market volatility is because not everyone wants to buy or sell at the exact same time. Or at the exact same price. At 9:00 AM, there might be a lot of buyers and few sellers. Between 10:00 AM and 11:00 AM, there might be a lot of sellers, but few buyers. During the entire period of time between 9:00 AM and 11:00 AM, the price increased from 9:00 AM to 10:00 AM, and then sold-off. The price might end up the same at 11:00 AM as it started at 9:00 AM, but there was a lot of movement in between. Markets move up and down all day long, and that's volatility.

There are many fundamental factors that contribute to Repo market volatility. There's clearly more volatility on quarter-end and year-end. But why? That's easy: window dressing. Remember the part about securities and cash being removed from the market? It creates dislocation and increases volatility.

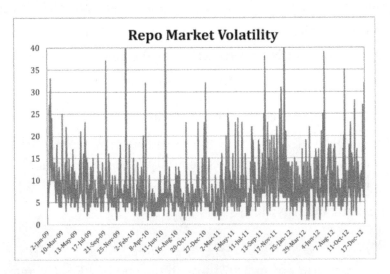

*Post-Financial Crisis Repo Market Volatility[31] Between 2009 and 2012*
*GC averaged an 8.7 basis point trading range each day*

Daylight Overdraft Charges (DOD) also contribute to Repo market volatility. Each morning, there's a rush to finance long positions between when the Repo market opens at 7:00 AM and when the Fedwire opens at 8:30 AM. Once securities are delivered to your box, there's a DOD charge ticking away minute by minute. Given the high DOD charges at the clearing banks, it's uneconomical to hold collateral throughout the day. There's a strong incentive to sell positions before they begin to arrive at 8:30 AM.

The rush to sell collateral creates a problem for West Coast cash investors. Due to the time difference, they don't begin to invest their

---

[31] I use a simple volatility measure for Repo market volatility: the high rate for the day minus the low rate. For example, when I calculate the volatility for General Collateral, I use the highest rate General Collateral traded for on a particular day minus the lowest rate it traded.

cash until the middle of the Repo trading day. If a bank already sold their collateral by 8:30 AM, they need to go back into the market to get securities to fill West Coast clients' cash positions. It's a perfect example of market timing issues. Banks sell collateral in the morning to avoid DOD charges, but buy it back in the afternoon. That's one reason why Repo rates tend to decline as the day goes on. Cash keeps coming into the market, and there's less and less collateral left.

Then, throw in all of the supply-and-demand effects and the calendar dates. They all add to volatility. Yes, GSE cash, quarter-end, and year-end all increase market volatility. Treasury issuance? Check. Fed tightenings and eases? Of course! Securities shortages? Why not! A good panic or crisis? That's a no-brainer!

Repo market volatility peaked during the Financial Crisis. For a full two year period from 2007 through the end of 2008, GC rates had a daily trading range averaging 31.4 basis points. It's incredible how many times overnight rates moved in excess of 200 basis points back then. Good times!

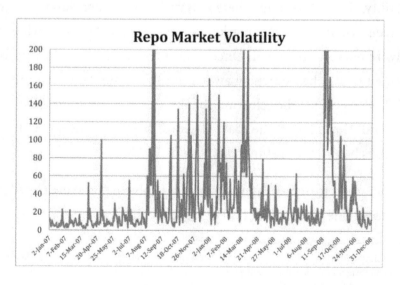

There was also significant Repo market volatility at the beginning of the COVID crisis. It almost felt like the glory days of the Repo market were back! There were incredibly large overnight rate swings in March 2020. However, once the Fed cut overnight rates to zero and expanded the QE buying, volatility collapsed. For a full two-year period from April 2020 to April 2022, the average daily trading range was only 6.4 basis points.

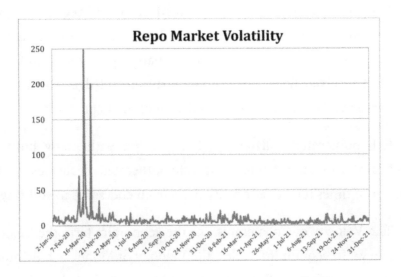

# The Velocity of Collateral (VofC)

What's the size of the Repo market? That all depends on how you measure it. There's no central exchange or registry of Repo transactions. Yes, there is a central clearing counterparty – FICC – but a large percentage of Repo trades are private. The Fed reports the size of Primary Dealer Repo positions weekly,[32] so much of the inter-dealer trades are measurable, but how do you measure the dealer-to-

---

[32] Available on the Fed's website. It's a start, but somewhat limited. FICC data is a better gauge, since it encompasses more counterparties in the market.

customer transactions? Wait until the end of the year and look at each bank's year-end financial statement?

In general, the U.S. Repo market is estimated to be $6 trillion of Reverse-Repo and $5.6 trillion of Repo. However, the true size of the market gets obscured by one thing: the Velocity of Collateral (VofC). What?

Rehypothecation is a bad word around regulatory and government circles for some reason. It occurs when an asset is borrowed and re-pledged to another party. It's when banks use collateral received from one counterparty and pledge it to another counterparty. Basically, it's the foundation of the Repo market!

Rehypothecated collateral is like a chain with many links. In practical terms, the amount of rehypothecated securities is the number of times it takes a security to go from end-seller to end-buyer.

The Velocity of Collateral is like the economics term the Velocity of Money.[33] In economics circles, the Velocity of Money is how much, on average, a single dollar is re-used over a period of time. It's how fast a currency passes from one holder to another. Think of the same principle, except in the Repo market.

The VofC is how much, on average, a security turns over before it gets from end-seller to end-buyer. The Repo market has a high velocity because there are many players making markets, speculating on interest rates, and borrowing and lending securities. In the diagram below, $100 million of securities is loaned from a leveraged portfolio to Bank A, then to Bank B, then to Bank C before it reaches

---

[33] Don't leave me! I promise this will be painless.

its final destination, the cash provider. Every time the security is re-used (rehypothecated), assets and liabilities are created by the velocity of the collateral.

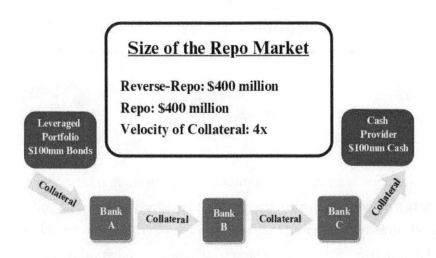

In the end, the $100 million of securities was rehypothecated three times before it reached its final destination. The total amount of assets in this Repo chain is $400 million, based on an initial $100 million; the Velocity of Collateral with three counterparties standing in the middle intermediating is four.

Here's another scenario in the diagram below, but this time there's only one bank doing the intermediation. The $100 million of securities is rehypothecated only once before it reaches the end-buyer. There's one market-maker (Bank B) and the Velocity of Collateral is two. The amount of assets in this Repo chain is $200 million. In this series of Repo transactions, it took half as many rehypothecations to get the securities from end-seller to end-buyer. The size of the Repo market in this chain just decreased by half.

Size of the Repo Market
Reverse-Repo: $200 million
Repo: $200 million
Velocity of Collateral: 2x

Leveraged Portfolio $100mm Bonds → Collateral → Bank B → Collateral → Cash Provider $100mm Cash

Now, below is an extreme example. There are no market-makers and there's no bank intermediation in this Repo transaction. The collateral goes directly from end-seller to end-buyer. Perhaps we can call it the "natural size of the Repo market." There's no rehypothecation, and the Velocity of Collateral is one. There's $100 million of securities, $100 million in Reverse-Repo, and $100 million in Repo transactions. If collateral rehypothecation were eliminated, this is what the market would look like. However, it's not realistic that a cash investor such as a money market fund would trade directly with a hedge fund.

## Size of the Repo Market

Reverse-Repo: $100 million

Repo: $100 million

Velocity of Collateral: 1x

| Leveraged Portfolio $100mm Bonds | Collateral → | Cash Provider $100mm Cash |
| --- | --- | --- |

Let's say the overall size of the U.S. Repo market is $11.6 trillion. As a mathematical formula, the true size of the Repo market equals the gross size of the repo market divided by the Velocity of Collateral. I've seen the Velocity of Collateral of the U.S. Repo market estimated to be between 2.4 and 3. That means, on average, the amount of times collateral goes from end-seller to end-buyer is between 2.4 times and 3 times. It also means there are, on average, between about 1.5 and 2 banks standing in between the end-sellers and end-buyers on each transaction. That appears about right.

Regulatory capital costs, securities haircuts, balance sheet restrictions, and a market crisis will all slow down the velocity. Wider Repo bid/offer spreads, booming markets, more Repo market-making, and larger bank balance sheets increases the velocity. Naturally, both the size of the Repo market and the amount of collateral available in the Repo market changes regularly. Therefore, the size of the Repo market also increases or decreases with more or less collateral velocity.

Rehypothecation is not risky in large Repo markets like U.S. Treasurys, but it becomes a potential problem in small securities markets. Think of small corporate or municipal bond issues. What happens if one of the counterparties defaults? Think of it like a break in the collateral chain. When one party defaults, the two counterparties on either side must liquidate their securities. One counterparty sells the collateral and the other one buys the collateral, but not necessarily to each other. For highly liquid and large issue securities, like U.S. Treasurys, this is easy. Problems arise when the collateral is non-fungible, a private-label issuer, or a small issue size. In these cases, when the entity in the middle goes bust, it's hard for the original seller to get back their securities.

The Velocity of Collateral (rehypothecation) creates assets and liabilities in the financial system, but it doesn't make the system any riskier. From a policy perspective, eliminating rehypothecation is the same as eliminating intermediation in the Repo market. It would force the Repo market to transactions between end-sellers and end-buyers. In fact, some collateral velocity is actually good for the financial system. It's not good to have a closed loop where end-sellers only trade with end-buyers, or when end-sellers and end-buyers are beholden to just one bank.

# Short Selling

*"He who sells what isn't his'n, must buy it back or go to prison."*

- DANIEL DREW

Short selling is a big part of the Repo market. In fact, if you broke down the Repo market into two distinct parts, there's General Collateral and Specials. The Specials market is all about shorts, and if you know about shorts, you understand a big part of the Repo market.

We've heard the definition of a short-sale many times before. It's the sale of an asset that the seller doesn't own with the expectation of buying it back in the future at a lower price. In some markets, like futures and options, the seller only needs a buyer to affect a short-sale. In the bond market, short-selling is a little more complicated because the seller must deliver a security. How do you deliver a security that you don't own? You borrow it. The seller borrows the security from a third party in order to make the delivery. And that's where the Repo market comes in!

To some, short-sellers are financial demons, betting against everyone's prosperity, like the creepy guy at the end of the craps table who bets the Don't Pass Line. To others, short-selling keeps securities prices from over-inflating. Many in the financial markets call the short-sellers financial detectives. They often sniff out fraud, corruption, and asset mis-pricing. In the Repo market, short-selling is just a part of our raison d'être.

The resentment toward short-selling extends back almost as long as there have been markets. The first known law banning short-selling appeared in Holland on February 24, 1610. The government called it "trading the wind" – which meant selling shares that you didn't own. The law was enacted when the East India Company complained that short-sellers were driving down the price of their stock. Sound familiar? When the SEC was created in 1933, one of the first items on the agenda was to enact short-selling regulation.

Sentiment against short-selling usually arises after price declines. Rather than blaming buyers for driving prices up, they blame short-sellers for driving prices lower! Here's an excerpt from Congressional testimony on the 1929 stock market crash:[34]

*Frank Oliver (New York Congressman): When the stocks collapsed from the high to the low, the public started to blame "the shorts" for that. Is that not a fact?*

*Richard Whitney (New York Stock Exchange President): I think from hindside point of view, they blamed "the shorts."*

*F.O.: They blamed the "shorts," whereas, as a matter of fact, if the prices were inflated, they should have blamed the "longs" for having inflated them?*

*R.W.: And themselves.*

*F.O.: But instead of being logical about it, and blaming those who inflated prices, they blamed those who might have deflated them had they the power at that time—that is, the "shorts?"*

---

[34] February 24, 1932 House Judiciary Committee Hearings on Short Selling. (Source: WSJ "Putting The Blame On The 'Longs'"; Dennis K. Berman, 8/1/2008, page C3.)

*R.W.: Yes.*

A 1963 SEC study concluded that short-selling rules did not prevent the harmful effects they were targeting. Another SEC study[35] stated that short-selling increases pricing efficiency and concluded that "efficient markets require that prices fully reflect all buy and sell interest." Another study concluded that markets with short-selling bans have relatively higher prices, but are subject to sharper downturns. That makes a lot of sense.

Most recently, in July 2008, just *before* the Financial Crisis, the SEC banned short-selling in the shares of 17 American banks, including Fannie Mae and Freddie Mac. A 2008 Credit Suisse study found that the ban made stock prices less efficient and trading in those stocks more expensive for investors. They found that bid/offer spreads doubled, on average, during the ban.

Time and time again, short-selling bans do more harm than good. The studies are pretty clear: limiting short-selling does not promote efficient markets. Regulation is counter-productive and results in less liquidity, greater volatility, and wider bid/offer spreads.

In that sense, it can be argued that short-selling increases market liquidity. That's right! Suppose someone wants to buy a bond but there are no actual owners looking to sell. Market-makers fill the gap between the time when customers are buying and when customers are selling. If a market-maker wasn't willing to sell, securities prices would be much more volatile. You could even say short-selling reduces the risk that someone buys an overpriced security! Short-selling quite

---

[35] Release No. 34-42037

possibly reduces the risk of market crashes, adding an element of pessimism to prices.

One thing is for sure: Short-selling is a big business on Wall Street. Prime brokerage, securities lending, Repo, and stock loan desks are all built around borrowing and lending securities. Clearly, short-selling employs a lot of traders and salespeople!

There are a number of reasons why someone short-sells a security. The first and most obvious is that it enables them to profit from a price decline. Markets go up and markets go down, so participants must be able to benefit from the market moving in either direction. Second, short-sellers are often hedging. They're long a security and are worried about the market declining. In order to reduce risk, they short-sell another security as a hedge. Third, arbitrage. As markets move, securities' prices become mis-aligned. That creates opportunities to buy securities that are relatively cheap and sell securities that are relatively rich. Though many in the public resent this type of speculation, it keeps the markets efficient and provides liquidity.

The derivatives market generates a substantial number of short positions in the Treasury market. Traders short Treasurys against OIS swaps and Eurodollar futures. When a trader is long a Treasury and short a futures contract, it's called being "long basis." Being short Treasurys against long futures is "short basis." Basis is a term to denote the spread between the yields in different interest rate markets.

*The U.S. Treasury yield curve versus the OIS swaps curve on 1/31/2022.*
*Close to the end of the Fed's QE program, the 2 year though 4 year sectors of*
*the Treasury curve were trading below the swaps curve by about 14 bps. The*
*Fed had inverted the Treasury curve relative to other interest rate curves.*
*Historically, Treasurys trade above the swaps curve.*

Agency and corporate bond hedging generates a lot of short positions. The term "agency" refers to the bonds issued by Fannie Mae, Freddie Mac, and Ginnie Mae, but not necessarily the mortgage-backed securities (MBS). Securities dealers, banks, hedge funds, and private investment funds all carry positions in these securities that are often hedged. Naturally, the best hedge for an agency or corporate bond is another agency or corporate bond. Even hedging a Fannie Mae with a Freddie Mac or Federal Home Loan Bank is a better hedge than with a Treasury.

First and foremost, there's less basis risk - the risk that yield spreads between the two markets diverge. Yes, agencies and corporates can be borrowed and loaned in the Repo market, just like Treasurys. There's even an active Specials market to cover shorts. However, agency and corporate bonds are difficult to borrow, though not impossible. The Repo market for these securities is much less liquid, issue sizes are small, they're difficult to find, and generally there's little available to borrow. Their Repo rates reflect the scarcity factor which means, as a general rule, there's a large premium to borrow them. Given the large issue sizes, liquidity, transparency, and efficiency of the Treasury Repo market, it's much more economical to hedge with Treasurys. On top of that, since most agencies and corporates are priced off of Treasurys, it makes sense to hedge with the same Treasury issue.

Mortgage-backed securities are also hedged with Treasurys, though the hedging is slightly more complex. The problem begins with the actual security itself. A mortgage-backed pass-through security is literally a giant pool of home mortgage loans, thousands of small loans packaged together into a security and issued by Fannie Mae, Freddie Mac, or Ginnie Mae.

MBSs are difficult to hedge because their duration changes as the market moves. That's because homeowners can prepay mortgage loans at any time. When homeowners move, refinance, or sell their house, they pay off their loans, and those prepayments are paid directly to the MBS bondholders. When interest rates decline, homeowners repay their mortgage loans faster. When interest rates rise, prepayments slow down and people stay in their homes longer. And therein lies the problem.

When interest rates decline, MBS bondholders get more of their original investment back sooner than expected. When interest rates rise, the securities are outstanding for a longer period of time. It's what's called negative convexity. When interest rates fall, MBSs become shorter-term securities. When interest rates rise, they become longer-term securities.[36]

During large bond market selloffs, massive short positions can accumulate in the 10 year sector of the bond market. MBS traders often struggle to hedge their positions when the market is declining fast. Think of June 2003, when the bond market sold-off and MBS traders sold massive amounts of the Treasury 10 Year Note (3.625% 5/13).

Short selling is also a big part of the Repo market. Repo traders actively speculate on interest rates by borrowing and lending securities in the term Repo markets. A Repo trader might loan a Treasury to another counterparty for a week, a month, three months, or even a year. They might speculate that overnight Repo rates will trade higher or lower in the upcoming days or weeks. At the same time, a customer might have a short position in a Treasury, and they want to cover with a term Repo.

When a Repo trader is long or short a term trade, they might take the term risk themselves, or they might go into the inter-dealer broker market to cover back their trade. There are many ways to speculate on interest rates in the Repo market. A Repo trader might loan a security to the customer for one month and borrow it back for two weeks, speculating that overnight rates will be higher during the last two weeks of the month. A Repo trader might be outright long or outright short in the term markets. The combinations are endless.

---

[36] Often called negative convexity.

It's important to note that short-selling in the Repo market is a little different than selling a security outright. In the Repo market, one party is loaning a security to another party, be it for overnight or for a year. A term Repo trade has a set maturity date. Long and short positions in the Repo market have a set expiration date as opposed to an outright short, which must be bought back at some point.

# SPECIALS THEORY

What determines the yield of a Treasury security? The market just doesn't make it up. It must be based on something fundamental. Theoretically, the yield on a Treasury should be the sum of its overnight Repo rates until it matures. If the market expects overnight interest rates to trade at 2.00% for the next two years, then the yield on the Treasury 2 Year Note should be 2.00%.

Consequently, if the market expects overnight rates to trade at 1.00% for this year and then at 3.00% for next year, the yield on the 2 Year Note should still be 2.00%. 1.00% for the first year and 3.00% for the second-year averages out to 2.00%. Except for short-term buying and selling imbalances, Treasury yields are based on the expected path of interest rates.

That's very basic and it's much more accurate in the short-end of the yield curve than in the long-end. However, there's another factor involved. There's a theory that Treasury yields can be broken down into two components: the expected future path of overnight interest rates and the "term premium." What's that?

Technically, the term premium is extra yield the investor receives for holding longer-term securities. The return is not just the average of the overnight rates, but a little extra yield just for holding the security for a longer period of time. Let's say you have the 2 Year Note yield from two years ago and you have the series of overnight rates for that security for the past two years. You have the market's expectation of overnight interest rates from two years ago – the yield on the 2 Year Note back then – and actual overnight rates for the past two years. It's unlikely the two interest rates will match. In fact, the expected yield is often priced higher than the actual rates. The difference between the expected rate and the actual rates is called the term premium,[37] in academic speak.

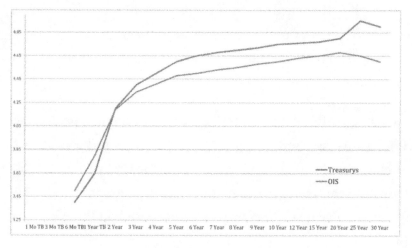

*If we assume overnight Repo rates will trade close to fed funds in May 2022, the market priced a negative term premium for securities with less than two years to maturity and a positive term premium for securities with greater than two years to maturity.*

*         *         *

In the Repo market, there's a big emphasis on break-evens and implied forward rates. Overnight Repo rates change each day as the overall market ebbs and flows, and term Repo rates are built on the expectation of overnight rates for a period of time. Just like in the

---

[37] Some might call this component a "fudge factor." Naturally, the term premium is more evident in longer-term rates because the market can price shorter-term securities more accurately.

Treasury market, if the term Repo rate[38] is 2.00% for a week, the market expects overnight rates to average 2.00% for the next week. It could mean the market expects overnight rates to trade at 2.00% every day. It could also mean the market expects overnight rates to trade at 2.10% for one day, 2.00% for five days, and 1.90% for one day. In the end, it's the same average, just more volatility in the second scenario.

That leads us to the big question. Is there a term premium in the Repo market? Believe me, there is not. I've tried to find biases in term rates for years and years. I can honestly say there are no unexplained biases in term Repo rates. Bottom line, there's no evidence of a term premium. However, there are factors that create distortions in term Repo rates:

1. <u>Cost of Balance Sheet.</u> Ever since Dodd-Frank, Basel II, and Basel III were born, assets on a bank's balance sheet have a cost on quarter-end, year-end, and sometimes even month-end. Repo capital charges and leverage ratios make it more expensive to carry Repo trades over a statement period.

2. <u>Transaction Costs.</u> There are costs associated with booking a Repo trade: Ticket costs, brokerage, credit risk, operational risk, and sales commissions, just to name a few.

3. <u>Minimum Spread.</u> If there's a cost for having a trade on the balance sheet and balance sheets have limitations, Repo desks must achieve a minimum return to justify

---

[38] I wouldn't be a good financial author without a formula in my book: $Rt = \sum Ro/n$. The Repo term rate equals the summation of the overnight Repo rates.

carrying a trade. The inter-dealer market might have a tight bid/offer spread, but a Repo desk still needs to make a minimum spread. "After all, we are not Communists."[39]

Taking these factors into consideration, it doesn't mean there are set biases, just factors that distort rates.

## The Theory of Supply

U.S. Treasury securities are created by the U.S. Treasury. The Treasury issues the new securities and the Fed auctions them to the public. The buyers of Treasurys come in many varieties. There are retail accounts, like mom and pop, domestic and foreign banks, foreign central banks, money market funds, Primary Dealers, hedge funds, states and municipalities, pension funds, and insurance companies, just to name a few. These days, the Federal Reserve is the largest owner of Treasurys.

The securities owned by leveraged investors, like the Primary Dealers and hedge funds, are loaned into the Repo market each day. You might say they're always "floating around" the market. These investors must lend their securities because they're leveraged; they need to borrow money to finance their purchases. The next set of investors are very close to the market. They are actively following the Repo market and are looking for opportunities. These are sophisticated investors who loan their securities into the market to earn incremental income. The next set of investors is a little more removed from the market. They partner with custody banks for securities lending. When an issue they own trades Special, their custody bank loans the security into the market.

---

[39] *The Godfather*, 1972.

Digging down a little deeper, the next kind of investor is much more removed from the market. They probably need a salesperson from a big bank to inform them that one of their securities is Special. Maybe the investor is located in Europe or Asia and just doesn't follow the market very closely. Their costs are higher; maybe they need a 25 basis point spread to loan their securities into the market.

The last kind of investor never loans their securities into the market. Maybe their positions are too small. Maybe they don't know what Repo is. Maybe they just don't care. These securities are gone from the market. Permanently gone.

At the bottom of the supply pyramid are securities that are all loaned into the market each day. These are the securities owned by the Primary Dealers, Prime Brokerage groups, and hedge funds. At the top are securities that are never loaned into the market. The rest are somewhere in between and need a certain spread to loan their securities.

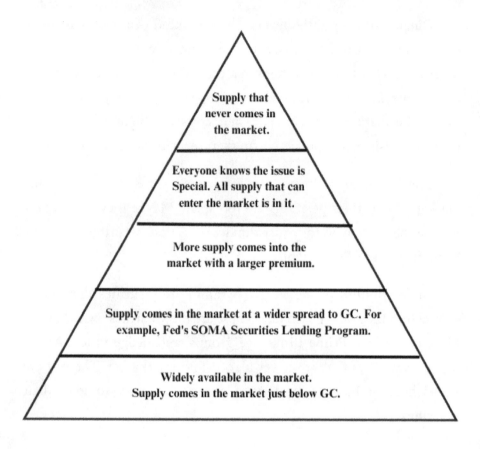

The supply pyramid changes under different market conditions. Here's a theoretical pyramid during a Flight-To-Quality [below]. Investors are worried about market risk, so they pull their securities from the market.

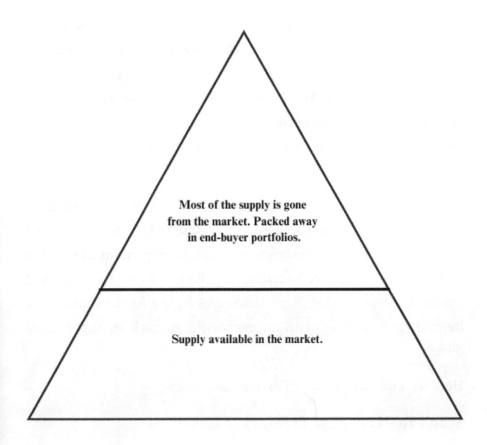

Most of the supply is gone
from the market. Packed away
in end-buyer portfolios.

Supply available in the market.

## The Theory of Demand

In the Repo market, demand creates supply. That's right. Who would have thought? Once a security is issued by the Treasury, the market can actually create more of it. New supply[40] is created when someone short-sells a security.

Let's take a look at a short-sale transaction. A hedge fund short-sells $100 million of a Treasury to a bank. The hedge fund is short the

---

[40] Technically, getting into the weeds further, perhaps it's more accurate to say short-selling creates more long positions. But the concept is still the same.

issue and the bank is long. The hedge fund now represents the demand for the security and must borrow it from a third party in order to deliver to the buyer. The bank who owns the security loans it into the Repo market. Maybe they loan it back to the hedge fund or maybe they loan it to someone else. Either way, there's more supply in the market. However, there's no net increase in supply. One entity has a new long position and one has a new short position.

The same holds true in the Repo market for Repo transactions. When a security is borrowed and loaned, it adds to the supply and demand in the market. However, because it's a Repo transaction, it's a little different. It's more like shuffling the longs and shorts around within the Repo market. Repo short-sales have a fixed maturity date (term Repo), so the securities eventually go back to the original owner.

Here are some scenarios to illustrate short sales:

## Scenario #1: A New Treasury is Issued

The Treasury issues $1 billion of a new security. In this scenario, there are no shorts. There's $1 billion of the security available in the market. The securities might be owned by end-user portfolios or leveraged investors, but who owns them doesn't matter. The amount of supply in the marketplace at the end of the day is $1 billion.

|  | Supply ($ Millions) | Demand ($ Millions) |
|---|---|---|
| Amount Issued | $1,000 | $0 |
|  | $1,000 | $0 |

## Scenario #2: One Short-Seller

A short seller enters the market and sells $100 million to another party. When the buyer purchases $100 million, it means there are now $1.1 billion worth of long positions. There are also $100 million in short positions. The net amount of supply is the same: $1 billion, the amount originally issued.

|  | Supply | Demand |
|---|---|---|
|  | ($ Millions) | ($ Millions) |
| Amount Issued | $1,000 | |
| New Buyer | $100 | |
| Short Seller | | $100 |
|  | _____ | _____ |
|  | $1,100 | $100 |

## Scenario #3: Many Short-Sellers

Starting with the same original issue of $1 billion, but now there are $2 billion in short positions. Yes, there are more shorts than the amount originally issued. There's $3 billion in long positions, though the net is still $1 billion. The shorts must cover $2 billion worth of short positions in the Repo market each day. As long as there are investors with $2 billion[41] worth of long positions to loan, there are no fails.

---

[41] Something to think about! How does $1 billion in actual issuance cover $2 billion in short positions? It's because settlement receives and deliveries can spin around the market back and forth between the original owners, the new buyers, and the short-sellers.

|  | Supply | Demand |
|---|---|---|
|  | ($ Millions) | ($ Millions) |
| Amount Issued | $1,000 |  |
| New Buyers | $2,000 |  |
| Short Sellers |  | $2,000 |
|  | ——— | ——— |
|  | $3,000 | $2,000 |

## Short-Selling Summary

- Because of short-selling, more securities can be sold to end-user portfolios than were originally issued.

- Short-selling increases both the supply and demand, but it does not increase the net number of securities.

- You can say a short-seller is selling a security *for* someone else. They sell the security and borrow it from an actual owner.

- Short-selling makes it possible for supply and demand imbalances to occur. Short-sellers must pay Special Repo rates to incentivize owners to loan their securities.

- If there isn't enough actual supply in the Repo market to cover all of the shorts, settlements fail.

- The shorts must eventually buy back their short positions. When a security is packed away in end-user portfolios, the security's price might trade at a premium in order to entice investors to sell, just like Special Repo rates are needed to get the securities into the Repo market.

## Specials Theory

On any given day, there are literally trillions of securities in the Repo market. With individual issue sizes in the tens of billions, there's a lot of supply out there to cover all of the short positions. However, from one day to the next, new shorts enter the market. Perhaps there's a market sell-off or a big market really or something related to the auction cycle, or maybe a large corporate bond issue came to market. Bottom line, there can be big supply and demand changes from day to day pushing Repo rates higher or lower.

What does it mean for a security to trade Special? The lowest Repo rate ever printed was -30.0%. That's right, negative thirty percent overnight. One counterparty paid -30.0% to borrow a security from another counterparty. As it turns out, the borrower needed a cheapest-to-deliver (CTD) Treasury issue to deliver to the futures exchange. For futures deliveries, they absolutely positively need to be delivered, otherwise the fine from the exchange is even more expensive! The trade occurred when we were holding the securities in our box for days in anticipation of the CTD trading Special. And it did!

If there are no shorts in an issue, it trades as General Collateral because no one needs to borrow it. Once someone has a short, they must pay a premium in order to borrow the security. A Special is a security that trades with a premium,[42] a rate that's somewhere below General Collateral.

The next logical question is: What determines the premium? If General Collateral is 2.00% and a security trades five basis points below General Collateral, it means there are some shorts, but not a lot. If the same security trades 100 basis points below General Collateral, there are a lot of shorts. What makes it trade five basis points below versus 100 basis points below? Naturally, more shorts mean lower rates because there's more demand. Still, what explains a Repo rate of 1.95% versus 1.00%? Here are some theories:

## Chance of A Fail Theory

One theory is that the Repo rate for a Special is a function of the percentage chance of a fail. That is, the premium below General Collateral is approximately the probability the Repo rate will drop down to the fail charge rate. Let's say General Collateral is at 2.00% and the fail charge rate is -1.00%.[43] If the Repo rate for a specific Treasury issue trades at 1.75%, it's trading 25 basis points below General Collateral. That 25 basis premium implies an 8.3% chance of a fail.[44] Repo traders are willing to pay a premium of 25 basis points to ensure they cover their shorts so rates don't drop to the fail charge rate. In this same scenario, suppose a Treasury security is actually failing and the market prices the overnight rate at -1.00%. That means the market believes there's a 100% chance the issue will fail. When Repo rates get very Special, there's a lot of validity to this theory.

---

[42] Way back in the early days, I believe the official definition of a Special was 50 basis points below General Collateral.

[43] The fail charge is 300 basis points below the bottom of the fed funds target range, though the charge is always at least 100 basis points.

[44] 8.3% = 25 basis points/300 basis points.

# The Theory of Supply Plateaus

Different kinds of investors make their securities available at different rates. Repo rates might be determined by how much supply is available at a certain level of demand. Let me explain. Let's say there are $3 billion in long positions floating around the market from the Primary Dealers, Prime Brokerage groups, and hedge funds. These securities are available to cover shorts at two to three basis points below General Collateral. As long as the short-base is less than $3 billion, securities are readily available to cover shorts at two to three basis points below GC.

Now, let's say the securities lending groups and the Fed have another $3 billion more securities available at five basis points below General Collateral. Here, as long as the short-base is between $3 billion and $6 billion, the issue trades at five basis points below GC.

As shorts continue to grow, the market needs to pull in more securities from more investor portfolios. Those portfolios require a larger and larger premium to loan their securities into the market. That pushes Repo rates lower and lower as short position grow. Let's say there is $12 billion in short positions in the market. The shorts suck up all of the securities from the Primary Dealers, Prime Brokerage groups, securities lending groups, Federal Reserve, and the owners who are slightly removed from the market. Because of the $12 billion in short-demand, it requires Repo rates at least 100 basis points below General Collateral to attract enough securities from owners.

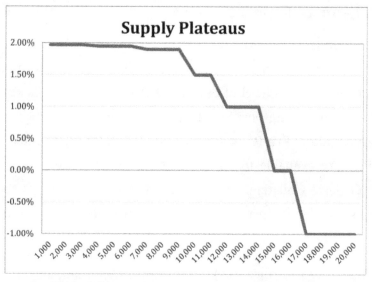

*The graph illustrates the Repo rate versus the number of short positions (in millions). Once the short-base reaches $17 billion, there is not enough supply to cover all of the shorts and the issue fails.*

## Short Covering Premium Theory

When there are large short positions, the market is willing to pay a larger premium to cover some of their shorts in order to reduce the size of their short positions. However, as the day goes on and more shorts get covered, Repo rates move higher because the number of shorts is smaller. For example, if the short-base is $12 billion at the beginning of the day and Repo rates start off at 1.00%, as more and more shorts get covered, the rate goes higher. When the short-base is down to $5 billion, the Repo rate is closer to General Collateral – maybe at 1.50% - because the shorts were covering through the course of the day. This theory can explain much of the overnight rate volatility in the Specials market.

# Term Repo Rates

### Insurance Theory

The market for term Specials is very different from the term General Collateral market. The on-the-run issues like the 2 Year, 3 Year, 5 Year, 7 Year, 10 Year, 20 Year, and 30 Year each have their own story, auction dynamics, buyers, short-sellers, and trading dynamics. These securities will usually trade Special at some point during their auction cycle. It just depends on how Special and when. Will the 2 Year Note trade 25 basis points under General Collateral or 100 basis points under? No one ever knows for sure. However, the market prices term Specials rates based on expectations.

When a trader is short a Treasury, there's always a risk it will trade Special, very Special, or extremely Special. Extremely Special implies rates close to the fail charge rate. Because of the propensity of on-the-run issues to trade volatile, it can be argued that term Repo markets carry a premium for protecting the buyer against lower rates. Think of the premium as a form of insurance. A trader covering a short position for one week, one month, or even three months, theoretically, should pay a premium for locking in the term Repo rate. In a way, they are buying protection from the chance of a decline in Repo rates.

### Option Theory

There's a similar theory that says term Repo rates are like options. If someone short-sells a term Repo, it's like selling an option. If someone buys term, it's like buying an option. Here's the thinking: If you borrow a security term, you are covered against the chance it trades Special. If you sell term, you are betting against it trading Special. One thing that's for sure, overnight rate volatility is *the* main factor that determines term Repo rates for Special issues. When there's more volatility, there's more risk and term rates move lower. Just like with options, a more volatile security commands a larger term market premium. Maybe the Option Theory carries some weight?

### Past Versus Future Volatility

One major flaw in the Repo market is the mis-pricing of past volatility versus future volatility. When pricing a new on-the-run Treasury issue, the market often prices the new issue to trade similar to the last issue. If the last 2 Year Note only averaged 10 basis points below General Collateral, then the market often prices the next 2 Year Note the same way. Assuming there are no changes in market conditions, this makes sense. However, because market conditions change over time, the market often gets this wrong. When the market is quiet, activity always picks up again eventually. Conversely, volatile Repo markets don't last forever. Eventually shorts get covered, bought back, or they remain in the old issues. Once again, it's about market volatility. Understanding rate volatility is important to understanding the Repo market.

# THE ERA OF THE SHORT SQUEEZE

Before 2006, short squeezes were pretty common in the Repo market.45 In fact, in many traders' eyes, short squeezes were the sole purpose of the Repo market! It was all about the squeezes. Who was squeezing what? Who was buying term? Are the shorts or longs buying? Psst, so-and-so is going to squeeze. Can it be done? It was like a soap opera!

Anyone on the wrong side of a squeeze often cursed the Repo market. To them, Repo market short squeezes cost them money. It made it more expensive to carry short positions. And because the squeezes were so common, it added another element of risk to the market. As we know, risk makes everything more expensive – more volatility and wider spreads.

Strangely, the Fed never knew what to do about the squeezes. Squeezes were mildly tolerated for years. Yes, every once in a while the Fed asked to see Primary Dealers' trading positions, but again it was like driving 35 MPH in a 25 MPH speed zone. Yes, it's over the limit, but no one's getting a ticket. The question eventually came up: Were Repo market squeezes legal? Maybe. Was it market manipulation? Maybe. Are they allowed? Not anymore!

Don't get me wrong. There were many legitimate securities shortages throughout the history of the Repo market. The Repo

---

45 Even though Repo market squeezes are a thing of the past, I wrote this chapter in the present tense.

market didn't play a role in every shortage. Most of the time, the shortages were short-lived, a temporary imbalance between longs and shorts, and most often related to the auction cycle. The real significant shortages were caused by one of the following:

1. **Cheapest-To-Deliver (CTD)** – A specific security must be delivered to the exchange (CME) to fulfill a futures delivery requirement. If the correct security is not delivered, it's a very expensive fine. This is a can't-fail scenario.

2. **Gone From The Market** – This was the case with the 3.625% 5/15/2013. There was no supply available and deep shorts.

3. **Settlement Distortion** – During the September 11, 2001, period, the entire settlement system broke down. BONY couldn't clear securities for days.

4. **Flight-To-Quality** – End-investors buy-up all of the Treasurys, pack them away in their portfolios, and don't loan them into the Repo market.

These are solid reasons for securities shortages. However, when you take these out, the rest can generally be attributed to the Repo market, assisted by the Repo market, or helped along by the Repo market.

A "Repo market squeeze" is a short squeeze that's orchestrated by someone in the Repo market. The squeezer could be a Primary Dealer, a bank, a broker-dealer, or even a West Coast money manager. The concept is simple: Buy or borrow as much of a Treasury issue as possible and hold that supply out of the market. Don't loan it to anyone. Then see how low Repo rates go. When the security begins to trade rich in the cash market or term Repo rates decline, sell the position. Or sell as much as possible.

One thing to remember: A Repo market squeeze is not an actual shortage. Yes, during a squeeze there are fewer securities available in the market. But it's artificial. The goal of the squeeze is to create the impression of a shortage. The squeeze fools the market into believing there are more shorts or less supply of the security in the market.

Here's the blueprint:[46]

In most cases, a squeeze is only possible if there's already a large number of shorts. The stage must be set before a squeeze is possible. No one will attempt a squeeze unless there's a good risk/reward. Keep in mind, there's a lot of risk associated with a short squeeze.

Step 1: *Accumulate a Large Long Position*

A big bank might see a growing short-base in a Treasury issue. Their cash desk and hedge fund customers might be short, while their portfolio investor customers are long. They're lending a lot of the issue into the market each day and they know it!

Step 2: *Hold Supply Out of The Market*

The next step is finding a place to put the securities. You could even go so far as calling it a hiding place. The securities must be placed somewhere outside of the actual Repo market, somewhere where the shorts cannot cover their positions. And guess what? The

---

[46] Hopefully this chapter isn't used like an *Anarchists Cookbook* (1971 version) for manipulation in other markets!

Repo market already invented the perfect tool: Tri-Party Repo! Remember that in Tri-Party, the cash investor delivers cash to the clearing bank, the securities dealer delivers the securities, and the clearing bank holds the cash and securities. Because the securities are moved into the account by the securities dealer, they have complete control of what goes in. Tri-Party accounts all but made short squeezes possible. I'm sure the money market funds and municipalities never knew how often their cash was used to help squeeze a Treasury issue!

Let's say there's a Treasury issue with a total of $10 billion outstanding. From the beginning, a lot of the issue is already packed away in end-user accounts that don't lend. Let's call it $5 billion permanently gone from market. Now, as the weeks go on, the short-base of the issue is growing. It takes longer and longer each morning for the shorts to get covered. Overnight Repo rates trade a little lower each day. Trading volume is increasing in the inter-dealer broker market each day. Clearly, the short-base is growing, but how large is it?

Let's say the short base is now at $5 billion. Using the Theory of Demand, there's now a total of $15 billion in long positions, $5 billion in shorts, and $5 billion permanently gone from the market. That leaves $5 billion[47] excess supply floating around the market.

## Scenario #1: The Bank Doesn't Lend Their Existing Long Position

What if the big bank is long a total of $3 billion from customers and from Repo desk positions? In this scenario, they choose not to loan

---

[47] $10 billion originally issued + $5 billion of longs created from the short sales - $5 billion permanently gone - $5 billion in shorts = $5 billion left (excess supply).

their long position. The removal of the $3 billion from the market doesn't make the issue fail, but it does push Repo rates lower. That's because deducting the bank's $3 billion position still leaves an extra $2 billion of supply available.

At this point, the bank knows that holding $3 billion out of the market moves rates lower, but it doesn't create a shortage. In fact, the bank didn't even benefit because they lose money financing their long positions at General Collateral rates in the Tri-Party accounts.

## Scenario #2: The Bank Accumulates a Larger Position

Holding $3 billion didn't result in a successful squeeze, but they know they're close. This time they borrow another $2 billion of the security in the overnight and term Repo markets. Now they hold $5 billion out of the market, all of the shorts can't get covered, and the issue fails.[48] Given the amount of fails, it's a big windfall for the traders at the bank.

Once the bank knows how much they need to hold out of the market, they know how to control the issue. They can move the Repo rates higher or lower just by adding and removing supply. They can sell their position overnight and back up overnight rates. When Repo rates move higher, they can start buying again. Once they have control, they can make a lot of money just by moving rates up and down all day. Once it feels like the shorts are rolling out of the issue, they sell as much as they can in the term Repo market.

All in all, when a bank sets out to squeeze an issue, there are a number of potential goals. The obvious one is financial: to make

---

[48] I realize, theoretically, there's just enough securities in the market to cover all of the shorts, but there's a lot of slippage.

money. Other goals could be to create fails, move term rates lower, or affect the price of the security in the cash market.

1. <u>Fails</u> - The immediate indication of a successful squeeze is when the issue fails. If enough supply is held out of the market, there will be fails. The squeezer makes a lot of money when they "pick up fails."

2. <u>Sell Term</u> – Remember that the squeezer must have a large enough long position in order to have sufficient control. In order to initiate the squeeze, they need to accumulate long positions. One goal is to sell those existing long positions at lower rates. By creating the impression of a severe shortage, term Repo rates move lower because market participants are willing to pay those lower rates. If overnight rates drop down to the fail charge rate, term Repo rates often become very attractive to the shorts.[49]

3. <u>Affect the Cash Market</u> - The squeezer might try to affect the security's price in the cash market. There's a close connection between Repo rates and a security's relative value on the yield curve. Once a squeezer makes the financing appear expensive, the security often trades at a premium in the cash market. If you scare enough traders with low Repo rates, the shorts will pay a premium to buy back their positions or roll their shorts into a different issue.

---

[49] Repo Maxim – Never buy term on a squeeze day. At the same time and conceptually the same, never sell term General Collateral on a day with funding pressure.

4. <u>Affect The WI Roll</u> - Shorts enter the market based on the auction cycle – often just when the When Issued (WI) security is announced. Short squeezes are common around this time. Where some dealers are trying to cheapen the price of the current issue by short-selling, other dealers see increasing shorts as an opportunity. Squeezing an issue during the auction period often forces the shorts to roll into the WI issue.

5. <u>Other</u> - There are other reasons for a squeeze. There are Cheapest-To-Deliver squeezes. Sometimes a squeeze is an attempt to test an issue. Let's call it a test squeeze - just see if there are shorts developing. Does holding some supply out of the market move the supply plateau lower? Or does the missing supply have no effect?

The Federal Reserve, the Treasury, FINRA, and even the Treasury Markets Practices Group have specific rules on how participants can interact in the market. Some practices are illegal and some that are not. There are grey areas, too. There are always some practices that regulators don't like, but it doesn't mean that they're illegal. Short squeezes are not necessarily illegal. If a shortage results from natural supply-and-demand imbalances, it's not illegal. However, market manipulation is, and always will be, illegal. Still, there's a grey area in between.

It's easiest to start with what's clearly illegal. Based on Salomon Brother's famous 2 Year Note squeeze, you cannot break the Treasury's auction rules to accumulate long positions. The Treasury's rules are very specific. However, after the auction, you can purchase as much as you want in the secondary market. There are no rules prohibiting large purchases. If that were the case, there would be several arrests at the Federal Reserve!

Collusion is also not allowed. Two market participants cannot coordinate their activities. If two separate entities are working together, it's collusion. You can't call your buddy at another bank and say, "Let's each buy $5 billion of the 5 Year Note and not lend 'um." That's certainly illegal. It's market manipulation.

Of course, shared market views are not collusion. Two traders can speak on the phone and decide the 5 Year Note is cheap. If this was illegal, I would have been arrested! The difference here is that they didn't agree to manipulate the market. They agreed that the 5 Year looked cheap, but they didn't agree to work together. It's impossible for regulators to ban market participants from discussing the market. If two traders have the same view on the market, they're allowed to take a position. They just can't agree to coordinate.

Here are some additional scenarios to ponder. If someone happens to own a security and a shortage develops, are they required to sell their position? What's the difference between being long and not lending your position and a short-squeeze? What's the difference between a successful trade and market manipulation?

- If a bank has a large position in a Treasury issue, is it illegal for them to buy more?

- Is a bank required to lend their long position to short-sellers so the shorts can cover their positions?

- As long as someone with a long position makes their supply available at some price or rate, isn't that sufficient?

- If a security is failing, is there a requirement to lend that position?

Whether or not Repo market squeezes were good or bad for the market, whether or not they served a purpose, they're gone. Eventually, the short squeezes that drove the Repo market for years and years were about to end. Regulators began to view the squeezes as market manipulation. At first, they let the dealer community know they didn't like the squeezes. Primary Dealers were called to submit large position reports in order to disclose how much of a particular Treasury issue they owned or controlled. This was supposed to be a flag that said, "We're watching you." However, it was still a game of cat and mouse. The cat chased the mouse around the market, but the mouse kept coming back.

Then, the Treasury Department got serious in 2006. James Clouse, a Treasury official, on September 27, 2006, called Repo market squeezes "an exercise in monopoly pricing." He clearly wanted to clean up the market. The Fed met with the 22 Primary Dealers in November 2006, and when the dust settled, there were big changes. No longer was anyone looking the other way. There would be serious regulatory issues for anyone who let Repo market squeezes continue.

Repo market squeezes ended right there and then. There was little pain in the market, except for a few unfortunate Repo traders. One Credit Suisse and two UBS Repo traders were fired as a show of support.

Shortages of Treasury securities still arise from time to time. It's a part of any market. It's impossible to have a free market without supply and demand imbalances from time to time. The shortages are usually temporary and relatively mild. They're most often self-corrected. Repo rates eventually get low enough to attract supply into the market. The price in the cash market develops a premium and investors sell their positions. The WI issue is announced as the shorts roll forward.

There have been no clear Repo market squeezes since 2006. A practice that was so common is pretty much dead. There are no large banks actively accumulating a security, holding supply out of the market, and causing settlements to fail. However, there are certainty market participants that help rates move lower. Maybe they're not buying billions and depositing them in Tri-Party accounts, but they're still trying to pick up fails. After all, you cannot ask a leopard to change its spots. Even in the Repo market.

# THE SALOMON 2 YEAR NOTE SQUEEZE

The Salomon 2 Year Note squeeze was the biggest short squeeze ever orchestrated. Ever. We can't call it the most successful squeeze because many of those involved lost their jobs, and, arguably, it led to the sale of Salomon Brothers to Travelers Insurance Co. But that wasn't even the end of it. More than just those at Salomon Brothers were impacted; there were widespread consequences.

Salomon Brothers was *the* bond trading shop in the 1980s. It was *the* place to be. The firm was run by John Gutfreund, who was declared by *Time Magazine* to be the "King of Wall Street." John Meriwether was the Vice Chairman and ran their storied arbitrage group. Paul W. Mozer ran the Government Bond Department. The firm was aggressive, profitable, and not afraid of risk. They were forever pushing boundaries, charging into new markets, and accumulating larger trading positions.

At the height of their prowess, the traders at Salomon Brothers hatched a plan to corner the U.S. Treasury 2 Year Note. Yes, they had many successful squeezes under their belt, but this time it was different. They invented a whole new kind of squeeze. Rather than accumulating the position in the secondary market, borrowing the securities from clients, or buying in the term Repo market, why not just buy the securities right from the start? Why accumulate securities in the secondary market and drive-up prices when you can just buy them directly from the Treasury? Buy the entire new Treasury issue and eliminate the middle-men! Not a bad idea!

It took a few attempts for them to get it right. The first strike came on February 21, 1991, when the Salomon traders submitted several bids for the new 5 Year Note, both for themselves and for a large client. Officially, the customer's name on the submission was Warburg Asset Management. Right from the beginning, Fed officials should have known something was wrong. Warburg Asset Management didn't exist. There was S.G. Warburg, a Primary Dealer, and there was Mercury Asset Management, a money manager based in London. Both firms were owned by the same holding company. When Salomon was questioned by the Fed, they admitted they made a mistake, and changed the customer's name to Mercury Asset Management. However, as a Primary Dealer, S.G. Warburg had submitted bids of their own. When the Fed totaled the bids from S.G. Warburg and Mercury Asset Management, the bids exceeded the Treasury's 35% bidding limit for a single corporate entity. This time, the Treasury allowed it, under the assumption that the two affiliates were legally separate companies. As it turned out, there was really no Mercury Asset Management bid. The bonds went straight into Salomon's house account.

From Salomon's point of view, they survived scrutiny from the Treasury. And such a close call might make someone think twice about attempting the same scheme twice. Once again, what's that saying about a leopard and its spots?

When the next set of auctions arrived one month later, two hedge funds got involved. It's unclear whether they knew about the previous Salomon trade or not. There's a high probability of a connection, since rumors fly around the market pretty fast. Steinhardt Management Co. and Caxton Corp – both large hedge funds of the time – submitted bids for the March 2 Year Note. By using multiple corporate entities, they were able to accumulate $20 billion of the issue between them. When adding up their purchases at the auction and those in the secondary market, they owned 158% of the total amount outstanding. Not only did they buy the entire issue, but they had an even larger long position courtesy of the short-sellers, a group that accounted for the additional 58% of their long position.[50]

With two parties in control of the entire 2 Year Note, the price of the issue became distorted; the price increased and the yield declined relative to similar Treasury issues. As the price of the 2 Year Note richened, it brought in even more short-sellers. The issue was ripe for a short squeeze, but a big Repo market squeeze never arrived. Repo rates were expensive, but the securities were available to borrow because the two hedge funds didn't have access to Tri-Party Repo accounts. They had to loan their positions into the market each day. Salomon was not officially connected to the trade, but they clearly knew what was going on. They saw the potential for an even better trade, yet one they knew was illegal.

During the month, Salomon's head trader, Paul Mozer, went out to dinner with a group of senior traders from Tiger Investments and the Quantum Fund, two other large hedge funds of the time. Quantum Fund was the fund run by George Soros before he converted it into a family office. At the dinner, they discussed the success of the Steinhardt and Caxton 2 Year Note trade, and everyone liked the idea. As luck would have it, there was another 2 Year Note

---

[50] The Theory of Demand in practice!

auction just around the corner. Working together, Salomon submitted bids for their own account, Tiger Investments, and the Quantum Fund.

The 2 Year Note auction was held on April 24, 1991. Salomon bid for $4.2 billion in its own name, $4.287 billion on behalf of the Quantum Fund, $2 billion on behalf of Tiger Investments, and $130 million for some smaller clients. Keep in mind, U.S. Treasury issues were much smaller back then. The total issue size was only $11.3 billion. All total, Salomon and the hedge funds bought $10.6 billion of the 2 Year Note at the auction – 94% of the entire issue. Officially, and on paper, Salomon owned just under 35%. However, once the issue settled, Tiger and Quantum agreed to have Salomon manage their positions. Salomon had complete control of the entire 2 Year Note.

By the middle of May, it was clear there was something wrong. The 2 Year Note's price was completely distorted; it was trading extremely rich and the yield was extremely low. There was no squeeze in the Repo market, however, because Salomon loaned the securities into the market each day. This created one of the strangest squeezes ever. There was no shortage in the Repo market, but there was a huge premium in the cash market.

As the squeeze in the April 2 Year Note continued, Salomon submitted large bids again for the next 2 Year Note settling at the end of May. They were able to accumulate an abnormally large position once again. Prices across the entire 2 year sector were now distorted. Prices were abnormally high and yields were abnormally low. Everyone knew that Salomon had the issue and Salomon was not selling. At this point, all of the trading in the market was from one short seller to another. There were no real owners selling. All of the buyers were existing short-sellers who had ridden their losses as far as they could go and got stopped out. All of the sellers were new short-sellers willing to take short positions and higher and higher prices. There was no way for the squeeze to end without Salomon selling.

What was Salomon's goal? They had already achieved a very successful squeeze. Prices moved in their favor and they had a huge win under their belt. The biggest short-squeeze of all time! However, in July things started to unravel. Market participants started complaining to the Fed. Everyone knew that Salomon owned the entire issue. The Fed passed the information to the Treasury Department. Treasury then passed it to the SEC, who immediately launched an investigation. By the end of July, it was all over.

Events moved pretty quickly from there. Within one month[51] of the squeeze becoming public, Salomon admitted to the SEC that they had submitted unauthorized bids in several auctions. They violated the Treasury's rule that no entity could purchase more than 35% of an issue at auction. John Gutfreund – the former King of Wall Street - resigned in August 1991 in disgrace. Five Salomon executives were fired, including John Meriwether and Paul Mozer. In 1993, Mozer pleaded guilty to two felonies of making false statements to U.S. officials. The firm was never the same after that. They were sold to Travelers Insurance Co. in 1997, and merged to become Salomon Smith Barney – a quiet and passive retail broker.

Regulators finally caught up to the two hedge funds a couple of years later. Steinhardt and Caxton were fined $76 million in order to settle the fraud and price-fixing charges. Steinhardt paid $40 million

---

[51] Early July 1991

and Caxton paid $36 million. A few years after that, they both settled class-action suits, with Steinhardt paying an additional $22 million and Caxton paying $12 million.

After these events unfolded, regulators realized the Government Securities Act of 1986 needed some updating. It had been several years since the market abuses of the small broker-dealers in the 1980s, and the Act needed some fine-tuning. Clearly the Treasury auction process needed reform.

- At the time, some government securities dealers were still not registered with the SEC. They had to register.

- The Fed started contacting customers directly about large auction purchases, just to spot-check the validity of their bids.

- The Treasury pledged to reopen issues that were experiencing shortages. The Treasury planned to break securities shortages by selling more of an existing issue, effectively increasing the supply in the market. In reality, the Treasury never reopened an issue due to market manipulation. Perhaps the threat of a snap Treasury reopening helped change the math for anyone pondering a squeeze.

In the end, Salomon Brothers was forever changed, traders lost their jobs, executives resigned in disgrace, and there were regulatory updates added to the market. These are the typical results of a Wall Street scandal. However, the impact across the market didn't end there. Many traders were hurt by the short-squeeze. Many were wiped out, lost their jobs, and entire trading groups shut down. Those who had shorted the 2 Year Note were "run over." Yes, there are always traders on the wrong side of the market who take losses. Sometimes significant losses. That's a part of the business when the game is assumed to be fair.

I was working for a Japanese bank at the time. It was my first job on a Repo desk. The bank had an arbitrage group, which was charged with taking proprietary risk – looking for mis-pricings across the U.S. Treasury and financial futures markets. They were all well-experienced and established Wall Street traders. However, they got caught in the squeeze. As the price of the 2 Year Note increased, they were one of the unlucky short-sellers. They suffered in the trade for about two months. Once they reached their maximum loss, they were stopped-out. They were forced to cover their position at the end of June.

When it came time to get out, the head trader called his salesman at Salomon Brothers. He said, "Please offer $500 million 2 Year Notes." Salomon offered the securities right on the spot. No hesitation and right on the offered side of the market. A couple of days later, the groups' desks were cleaned out and I never saw them again.[52]

---

[52] I heard they blew up a second time during the Asian crisis in 1997.

# CTD Squeezes

As the COVID-19 virus spread across the globe in 2020, governments initiated lockdowns to slow the spread of the virus. People stayed local and mostly travelled only as far as their local supermarket. With less driving, the consumption of gasoline declined. As the demand for gasoline ground to a halt, oil inventories continued to grow. And grow. And grow.

Oil storage tanks filled up one after another. At the beginning of 2020, oil was trading at nearly $60 a barrel. On April 20th, the price of the West Texas Intermediate (WTI) opened at $18 a barrel. By all standards, oil was cheap. The price was down over 70% for the year.

As the day went on, the price continued to fall. At 2:00 PM, it dropped to zero. That meant someone was willing to give you a barrel of oil for free. Just take it! A few minutes later, the price dropped below zero and went into free-fall. By the end of the day, oil settled at -$37.63. That's a negative thirty-seven dollars and sixty-three cents, just in case you missed the negative sign. Anyone long a futures contract was saying, "I'll pay you $37.63. Just take it off my hands!"

April 20, 2020, was an important day in the oil market because it was the last trading day for the WTI futures contract on the CME exchange. If you were long any contracts at the end of the day, you had two choices: Take delivery or sell the position. Anyone long the contact was obligated to take possession of 1,000 barrels of light sweet crude oil in the town of Cushing, Oklahoma. Given the oil glut, all of the storage facilities were already full. Even if you wanted to take possession, there was nowhere to store it. That left the other option: Sell the contract at any price!

Not surprisingly, there were big winners and losers that day. A small group of traders who called themselves "The Essex Boys" worked at a traders' arcade called Vega Capital London Ltd. They were short oil all month, and pressed their shorts further on the last day. Industry experts estimate they made $660 million. The big loser was China's Crude Oil Treasury Fund. The owners closed the fund shortly thereafter, informing investors: "It didn't occur to us that oil could go negative."

No one in the oil industry ever expected the price of oil to go negative! Negative numbers are foreign to the commodity markets, but they're nothing new to the Repo market. WTI oil futures were squeezed that day. And, again, squeezes are nothing new to the Repo market either. In fact, a squeeze in the oil futures market is not too different from a squeeze in the Treasury futures market, except, ironically, the Covid crisis presented the oil market with something virtually unheard of: A long squeeze instead of a short squeeze.

Squeezes in the futures market can occur because the futures exchanges have very specific delivery requirements. A specific commodity or security must be delivered at a specific time and place on a specific date. Anyone who can't meet the requirements faces a severe fine. Even if the commodity or security is in short supply, it still must be delivered at any price.

Speculation in the futures markets is compounded further because traders bet on the difference between prices in the cash market and the futures market. The difference in prices between the two markets is call "the basis." There's a basis for spot oil and oil futures, a basis for bushels of corn and the corn futures. And, of course, there's a basis for U.S. Treasurys and the Treasury futures contracts. A basis trade can involve any interest rate futures contract, not just Treasury Note/Bond futures, but also Eurodollar, fed funds or SOFR futures.

However, there's an important difference between basis and "the basis." "The basis" is still the price difference between a security and the futures contract, but not just any security. It's the security that's deliverable to the futures contract, also known as the cheapest-to-delivery, or CTD.

Because every futures contract has settlement specifications, it's pretty import to know what you'll receive or are required to deliver. If you own a contract to purchase corn at a future date, how many bushels of corn are you going to receive? Where are you going to receive them? Do you send a truck to a storage facility in Chicago? When does the truck pick up the corn?

The concept is the same for the Treasury note/bond contracts. Which security is eligible for delivery? What maturity dates are possible? What day of the month will it be delivered? The contract specifications have a large impact on the pricing of the futures contract and the deliverable security. The contract specifies the allowable maturity range, the eligible delivery days of the contract month, and a formula to convert the price of the security to the price of the futures contract. Taking these factors into consideration, there's always one Treasury security that's the "cheapest-to-delivery" for every futures contract.

Repo financing also plays an important role in the basis market. Just think of the definition of a futures contract. It's an agreement to buy or sell an asset in the future. If someone is long the basis, they own a security today with an agreement to sell it at a future date. That means there are really three components to a basis trade: the Treasury security, the futures contact, and the Repo financing between today and the future date.

Theoretically, the difference between the current price of the security and the futures price should be equal to the cost of financing. Theoretically. If one of the components is mispriced, there's an arbitrage opportunity.[53]

There are a number of Treasury futures contracts that trade on the Chicago Board of Trade (CBOT), including the Two Year Note, Three Year Note, Five Year Note, Ten Year Note, Ultra Ten Year Note, Bond, and Ultra Bond futures. The contracts settle in the months of March, June, September, and December. If a trader is long the March basis, they're long the Treasury that's cheapest-to-deliver for the March futures contract and short the March futures contact. Assuming they hold the trade into March, they must deliver the security to the exchange. A trader who is "short the basis" is short the security which is the CTD and long the futures contract. They expect to receive the security sometime during the month of March. But they

---

[53] Basis trading is much more complicated than the future price less the current price less the financing. The futures contracts have "switch" options, "wild card" options, delivery specifications, margin, and balance sheet implications. Did I miss anything?

don't know when they'll receive it. The trader making the delivery chooses when.

In the Treasury Note/Bond futures contracts, the delivery period begins at the beginning of the month and ends on the last day[54] of the month. There are factors which dictate whether the delivery occurs at the beginning of the month or at the end. The main factor is "carry." Positive carry means the coupon accrual of the bond is greater than the Repo financing cost. Because the owner of the security makes money each day holding the position, the delivery is usually made at the end of the month. Conversely, if there's negative carry – meaning the Repo financing costs are greater than the coupon accrual – the delivery usually occurs at the beginning of the month. Why pay to hold the security any longer than is required?

When it comes time to make a futures delivery, there are a lot of things that can go wrong. The trader who is long the security (short the futures contract) must give notice to the exchange. The exchange requires two days advance notice. If the delivery is scheduled on a Wednesday, notice must be given on Monday. When the delivery date arrives, the securities must be delivered by 9:30 AM New York time (8:30 AM Chicago time). There's something very important about this cut-off time. It's not the same as the Fedwire. The Fedwire cut-off time is 3:00 PM. The futures exchange requires the securities to be delivered 5 ½ hours earlier. That means anyone buying the security specifically to settle on the delivery date is out of luck. There's no guarantee the securities will arrive in time. Thus, the complication in the futures delivery process.

---

[54] Most contracts, but not all.

Anyone making a futures delivery must have control of the securities, at a minimum, the day before. They must make sure the securities can be delivered promptly in the morning, so the securities must be held in their box or in a Tri-Party account the night before. Remember, a late delivery to the exchange is extremely punitive. You absolutely positively cannot fail to the exchange.

Over the years, many firms developed policies to minimize and eliminate CTD fails and late deliveries. Here's how it goes: If a basis trader is looking to make a futures delivery, they notify their Repo desk two days in advance. Most firms have rules that the securities must be in the box or in a Tri-Party account before the delivery notice is given. Once and only once the securities are received, the trader can give notice to the exchange. Note, this means the securities are held out of the Repo market for a total of two days. From the firm's point of view, they control the securities and can safely deliver on the delivery date. The procedure is solid. However, this has a big impact on the Repo market. If there are $5 billion futures deliveries scheduled, it's means there are $5 billion fewer CTD securities in the market for two days prior to the delivery. Picture the impact of $10 billion of futures deliveries! The traders who are short the basis need to borrow the CTD and have to scramble to cover their shorts. During the delivery period, CTDs can get very Special.

CTD squeezes have been around as long as futures contracts, but the frequency and severity increased in the early 2000s and abruptly ended in 2005. The Repo market is well accustomed to futures-related supply shortages. And if you know that supply is restricted, it is the perfect time for a short squeeze. If the longs can't get their securities delivered to the exchange, they're faced with the age-old dilemma:

Find a way to make the delivery or buy back the position. In order to make the delivery, they're often required to pay extremely punitive Repo rates. If they buy back the position, they pay an inflated price.[55] Once someone is caught in a CTD short squeeze, their prospect of getting out unscathed is not good.

One of the most severe CTD squeezes occurred in the aftermath of September 11. Lehman Brothers took advantage of both the securities settlement problems and year-end. Although most of the settlement problems had cleared up by November 2001, as year-end approached, securities started failing again. It looked like there would be a lot of fails over year-end. At the time, the Five Year Note futures contract had two CTDs: The Old 5 Year Note, which was still in short supply from the settlement problems, and the current 5 Year Note. Since the 5 Year Note was a current, it already had a large short-base.

Knowing both CTD issues were in short supply, Lehman boxed both the 5 Year Note and the Old 5 Year Note, and both issues failed during the final days of the delivery period. Unless someone already had them in their box, no one could get either 5 Year Note to make a futures delivery. Many firms failed and large fines were levied by the exchange.

Fast forward to March 2004. The bond futures contract had a problem. The size of the futures delivery was greater than the amount of the CTD available in the market. That's right, there were only $3.9 billion of the 8.75% 5/2020 available in the market. By the end of March 2004, the open interest called for $5.3 billion to be delivered to the exchange. On the surface, it appeared that a security with $6

---

[55] Let's assume paying the fine is not an option!

billion originally issued would not have a settlement issue. However, fifteen years after it was issued, $1.4 billion of the issue was stripped. That left only $3.9 billion left in the market, and not enough to fulfill the futures deliveries. The issue failed at the end of March. Knowing supply was mostly unavailable, many shorts were forced to buy back their positions.

In December of 2004, the fail problem returned. The CTD for the Ten Year Note futures contract was the 3.0% 2/2009. Two weeks prior to the delivery date, the issue began failing, though no one was specifically squeezing it. In its aftermath, traders re-examined their two day boxing rule, and it prompted many to begin holding securities for three or four days prior to the delivery date.

Three months later in March 2005, the CTD for the Ten Year Note futures contract was the 3.875% 5/2009. The basis traded at a large discount during most of March and many traders increased the size of their positions. Curiously, at the end of March, there were no fail issues. However, the size of the delivery to the CBOT was huge; a total of $11.9 billion was delivered. The basis market was clearly growing, and risks from both fails and large deliveries were increasing.

In June of 2005, it really hit the fan! Yes, there had been CTD squeezes on and off for years, but never something of this magnitude. The June 2005 CTD squeeze was not only the largest CTD squeeze of all time, but its consequences changed the basis market forever.

After the large futures delivery in March 2005 and the fails in December 2004, there was nervousness going into the June delivery month. Surprisingly, the basis for the June Ten Year Note futures contact (4.875% 2/2012 CTD) was extremely cheap. Though the CTD was a large issue with $25 billion outstanding and there was seemingly plenty of supply in the market for deliveries, the spread between the CTD and the futures contract was very wide. It looked like a June futures delivery was going to be a very profitable trade! Yet, something was amiss. Someone kept buying as much of the futures contract as they could, widening the spread and positioning themselves to receive a massive number of the deliveries.

As June went on, no one was sure what was going on. Buying continued in the futures contract. No one knew who was behind it. In fact, no one knew if it was a squeeze or not. The effect, however, made the basis even cheaper.

As it turned out, PIMCO – the Pacific Investment Management Company – was behind the large purchases. They were a West Coast money manager with over $500 billion in assets. They were run by legendary bond market investor Bill Gross, who was later dubbed "The Bond King."[56] PIMCO would never officially comment on the trade, but news eventually came out that PIMCO was the one short the basis. They bought most of the Ten Year Note futures contracts and were daring the market to deliver them!

At the beginning of June, the basis was trading at an unprecedented discount, and the issue was completely gone from the market. Smart traders had quickly locked up[57] as much as they could in their box or in a Tri-Party account. The security was impossible to borrow. The open interest of the contract reached a high of $19.4 billion. Out of a $24 billion issue, $19.4 billion was scheduled to be delivered that month. Even with the Fed loaning $2 billion of the

[56] Note to self: If ever dubbed the "king" of anything, it's time to retire!
[57] Traders began boxing the issue an unprecedented four weeks before the final delivery date!

4.875% 2/12 from the SOMA portfolio into the market, it was not enough to eliminate the shortage. The issue went dead fail. Nothing moved. Anyone with a long position kept it locked-up in their box. Anyone who was short was scrambling to borrow them. The stage was set for the largest futures CTD squeeze of all time!

Traders were once again faced with that age-old choice: find the securities in the Repo market to make the delivery or buy back the position. Many traders took the loss and rolled their short position into the next contract. Rolling forward meant locking in a huge loss. However, knowing how well the Prompt Delivery Repo[58] trade worked two years earlier to settle the 3.625% 5/2013, the Repo market brought it back.

The Prompt Delivery Repo trade effectively priced the value of actually receiving the securities. With traders desperate to get their hands on as many 4.875% 2/2012 as possible, negative PD Repo rates began trading. At first, the negative rates were between -1.00% and -5.00%, but they kept going lower and lower. After a few days, the issue bottomed out at -30.0%. Not negative 30 basis points, negative thirty percent – the lowest rate that ever traded in the U.S. Repo market. Settlements continued to fail, but traders who really wanted to get out now had a mechanism to do so. At this point, the Ten Year Note futures basis was able to trade again.

By the end of the month, $14.1 billion of futures deliveries were made to the exchange, indicating the market was boxing $14.1 billion of the issue during most of June. PIMCO had taken delivery of $13.3 billion, almost the entire open interest. PIMCO had attempted to

---

[58] Prompt Delivery meant the securities had to be delivered within a short period of time or the trade was cancelled.

squeeze the CTD, but they didn't expect the market to be able to deliver the full open interest. PIMCO was later charged with market manipulation.

By the end of 2005, the CME had enough of the CTD shortages and decided to do something about it. They issued new position size limits beginning in December 2005, including a limit of 50,000 contracts ($5 billion) for Ten Year Note futures and 35,000 contracts ($3.5 billion) for Five Year Note contracts. Even more importantly, they changed the calculation for determining the CTD. They made it easier for the CTD to switch from one Treasury to another. It was no longer so expensive to deliver the second most CTD as it was in the past. If there was a squeeze, the next cheapest issue could be delivered with a minimal loss. Since then, there have been no CTD squeezes. There have been shortages, but nothing close to the magnitude of the PIMCO CTD squeeze.

# NEGATIVE RATES

It took high interest rates to break the back of the inflation in the 1970s and early 1980s. By the late 1980s, interest rates were still high by today's standards, but continued trending lower. When recession struck in 1990, the Greenspan Fed cut the fed funds rate from 8.25% in January 1990 down to 3.00% in September 1992, ushering in a new world of low rates. At the time, 3.00% seemed incredibly low, but it worked. Economic activity picked up and the economy began moving again.

Ten years later, the economy was faltering again, and the Fed pushed the fed funds rate even lower. This time, the rate bottomed-out at 1.00% in June 2003. It was the lowest fed funds rate in 45 years and seemed incredibly low once again. Almost irresponsible.[59] At the time, no one thought rates could go any lower. It was believed the negative effects of extremely low rates would be too damaging. For one, the money market fund (MMF) industry would be devastated. Completely gutted. MMFs would suffer huge capital outflows and be forced to shed their assets in a fragile market.

Fast forward five years later, and the Fed finally crossed the 1.00% barrier! In December 2008, during the depths of the Financial Crisis, the Fed cut the fed funds target range to 0.0% to .25%, ushering in the first so-called Zero Percent Interest Rate Policy (ZIRP). Zero percent

---

[59] Did the ultra-low 1.00% overnight rate help fuel the housing boom? Maybe!

overnight rates were unprecedented. It had never been attempted in the U.S. before. Of course, it was assumed the fixed income and MMF businesses were all but finished. Not to mention the Repo market! All told, it took three interest rate cycles and 25 years for interest rates to peak in the 1980s and drop to 0% in 2008.

No one knew what would happen next. What happens after zero? Is the Fed done? Out of ammunition? Do they sit and wait for 0% rates to stimulate the economy? As it turns out, interest rates *could* drop further.[60] Taking them negative. Negative interest rates are a whole different animal. They require a new level of thinking.

There are really two kinds of negative interest rates. The first is an extension of the interest playing field. It's like pushing the endzone back ten yards in football. The entire playing field is now 120 yards long, adding yards -1 to -10 between the zero yard-line and the goal on each side. The second kind of negative rate is punitive, the cost of obtaining something that's hard to get.

Until recently, negative rates were mostly a Repo phenomenon. There were only a few instances in the past when securities traded at negative rates. Treasury bills occasionally traded negative during the Great Depression and World War II. In the 1970s, the Swiss National Bank imposed capital controls and negative rates to keep their currency from appreciating. However, it was the Bank of Japan that first went full-throttle with a negative policy rate in 1998. The European Central Bank (ECB) dropped its overnight deposit rate to 0.0% in July 2012, and took it to -.25% in June 2013.[61] The ECB was soon joined by the Bank of England and the Danish Nation Bank. The

---

[60] Luckily not in the U.S.
[61] The ECB kept negative rates until July 2022.

Swiss National Bank then set their overnight rate to 0.0% just to stop Swiss Franc from appreciating. It became a Flight-To-Quality currency once again.

When central banks cut their policy rate, it's supposed to be an incentive for people to take cash out of their bank accounts. Stop saving and start spending! It also encourages banks to make loans and spur investment. More spending and investing stimulates aggregate demand, according to the economics textbooks.

Negative rates go one step further. They're like monetary policy on steroids. Negative rates have the added incentive of penalizing cash savings, because people are literally paying a bank to hold their cash[62]. In a way, negative rates are a tax on holding money.

From a bank's perspective, they just pass negative rates on to their customers. Let's say the central bank policy rate is -.75% and the savings bank marks up their customers by 25 basis points. That means the depositor receives an interest rate of -1.00% on their savings account. Yes, paying 1.00% a year to keep money at the bank! For a depositor with $1,000, their savings are trickling away by $10 each year. So why not just leave the cash uninvested somewhere and receive no interest? That's the equivalent of a 0% rate. Of course, someone already thought of that.

One of the first instances of negative rates in the U.S. arrived during the Debt Ceiling Crisis of July/August 2011. At the time, many cash investors didn't want to invest in the Repo market for fears of receiving a defaulted U.S. Treasury as collateral. Instead, they just left

---

[62] The global amount of negative yielding debt peaked at $18.4 trillion in December 2020. Source: *The Wall Street Journal*; "Investors Wave Goodbye to Negative-Yielding Debt"; July 27, 2022.

cash in their account at the Bank of New York (BONY). For a bank, uninvested funds are technically deposits, and deposits cost[63] the bank money. When interest rates are 5%, those costs are nominal, but they're significant when rates are zero. In August 2011, BONY announced a fee for keeping uninvested cash deposits in securities accounts. Money market funds, corporate treasurers, and broker-dealers were all charged 13 basis points for uninvested cash balances over $50 million.

In the Repo market, negative rates developed as the price to borrow a security that was in short supply. Eventually, the market evolved into the first kind of negative rate: an extension of the playing field.

In some respects, negative rates in the Repo market don't make much sense: Pay me to hold my Treasury security overnight. Now that's a good business! Consider it this way: In a normal Repo transaction, a cash investor gives their counterparty cash in exchange for a Treasury to hold as collateral. The investor receives interest on the cash. Basically, they get back a little more money than they invested. Now, think of the upside-down world of negative interest rates. The cash investor gives the Repo counterparty cash and receives collateral. This time, they don't receive interest, but instead *pay* interest. The investor pays a counterparty to hold the counterparty's security.

---

[63] Banks were required to pay an FDIC tax of .10% for deposit insurance, which meant banks were losing 10 basis points a day on uninvested cash balances. BONY was the first to institute the .13% charge for funds above $50 million, thus creating the first negative rate for cash.

In general, there are several reasons why someone is willing to pay a negative rate on a Repo. As we know, negative rates most often occur when there's a shortage. Paying the negative rate is the only way to borrow the security.

Negative rates can also occur during a market panic or a Flight-To-Quality. When investors are buying ultra-safe securities, they don't care about the rate. If you're worried about getting your money back, you care about return *of* investment rather than return *on* investment!

Some investors have internal rules which require them to invest in specific types of securities. The rules might specify that 10% of a fund must be invested in U.S. Treasury bills. If bills are in short supply, it doesn't matter. The investor can get stuck with a negative rate.

Sometimes there's no better alternative. If the investor doesn't invest, the alternative is even worse. For example, the BONY cash balance fee of August 2011. Or maybe the Prime Broker charges a very low rate for cash balances. The cost of not investing might outweigh the cost of the negative rate.

Of course, during quarter-end and year-end, all bets are off. Window dressing is not rate sensitive. Many investors want to show Treasury bills on their balance sheet over quarter-end. If bills are trading at negative rates, that's the cost of window dressing!

There were several times when General Collateral even traded negative, though it was mostly a quarter-end or year-end phenomenon. There were also times when Treasury collateral was just in short supply at the end of the day.

Before 2003, negative Repo rates were quite rare. Before the fail charge, market participants had the option of failing. Fails had no costs, or at least the costs were considered nominal. If a trader was unable to cover a short, it was the equivalent of a 0.0% rate. Securities shortages were relatively short lived, so there was no reason to borrow at a negative rate except under extreme circumstances.

In the 1980s and 1990s, if a security shortage arose and someone desperately needed to cover the short, the market created a negative rate with a bonds-borrowed style transaction. Thus, the first negative rate Repo trades were booked by swapping one security for another. The borrower received the security they wanted and loaned General Collateral. The rate on the special might be 0.0% and the general collateral side was booked at a rate of 4.00% when general collateral was trading at 3.00%. *Voila!* The equivalent of -1.00% (negative one percent). Trades were booked this way mostly because the trade processing systems at the time couldn't handle negative rates.

When the 3.625% 5/2013s rolled around in 2003, negative Repo rates still didn't officially exist. It took an extreme event to illustrate the true cost of fails, or at least to show the costs of fails over a long period of time. In order to help traders who desperately needed the 3.625% 5/2013, the Repo market devised the prompt delivery (PD) Repo trade. This was the initial incarnation of negative rates. The market needed a mechanism for someone to pay extra to guarantee they'd receive the securities. PD Repo meant the seller had to deliver the securities promptly. They needed to have the securities in their box.

However, prompt delivery Repo quickly evolved into guaranteed delivery (GD) Repo. In this incarnation, the seller had to guarantee delivery by the end of the day. The rate on a GD Repo trade was always negative, but it had a drawback: There was no penalty for failing. The trade was merely cancelled if the securities were not received. On top of that, the borrower didn't know for hours whether the securities would be delivered or not. During the depth of the PIMCO CTD squeeze in 2005, the Repo market brought back the prompt delivery trade instead of the GD trade.

After the market experienced a full year of CTD squeezes in 2005, the Bond Market Association officially proposed negative Repo rates. It was called Negative Rate Repo (NRR) and was formally adopted in April 2006. The new system attempted to solve the problem with both the PD Repo and GD Repo: the lack of penalty for failing. In the new NRR, the seller received the negative rate only if they delivered the security within 15 minutes. Otherwise, the seller owed the buyer the equivalent of the negative rate. It served as a good incentive for sellers to make sure the securities were delivered promptly. It gave buyers confidence they were getting what they paid for. Over the next few years, NRR trades were almost exclusively used for futures deliveries.

Keep in mind, this was still 2006. At this time, no one imagined a zero percent fed funds rate. Negative Repo rates were still the means to borrow a security that was in short supply, clean up a fail, or get a CTD. NRR was merely the mechanism to facilitate a settlement.

The NRR only lasted until the Financial Crisis. In response to the unprecedented number of fails in September and October 2008, regulators pressured the Treasury market to solve the fail problem. The fail charge solution basically expanded the interest rate playing field by 300 basis points. Where the previous lower boundary of the Repo market was at 0.0%, after the fail charge, Repo rates could trade anywhere in the negatives. It marked the end of PD, GD, or NRR Repo trades for guaranteed deliveries. When a security is in short supply, the negative rates just keep going lower and lower!

# Risk Management

I remember a story floating around the Repo market after the Russian Debt Crisis and the collapse of LTCM in 1998. Several South Korean banks had lost access to funding and desperately needed cash. With no one to buy their CDs, they came to the Repo market, pretty much hat in hand. The banks owned plenty of stocks and bonds issued by South Korean corporations, but they had never used Repo for funding. A large Swiss bank stepped in and offered to fund their entire securities holdings, which amounted to over $1 billion. There was one catch: The bank wanted a 50% haircut on all of the collateral. Maybe it wasn't such a surprise, but the South Korean banks quickly said, "Done!" Soon after, the Swiss bank grabbed two of its Repo traders from London and flew them to Singapore to set up a temporary shop at the bank's local office. At the time, the fed funds rate was trading at 4.75% and the bank had access to cash at 5.00%. They charged the South Korean banks a Repo rate of 10%, earning 500 basis points and generating $140,000 a day in revenue.

The two Repo traders' only task was to price the securities throughout the day and make margin calls. They knew that as long as they had the securities priced accurately and kept the 50% haircut, the transaction had very little risk. So that's what the traders did all day every day for six months; they priced the securities and made margin calls. After about 6 months, the South Korean banks started getting their funding back and the trade wound down. The Repo traders closed out the transactions and flew back to London with over $25 million in their trading book.

Moral of the story: If you have accurate prices and take the right haircut, you can safely Repo anything!

In a Repo transaction, there are two layers of security: the credit of the counterparty and the value of the securities. It's kind of like wearing both a belt and suspenders. If the counterparty is in trouble, the underlying securities can be liquidated. As long as risk is managed well, Repo transactions are very safe, however, there are still four forms of risk:

- Counterparty Risk

- Collateral Risk

- Interest Rate Risk

- Liquidity Risk

## Counterparty Risk

A central bank, a government-sponsored enterprise (GSE)[64], an exchange, and a handful of the top global banks are considered risk-free counterparties. Hedge funds, banks, investment funds, money funds, and broker-dealers all have counterparty risk. There's a risk they can go bankrupt, default, or become insolvent. At one point, every kind of Repo counterparty has defaulted, gone bankrupt, or needed a bailout – banks, broker-dealers, hedge funds, etc. But note, there was only one instance when a firm was brought down by U.S. Treasury Repo transactions. That was Drysdale.

---

[64] Like the World Bank, Fannie Mae, Freddie Mac, Ginnie Mae, Federal Home Loan Banks, etc.

If there *is* counterparty risk, it's important to understand how much. Exposure is the amount of excess margin or deficit with a Repo counterparty at any given time. If all of the Repo transactions were liquidated immediately, how much money would be left? More technically, exposure is how much the value of the underlying securities moved since the original Repo transactions were booked. The value of the securities change literally minute-by-minute with movements in the market. Most companies mark-to-market their positions at the end of the day, and then compare the original prices to the end-of-day prices.[65] One counterparty always has an excess and the other always has a deficit. The counterparty with the deficit makes a margin call on the one with the excess.

Every company assigns a credit line to each of its counterparties. It's a limit as to how much risk they will allow with that counterparty. The goal is to assign a volume of business that is safe without undue risk. Basically, something that maximizes revenue without too much risk. In Repo, credit lines are usually based on a gross limit, net limit, and/or value-at-risk (VaR).

A gross limit caps the overall amount of business that's allowed with a counterparty. The gross is generated by adding up all of the Repo and Reverse-Repo trades. Keep in mind, every kind of limit has its drawbacks. For example, let's say the gross limit is $500 million. There's a big difference in risk between a Repo of $500 million 3 Month Bills versus $500 million 30 Year Bonds.

---

[65] Repo desks make margin calls each morning, based on the previous night's closing prices. Some companies have systems that use current market prices. Note, by the next morning, the end-of-day price is already half a day old. Markets can move a lot in 12 hours!

A net limit looks at the difference between the total long and total short positions. In terms of managing risk, it's better to have both long and short positions combined. If it ever comes to a liquidation, having both longs and shorts reduces the chance of additional losses due to market movements. Once again, net limits also have drawbacks. Suppose the net limit is $100 million. That could mean a total of $200 million in long positions and $100 million in short positions, or as much as $2 billion in longs and $1.9 billion in shorts. There's a big difference between the two!

Clearly, there are risks that gross limits do not capture and risks that net limits do not capture. Overall, gross limits are better with high quality counterparties, and net limits are better with smaller counterparties.

There are many VaR models available in the market. The calculation takes a portfolio of securities and/or derivatives and returns a Value-at-Risk number. VaR can be generated based on the counterparty, the type of counterparty, the collateral type, or by long or short position. Models take into account current market volatility, historic market volatility, the maturities of the underlaying securities, and the liquidation period. If faced with a liquidation, the VaR model best reflects the liquidation risk. However, the best way to manage counterparty risk is a combination of all three: gross, net and VaR.

## Collateral Risk

Here's the second form of security, the one we called the suspenders: the collateral. When Repo and Reverse-Repo transactions are booked, the two counterparties exchange cash and securities. One counterparty has cash and the other has securities. Luckily, in case of a default or a bankruptcy, the *automatic stay* of the bankruptcy law does not apply. That was established thanks to David Heuwetter and Drysdale. If the non-defaulting counterparty is the securities borrower, securities are sold. If the non-defaulting counterparty is the securities lender, the securities are repurchased. The important thing is that the liquidation process is immediate and absolute.

In order to cushion the impact of a counterparty default, one counterparty generally asks the other for a haircut, or margin.[66] The entity with the better credit is usually the one doing the asking. A sovereign requires margin from a bank, a bank requires margin from a broker-dealer, a broker-dealer requires margin from the hedge fund, and so on. The trick is to figure out the appropriate amount of margin. For example, the risk on a 3 Month Bill Repo is much different than the risk on a 30 Year Bond Repo. One-size-fits-all margin should be a thing of the past, but it's generally not.

If it ever gets to the point of liquidation, here's how a typical liquidation works: On the first day, the value of the securities declined and there's a margin call. The money wire cutoff time is 6:00 PM EST, so the counterparty has the entire day to deliver the funds. If the counterparty misses the margin call, there could be a number of reasons why. Perhaps the funds were mistakenly sent to the wrong account, perhaps there was an operational error, or perhaps the margin call was in dispute and the party ignored it. Worst case, the counterparty doesn't have enough cash to make the call.

---

[66] Repo Principle – There's always an appropriate haircut that can make a Repo transaction almost risk-free.

The next day, the original margin call remains in effect. A second margin call is issued with a notice that if the call is not met, a liquidation could begin the next day.

On the third day, a legal notice is sent to the defaulting counterparty.[67] It says that unless the margin call is received immediately, a liquidation will begin. Once the liquidation begins, the liquidator makes sure to receive the best prices available and documents the entire process. Once the securities are liquidated,[68] there's either an excess or a deficit left over. If there are excess funds, they are returned to the defaulting party. If there's a deficit, the liquidating counterparty becomes a creditor of the defaulted entity.

The three-day liquidation process has significance in the Repo market. It's why VaR models use a three-day assumption. It's assumed that it takes three days for a liquidation to occur, start to finish. The VaR model estimates how much the price of the security can move in three days. That's the risk. If it takes three days to liquidate a counterparty, then the value that's at risk is how much the securities can move in three days.

Some markets look at VaR differently. When VaR is calculated for futures contracts, the models assume a one-day liquidation period because they assume it will only take one day to liquidate futures positions. That makes sense, given the standardization of futures contracts and the liquidity in most futures markets. As of recently, the CFTC proposed a five-day liquidation period assumption for interest rate swaps. This has a large impact on the economics of that market. If the margin requirement reflects how much the price can move in five

---

[67] There must be proof the counterparty received the notice.

[68] Assuming liquidity is good and there are no unexpected market moves.

days rather than three days, there's inherently more margin required to trade in the market.

## Interest Rate Risk

Repo transactions are money market investments, just like CDs, commercial paper, or Treasury bills. Term Repo transactions carry interest rate risk. If a term Repo trade is booked for three months, interest rates can change. Suppose the Fed unexpectedly raises rates by 50 basis points? Term Repo and Reverse-Repo transactions have interest rate risk which is not related to the value of the underlying securities.

## Liquidity Risk

The term liquidity has different meanings and applications in the financial markets. When used in relation to a liquidation, it means how easily a security can be sold. The Treasury market has razor-thin bid/offer spreads, and hundreds of millions can trade at any given time. The Treasury market is very liquid. Liquidity also means how easily a company can meet its financial obligations. A company can be well capitalized and be worth billions of dollars, but it still needs enough cash on hand to pay its bills.[69] Liquidity risk can arise in the Repo market due to the timing of margin payments.

Because the Treasury market is a global market that trades 24 hours a day, the value of the underlying securities moves during the course of the day <u>and</u> night. On top of that, different market participants issue margin calls at different times. For example, FICC uses end-of-day prices for a morning margin call and mid-day prices

---

[69] It can be argued that MF Global was sufficiently capitalized and became illiquid due to margin calls.

for an afternoon call. Repo counterparties generally exchange margin in the morning by 10:00 AM based on end-of-day prices. The futures market uses end-of-day prices for an end-of-day margin call. Many European entities prefer to settle margins before the U.S. opens and based on European closing prices. With margin calls at different times during the day and a 24-hour market, it's no surprise there are all kinds of scenarios of mis-matched margin call payments. A bank might satisfy margin calls with its clients based on the previous day's closing prices and have an FICC margin call in the afternoon. In a quiet market, this risk is nominal. In a volatile market, there's much more liquidity risk to worry about.

## Herstatt Risk

Back in 1974, a small German bank named Bankhaus Herstatt was in trouble. After a thorough review of their financial condition, their regulator forced them into liquidation on June 6, 1974. Given that Herstatt had an active foreign exchange trading business, they were settling a number of foreign exchange transactions with other banks that day. Herstatt had bought German marks and sold U.S. dollars. Their counterparties paid Herstatt the German marks during normal European settlement hours – a 4:30 PM cutoff-time in Germany (10:30 AM in New York). However, Herstatt was only open long enough that day to collect the German marks, but not pay the dollars. By the end of the day, Herstatt was left holding both the marks and the dollars, and then their accounts were frozen.

Ever since then, the risk of mismatched payments is known as "Herstatt risk." Even today this risk is still real. There are several different clearing facilities for settling cash and securities across Europe, the U.S., and Asia. On paper, a settlement might show up as a single day, but in fact there are 24 hours within the day and three major trading zones.

Herstatt risk also showed up just recently. It occurred in the Treasury market during the Covid Crisis of March 2020. There were incredibly large swings in the bond market that month, perhaps some of the largest moves ever. One morning, FICC added a morning margin call based on morning prices. It sounds like a prudent request from their perspective. However, banks and broker-dealers were still using the previous night's closing prices for margin calls with most of their clients. This meant additional margin had to be delivered to FICC, but it could not be collected from clients. Naturally this occurred on the day with one of the largest price moves in bond market history. Changing the FICC margin call from using end-of-day prices to morning prices was worth hundreds of millions of dollars to the dealer community. In the end, nothing could be done, because you can't miss a margin call with FICC!

# Accounting Rules and Scandals

A Repo matched-book is a great business. It's low-risk and generates a great return on capital. There's one drawback though: It generates a lot of assets. If you're looking for a great return-on-equity (ROE), Repo is the business for you! If return-on-assets (ROA) is important, keep walking, because Repo is not for you. Given the high balance sheet usage of Repo, it's no surprise the market is always looking for ways to reduce it.

The first iteration was the creation of FICC. The Central Clearing Counterparty allowed a significant increase in Repo netting. The ability to net is based on an accounting rule called Financial Accounting Standards Board (FASB) Interpretation No. 41.[70] Under this rule, a Repo and Reverse-Repo transaction can be netted if they're both with the same counterparty, they're the same type of security, and they have the same Repo end date.[71] International accounting rules are a little different. They allow netting Repo transactions with the same counterparty, the same Repo end date, just like the U.S. However, they require the exact same security. By allowing the broader same *type* of security, the U.S. allows hundreds of billions of dollars of additional balance sheet netting.

---

[70] In no way should you take this as accounting advice. Consult your accountant.
[71] The maturity of the underlying securities does not matter.

For example, suppose a U.S. bank borrows $100 million of the U.S. Treasury 5 Year Note from a hedge fund and loans the hedge fund $100 million 10 Year Notes in an overnight Repo transaction. In the U.S., the trades completely net off of the bank's balance sheet. Wiped clean. Gone. Globally, they're still there.

Over the years, the rule was stretched even further. The next change was to allow all securities that settled in the Fedwire system to net. That added federal agencies, like Fannie Mae, Ginnie Mae, and Freddie Mac, alongside Treasurys. They're all obligations of the U.S. government, so there's no reason why agencies wouldn't be included.

The next move took it one step further. Some banks began interpreting the "same type of security" to include all securities that settle within the same depository. For example, anything that settles in the Fedwire, like U.S. Treasurys and agencies, or all securities that settle within DTC, like corporate bonds. They began netting the bonds issued by Exxon with the bonds issued by Microsoft. Yes, it pushed the rule a little further, but there was still an argument to be made.

Netting U.S. Treasurys and agencies is pretty solid. There are good arguments to net corporate bonds. However, these are all minor expansions compared to how MF Global and Lehman Brothers pushed the rule. There's a big difference between aggressively reducing assets and outright hiding assets. It reminds me of the old saying: What's the difference between tax avoidance and tax evasion? A good lawyer. In the case of MF Global and Lehman, it was a cooperative accountant.

MF Global and Lehman both knowingly exploited the accounting rules to hide assets, and those hidden assets played an important role in the downfall of each firm. At first glance, it appears they used accounting gimmicks. However, there are important distinctions between the loopholes for Repo-To-Maturity and the so called "Repo 105."

Getting back to Repo market basics, a Repo transaction is the sale of an asset with an agreement to buy it back. The forward purchase is a key element of a Repo transaction. Without the forward transaction, it's purely a sale. That means the definition of what's a "sale" and what's not a "sale" is a critical part. FASB 140 is the accounting rule that governs whether or not a transaction is a "true sale."

If FASB 140 were a standardized set of rules, there would be no issue with its implementation. However, there were multiple interpretations that allowed those companies to manipulate the numbers for their benefit. A "true sale" is defined as "a transfer of a financial asset in which the transferor surrenders control over the asset."[72] The key word is "control." If one party gives control to another party, the original party relinquishes ownership. But then again, how do you determine if someone has "control" or not? An outright sale is definitely a loss of control. It gets a little more complicated when it comes to the control of securities under repurchase agreements and securities swaps.

Case in point: What if the securities are "loaned" to maturity, as in the case of MF Global? Does a Repo-To-Maturity constitute a "true sale"? Does a one-week sale with a quasi-option to repurchase the

---

[72] Once again, do not take accounting advice from me. Consult your accountant.

securities constitute a "true sale," as in the case of Repo 105? Oh, and by the way, that week always coincided with quarter-end.

A Repo-To-Maturity occurs when one party loans a security to another party until the security matures. Suppose someone owns a Treasury bill that matures on August 15. Instead of selling the bill, they Repo (loan) the bill until August 15. Instead of actually selling the bill, they loaned it to maturity. If a Repo-To-Maturity constitutes a "true sale," then it's pretty much the same as selling the bill. On one hand, the original owner is relinquishing control of their bonds. On the other hand, as part of a repurchase agreement, they will buy back the bonds on the maturity date. On the one hand again, the bonds mature on the Repo end-date, so they don't really didn't exist anymore. It was definitely a rule that needed interpretation.

In the case of Repo-To-Maturity, most banks kept them as "on-balance sheet transactions" where they were recognized as assets. However, some companies treated them as "off-balance sheet." Up until MF Global, the securities involved were all risk-free U.S. Treasurys settling at a risk-free central clearing counterparty. There were good arguments either way, but it was still a matter of interpretation.

MF Global took the whole transaction one step further. Actually, let's say two steps further. They entered into Repo-To-Maturity trades with non-risk-free securities, like the sovereign bonds of Italy, Spain, Portugal, Ireland, and Belgium. Then, since LCH.Clearnet did not allow Repo trades to mature on the same day as the underlying collateral, MF Global settled the Repo trades two days before maturity. Technically the MF Global transactions were not risk-free and therefore were not exactly Repo-To-Maturity.

Luckily for MF Global, their accounting firm allowed the trades to be removed from their balance sheet. As of December 31, 2010, there was about $5 billion in European sovereign debt that did not appear on the firm's balance sheet. By June 2011, they had jacked it up to $11.5 billion. The firm enjoyed a very favorable accounting interpretation.

The downfall came when both their accounting firm and FINRA began to question the regulatory capital requirements. Then it was discovered that MF Global's Repo-To-Maturity trades ended two days before the bonds matured. Getting the securities back two days before maturity clearly did not constitute giving up control. It was that fact that eventually led to the change in the accountant's FASB 140 opinion. In July 2011, the decision was handed down that MF Global's "sale" really didn't qualify as "true," at least as far as the accountants were concerned. When that happened, $11.5 billion in European sovereign bonds magically reappeared on their balance sheet.

After that, the regulators began taking a closer look, which then led to a capital charge on the trades, which led to the restatement of their July 31, 2011 FOCUS report. All of a sudden, it appeared the MF Global broker-dealer was undercapitalized. After a disastrous earnings report, when a loss of $191.6 million was announced in October 2011, it led to the "run on the bank." The rest is history.[73]

Whereas MF Global exploited a grey area of accounting, Lehman's use of Repo 105 was outright hiding assets. Repo-To-Maturity is kindergarten compared to how Lehman Brothers under-

---

[73] See my book, *The Money Noose*, for the whole MF Global story.

reported its balance sheet. Where MF Global enjoyed a favorable interpretation of FASB 140, Lehman was downright exploiting it. In total, the use of Repo 105 allowed Lehman to move between $40 billion to $50 billion of assets off of their balance sheet each quarter-end.

In 1998, I was working for a Dutch bank and our salesman from Lehman called me one day. He proposed a transaction where I could make an easy 15 to 20 basis points. All I had to do was to finance some of Lehman's assets over quarter-end. Just for a few days, maybe a week. Lehman's securities would be "sold" to me via a "total return swap." The easy basis points were intriguing. However, after examining the swap agreement, I understood how it worked. On the end-date of the transaction, I had the right, but not the obligation, to sell the securities back to Lehman. I was allowed to sell the securities to another party at current market prices. But that was only if I wanted to. That, of course, would never happen, since Lehman's repurchase price was always going to be higher. There was no way anyone would sell the securities to anyone besides Lehman.

I declined doing the trades, feeling there was no reason to bulk up the bank's balance sheet over quarter-end for just 15 to 20 basis points for a week. I really felt it was a sucker's trade. A lot of time and effort – and balance sheet – for only a few basis points. I remember the salesman at Lehman Brothers coming back to me and saying, "I thought you'd do the trade." Why? Because they were already doing it with another trading desk at my bank! I later learned that Lehman was doing it all around the Street.

The total return swaps, however, did not last much longer. There was a new accounting rule scheduled to take effect in September 2000.

Senior executives at Lehman began meeting to discuss ways of "window dressing" for quarter-end. With the size of their balance sheet growing, it left Lehman shopping around for a new way to hide their assets. They were looking for an accounting firm to approve a transaction similar to the "total return swap." The new incarnation would be called "Repo 105." The term Repo 105 got its name from the fact that the counterparty received 5% in excess securities as margin, and was taken from the Repo term "1.05% pricing." The assets and the 5% margin were frozen for the life of the trade. Lehman claimed they were losing control and that naturally meant it was as a "true sale."

As Lehman shopped around for a favorable opinion on Repo 105, every accounting and law firm except one refused to classify it as a "true sale." The law firm of Linklaters LLP in London agreed to write a favorable opinion for Lehman Brothers International. They declared that Repo 105 could be classified as a "true sale," but only under English law. Lehman was faced with a dilemma: Repo 105 was a "true sale" in London, but not in New York. In order to exploit the opinion, they had to move their assets from New York to London, and then book them with clients in Europe. That meant the counterparties for Repo 105 all were European banks. When it was time for Lehman in New York to be audited, their accounting firm conveniently looked the other way when massive amounts of securities left for London every quarter-end.

FASB eventually published an update[74] for the Repo-To-Maturity rules, which revised the accounting. Technically, Repo-To-Maturity is no longer considered a sale with a forward purchase. Instead, it's now a "secured borrowing" transaction. Thus, banks can no longer remove

---

[74] Update No. 2014-10

Repo-To-Maturity securities from their balance sheets. Naturally, Repo 105 ended when Lehman collapsed on September 15, 2008.

# FIRE SALES

*"When blood is running in the streets of Paris, that's when I buy."*

-BARON JAMES DE ROTHSCHILD

The first recorded instance of the term "fire sale" came from an advertisement posted by Maraton Upton, a resident of Fitchburg, Massachusetts. He suffered a massive fire at his home in December 1856. Following the destruction, Upton needed money, so he took out an advertisement that read in part, "Extraordinary Fire Sale; customers are invited to call and examine goods which are still warm."

These days, the term fire sale is still common in American life. Regardless of the setting, the meaning is always the same: Something is for sale, condition notwithstanding, for significantly less than it would cost new. For that matter, not only is it a discounted price, it's available at a drastically reduced price.

The financial markets are rife with fire sales. You could say it's a part of the business, the nature of the market. Rarely have a few years passed without some kind of liquidation that constituted a forced sale at a distressed price.

The rise of shadow banking added to the frequency of fire sales. No matter how you slice it, it comes down to one thing: leverage. Companies borrow money to buy assets to amplify their returns; at the same time, that borrowed money also amplifies risk. As long as the markets are stable, life is good. But when a company is highly leveraged and the market peaks, the end of the story is never a good one. Once the market declines, it leads to margin calls, margin calls lead to sales, sales lead to more price declines, which ultimately lead to liquidations. It's a downward spiral.

One of the best examples of a fire sale occurred at Bear Stearns Asset Management (BSAM) during the subprime housing bubble. As it turned out, they were one of the first dominos to fall in the period leading up to the Financial Crisis. Though at the time, no one realized what was to come. BSAM was caught highly leveraged just at the peak of the market. Once the market declined, they didn't have a chance. The declining market led to margin calls, which led to sales, and eventually they were liquidated.

BSAM was an affiliate of Bear Stearns, the investment bank. The asset management group was composed of two hedge funds that invested in the subprime mortgage market. No, they weren't like the heroes in *The Big Short* who were shorting the overinflated housing market. These were the guys still buying mortgage-backed securities at the peak. They owned a massive amount of CDOs (collateralized debt obligations) and were leveraged to the hilt.

The hedge funds were set up in 2003 when two traders from the Bear Stearns mortgage desk – Ralph Cioffi and Matthew Tannin – were sent over to start the business. Back then, CDOs were the new big thing and hedge funds that invested in mortgage-backed securities were popping up everywhere. The funds were billed as investing in "low-risk, high-grade debt securities." They had a great start, generating a 46.8% annualized return from 2003 to March 2007, exclusively from CDO investments.

Looking back, one might wonder why a sophisticated investor would buy something like a CDO. Here's the hook: The securities often paid a higher than market yield for the first few years. Just like offering a toaster to someone willing to open a savings account, the Street understands how investors can be short sighted. They pump-up the initial yield to attract buyers. The investor knows there's risk, but the incremental returns look great today!

The subprime loan market peaked sometime at the end of 2006. By the time 2007 rolled around, the market was toppy and was beginning to decline. The assets of BSAM had grown considerably since 2003, reaching $20 billion.[75] Of course, the funds didn't have $20 billion of investor money; the larger fund had $925 million and the smaller fund had $638 million. That's about $1.563 billion combined. So how did they leverage themselves to $20 billion in assets? That was done was courtesy of the Repo market! Back then, every large bank was eager to sell the CDOs they originated. Many investors only purchased the securities because the bank agreed to finance them. In order to keep the underwriting machine rolling, the banks offered very sweet financing terms. BSAM paid relatively small 10% haircuts.[76] Yes, they borrowed 90% of the money used to purchase some of the most volatile and illiquid securities ever created!

During the month of March 2007, cracks appeared in the market. Twenty-five subprime mortgage lenders went out of business. At first, the Street's reaction was muted. BSAM's Repo counterparties

---

[75] $11.5 billion in long positions and $4.5 billion in short positions in one fund and $9.7 billion in long positions and $4 billion in short positions in the other fund.

[76] Margin.

demanded monthly performance statements and issued more frequent margin calls. As the subprime market worsened, the margin calls became larger. Given that BSAM was already fully leveraged, they were forced to sell securities every time there was a margin call. In April 2007, the cracks widened further when the funds posted a loss of 6.75%. After the announcement, some investors demanded their money back. The funds had to sell more securities to pay off investors. All of this put additional downward pressure on the CDO market.

In May, the funds lost another 18%, and they still didn't have enough capital to meet the margin calls. Little did they know, the situation was about to get worse. Goldman Sachs, which was one of their largest Repo counterparties, had been marking their positions between 98 and 97 cents on the dollar. Just one month later, Goldman marked the securities to between 50 and 60 cents on the dollar. On a mark-to-market basis, the securities had lost half of their value in a month. Talk about a sell off!

Luckily for Cioffi and Tannin, not all of the Repo counterparties were as aggressive as Goldman. Yes, the others marked down the positions and issued margin calls, but it was about to get even worse. The Repo counterparties all jacked up the margin requirements. Whereas BSAM was charged 10% in the past, most of their counterparties increased it to 20%. Some even wanted 50%. Talk about being stuck between a rock and a hard place! Just when prices were falling, the Street issued margin calls, investors demanded their money back, and the Street increased their margin requirements. It doesn't get much worse.

On June 15, 2007, it was all over. The funds were declared in default and the liquidation began. Merrill Lynch, Goldman Sachs, and

JP Morgan liquidated most of the collateral. However, Merrill made a catastrophic mistake during the liquidation. When they couldn't sell the securities at prices they deemed acceptable, they held on. They took the securities into their own account, figuring the market would eventually recover. Down the road, they exposed themselves to larger losses.

Not too surprising, the Street expected Bear Steans to bail out the funds. The funds were named "Bear Stearns Asset Management" after all! Everyone expected Bear to do something. Bear, on the other hand, looked at it differently. They had invested only $40 million of their own capital in the funds and figured a bailout would expose them to larger losses. They were right. Though they had no legal responsibility to bail out the funds, in the end, under intense pressure from the Street, Bear loaned the funds $3.2 billion.

Once the dust settled, it was time to assign blame. The SEC claimed Cioffi and Tannin misled investors. They were charged with securities fraud. Prosecutors relied on internal emails which showed that Cioffi and Tannin reassured investors in public while panicking internally. The two principals maintained to the end that the banks had propped up the value of their CDOs to protect the banks' own positions. Once the banks unloaded, they started marking down their clients. Cioffi and Tannin were acquitted in 2009 of criminal charges.

Let's put it bluntly: Regulators don't like fire sales![77] Over the years, there's been a lot of time and energy spent trying to find a

---

[77] I attended the Federal Reserve's conference on "Fire Sales as a Driver of Systemic Risk in Tri-Party Repo and Other Secured Funding Markets" on Friday, October 4, 2013. The Fed's definition of a fire sale is when an entity is forced to sell quickly and at a low price. The key part here is that others must be harmed by the fire sale. As one official noted, "We don't care if people run, as long as it's not systemic."

solution to the problem. It's one thing when private capital loses money based on bad decisions, but it's a much bigger problem when a liquidation affects other companies' assets. That's contagion. And no one wants contagion.

The technical term for this is a "collective action problem." If everyone sells at once, it drives prices down further than if everyone coordinated their sales. It's kind of like the prisoner's dilemma, but in the financial markets. The first one to talk (sell) gets the best deal. However, if the prisoners (dealers) all cooperated, they'd get a better deal as a whole.

Regulators have always loved the idea of an industry consortium that comes together to liquidate defaulted financial companies. Many proponents of the industry consortium use Long Term Capital Management (LTCM) as the showcase. When LTCM failed, their counterparties pooled funds together, took over LTCM, and unwound their positions over time at a pace which did not stress the market. The consortium was successful.

Right now, there's no industry mechanism to coordinate liquidations during a market crisis. This is a valid concern. Regulators have pushed for a consortium of dealers, a central clearing counterparty, or an industry group to take over defaulted counterparties during a crisis. However, such a consortium has more than a few major problems. The Repo market's exemption from the automatic stay provision of the bankruptcy code would have to be changed. The structure is best for the prisoner who talks first or the dealer who sells first. Imagine waiting weeks or months to get your cash or securities back. Another problem is the source of the capital. How do you get market participants to contribute and how much?

In the end, it's a problem that's hard to solve. In the Treasury market, regulators are pushing to get the entire market into FICC. The central clearing counterparty has a default fund and experience to mutualize members' risk. However, importance of solving contagion in the U.S. Treasury market is small compared to something like the CDO market. For now, there's no good solution. Bottom line: Everyone would like to eliminate fire sales, except of course, those luckily enough to buy cheap assets "when blood is running in the streets."

I had the opportunity[78] to liquidate a large Repo customer. They were a well-known name in the financial markets, and the liquidation came at the worst time, right in the middle of the Liquidity Crisis of August 2007. This customer was leveraged with well over a billion dollars of corporate bonds, structured corporate bonds, CDOs, and a small amount of U.S. Treasurys and federal agencies.

One of the hardest parts of a fire sale liquidation is that you're unsure of the outcome. As soon as you legally take over the customer's positions, you're in a no-win situation. If you sell the positions and there's excess cash, you must return the funds to the bankrupt entity. If you lose money, you stand in line at the bankruptcy and might not get a settlement for years. When the bankruptcy gets resolved, you'll probably receive a fraction of what you're owed.

The key to a liquidation rests on not losing money. Makes sense, right? That means mark-to-market prices must be as accurate as possible and the margin must cover market volatility. If both the

---

[78] I'm not sure if this is the best word!

prices and margin are accurate, there's a good chance of getting out unscathed.

Here are recommendations for handling a liquidation:

1. **Devise a plan** Determine how much to sell each day, the maximum loss you'll accept on a security, who you're going to speak with, and who you can trust.

2. **Counterparties** Determine who is the best bid for different types of securities. For example, individual banks will be the best bid for their own paper.

3. **Keep a low profile** The key is to not to let the Street know about the liquidation and the size. If the Street has too much information, they'll front-run you.

4. **Stick to the plan** When prices are lower than expected, sell them and don't try to trade out of a bad market. Holding can work sometimes, but as a rule of thumb, it's the worst strategy. Holding positions too long will also open up questions from the bankruptcy trustee down the road.

# FLIGHTS-TO-QUALITY

*"When you go from a seller's market to a buyer's market, there's a lot
of pain. But going forward, there's a lot of opportunity."*
- MICHAEL VRANOS[79]

A financial crisis and a Flight-To-Quality[80] go hand-in-hand. The
crisis might be an economic slowdown, a panic, a stock market crash,
a terrorist attack, a liquidity squeeze, or even a global virus. When the
crisis begins, the Flight-To-Quality is the market's first reaction.
Investors quickly sell risky and illiquid assets and buy the safe and
secure assets.

During this time, the spread between credit products and risk-
free assets widens. Leveraged investors reduce the size of their balance
sheets, and the market builds in the expectation of Fed rate cuts. At
this point, it's hard to determine how much of the declining rates are
due to investor panic or expected rate cuts. Lower yields could be the
market pricing an aggressive Fed, or it could mean investors have
over-bought. You don't really know until the market settles down

The tool commonly used to gauge the severity of a financial crisis
is the spread between bank CDs and the Fed funds rate. The
LIBOR[81]/OIS spread is the rate difference between term bank deposits
and the effective Fed funds rate. When there's stress in the financial

---

[79] The legendary head of Ellington Management Group; Institutional Investor; September 1998; Page 39.
[80] Sometimes called a Flight-To-Safety and sometimes called a Flight-To-Liquidity.
[81] London Inter-Bank Offered Rate.

system, banks must pay more to borrow money. In the Repo market, the spread between General Collateral and fed funds is the equivalent gauge. General Collateral rates decline relative to fed funds when there's an increase in demand for safe assets.

During a panic, U.S. Treasurys are the investment of choice. When risks are high, investors want U.S. Treasurys. Investor buying removes Treasurys from the Repo market as they pack them away in portfolios. This creates premium for Treasury collateral. Panicked investors don't loan their securities either. They're worried their counterparty might go bust.

The Repo market itself is very resilient during a crisis. For one thing, FICC is a secure counterparty for Repo transactions. Banks and broker-dealers don't face each other directly; they have a AA-rated, central clearing counterparty standing in between. Because of this, the inter-dealer Repo market doesn't shut down.

It may sound surprising, but different types of Treasury collateral can trade at different rates. Treasury bills have the most demand and trade at a premium. TIPS, floating-rate-notes, and bond collateral trade at a discount. The difference might only be a few basis points, but there's a difference nonetheless.

And just like in the broader market, anything with credit risk is more difficult to finance. Cash investors often stop taking lower quality paper, which makes that paper harder to finance. Federal agencies, agency mortgages, and investment grade corporate bonds hold up well, but no one wants high-yield, CDOs, ABS, or CMOs.

Another effect is that banks and broker-dealers cut back on the credit they extend to their customers. When the market is deleveraging, they are already worried about client liquidations, so they often increase the haircuts and cut back on the size of credit lines. They see this as the best way to reduce risk.

Customers act differently during a crisis. Hedge funds and leveraged investors have no choice but to accept the more restrictive financing terms they are given. But customers, like corporate treasurers and money market funds, have leverage because they're the ones supplying the market with cash. When risks are high, they would never say to their management, "Let's keep trading with Lehman, but just charge them a larger haircut." During a panic, people are nervous and panicky. They just stop doing business with the Street, waiting for the market to settle down before they get back in.

There's more demand for on-the-run issues during a crisis. When the market is moving fast, there's a preference for liquidity, and off-the-run issues have either wide bid/off spreads or no market at all. The current, on-the-run issues have all the liquidity. Increased demand for current issues means more hedging shorts which tends to drive Repo rates lower.

Once it's all over and the crisis subsides, Treasurys start filtering back into the market. Sometimes the Repo market shows the first sign of a crisis ending. The spread between General Collateral and fed funds begins to return to normal.

Here's a look at some financial crises and how they impacted the Repo market:

## LTCM/Russian Debt Crisis 1998

When Russia defaulted on its sovereign debt on August 17, 1998, the event put the financial markets in a tailspin. Global markets sold-off and spreads began widening. Hedge funds were in trouble, and the biggest of them all, Long Term Capital Management (LTCM), collapsed.

- Number of years since the previous crisis: 4[82]

- Months when it occurred: September-November

- Number of Fed eases during the crisis: 3

- Total basis points of Fed cuts: 125

- Duration of the crisis in the Repo market: End of September to the beginning of November. About six weeks

- Depth of crisis: GC/fed funds spread hit -45 basis points on October 21

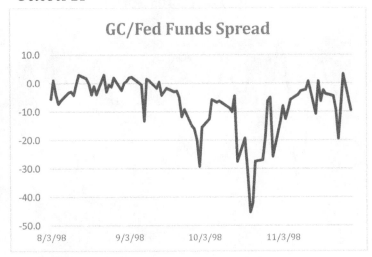

---

[82] Take your pick: Mexican Peso crisis, aggressive Fed tightening, Orange County bankruptcy.

# September 11, 2001

After the terrorist attack on the World Trade Center, the financial markets were frozen and unable to process trades because all of downtown New York City was without power.

- Number of years since the previous crisis: 3

- Months when it occurred: September, October

- Number of Fed eases during the crisis: 2[83]

- Total basis points of Fed cuts: 100

- Duration of the crisis in the Repo market: From September 11 to October 15. About four weeks

- Depth of crisis: GC/fed funds spread bottomed at only -25 basis points

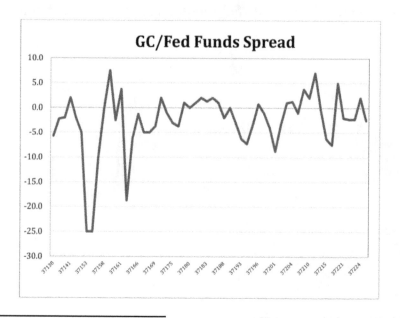

---

[83] The Fed was already in an easing cycle, so they continued to cut rates even after the crisis was over.

# Liquidity Crisis of August 2007

The Liquidity Crisis of August 2007 is sometimes referred to as the beginning of the Financial Crisis. It was a crisis of corporate and bank credit more than anything in the Treasury market. Though the crisis was mostly over within a month, September quarter-end pushed it out further.

- Number of years since the previous crisis: 6

- Months when it occurred: August, September

- Number of Fed eases during the crisis: 2

- Total basis points of Fed cuts: 75

- Duration of the crisis in the Repo market: August 15 to the beginning of October. About 6 weeks

- Depth of crisis: GC/fed funds spread hit -277 basis points on August 22, 2007

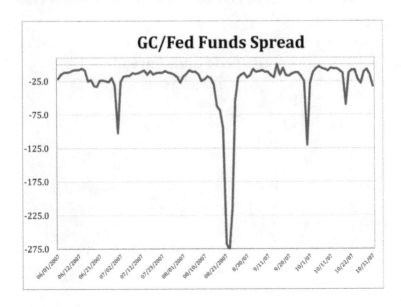

# The Financial Crisis 2008

The "GCAT" – Greatest Crisis of All Time! Officially, it began with the collapse of Lehman Brothers on September 15, 2008. The crisis in the Repo market started quickly thereafter; the GC/fed funds spread dropped to -195 basis points on the first day.

- Number of years since the previous crisis: 1

- Months when it occurred: September, October

- Number of Fed eases during the crisis: 3

- Total basis points of Fed cuts: 200

- Duration of the crisis in the Repo market: September 15 to the end of October. About 5 weeks

- Depth of crisis in the Repo market: GC/Fed funds spread hit -500 basis points on September 30 quarter-end. During the crisis, General Collateral averaged 155 basis points below fed funds

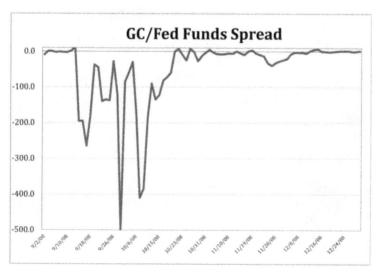

# COVID Crisis 2020

The COVID-19 virus began to filter into the U.S. at the end of February 2020. By the middle of March, a crisis was in full swing. Many financial companies, such as hedge funds and REITs, were highly leveraged with Treasurys and mortgage-backed securities. When liquidity left the market, spreads widened, generating losses and forced sales.

This was a much different crisis in the Repo market than any other crisis. In the past, General Collateral always traded at a premium. During the depth of this crisis, General Collateral traded well above fed funds.

- Number of years since the previous crisis: 12[84]

- Months when it occurred: March, April

- Number of Fed eases during the crisis: 2

- Total basis points of Fed cuts: 150

- Duration of the crisis in the Repo market: Middle of March 2020 to beginning of April 2020. About 3 weeks

- Depth of crisis: GC/fed funds spread hit +46 basis points[85] on March 17, 2020

---

[84] Nine years if you count the European Debt Crisis in 2011.
[85] Notice the plus sign and not a negative sign.

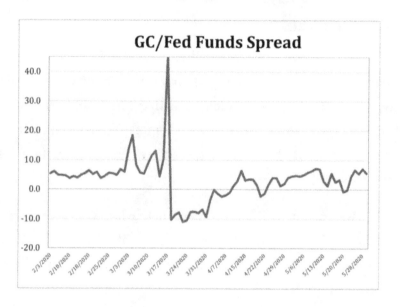

It used to be called the Greenspan Put,[86] but now the market realizes it wasn't just former Fed Chairman Alan Greenspan who aggressively added liquidity at the first sign of trouble. It's now the standard operating procedure in every central bank's playbook. But there are some detractors. Some call the Fed's easy lending policies during a crisis moral hazard. It's true, every time markets crash, the Fed supplies so much liquidity that it makes it look like the government is bailing out Wall Street. Should the Fed bail out Wall Street every time there's a financial crisis? On one hand the answer is yes, because the Fed *is* the lender of last resort, after all. On the other hand, there should be consequences for risky mistakes.

---

[86] I believe the term was originally called "The Greenspan Put" because Fed Chairman Alan Greenspan was very quick to provide liquidity to the financial system after the stock market crashed in 1987 and throughout the 1990s. These days people use the term Fed Put.

Let's take it one step further: Does Wall Street consciously engage in risky behavior because they know the Fed will provide liquidity? I can safely say no. No one I ever met wants to go through weeks and months of losses, panic, and worry during a crisis. The Street just doesn't think that way. A better prescription is to use preventative medicine when the patient is healthy. Tough love when the patient is on the operating table only serves to kill the patient.

# THE LIQUIDITY CRISIS

# 2007

It might have been called The Great Liquidity Crisis of 2007 or maybe even The Liquidity Crisis of August 2007, but unfortunately, it's mostly forgotten. In fact, there's very little written about it. It's just like how no one cared about Bear Stearns once Lehman collapsed.

The Liquidity Crisis is relevant because it illustrates how the cracks in the financial system began. Some believe the Financial Crisis really began in August 2007. At that time, the run on the banking system had started and, they argue, the financial system was already insolvent. It might even be argued that the demise of Bear Stearns began in August 2007.

Subprime mortgage loans were never the asset that buy-and-hold investors wanted on their books. Sure, mortgage originators loved the idea of underwriting these loans, but the problem was that no one wanted to hold them. As financial innovation progressed over the years, Wall Street found a solution: Mortgage banks, S&Ls, and community banks could underwrite the loans and sell them to the investment banks. Wall Street took risky loans that banks didn't want and pooled them into securities. While owning a single subprime loan carried a lot of risk, owning one share of thousands was considered diversified. Or at least that's how the theory went. For everyone involved, this was a great solution, and suddenly subprime debt was a hot commodity.

As the years went on, the Street securitized everything they could get their hands on: credit cards loans, auto loans, student loans, home equity loans, and more. The debt was cobbled together, sliced into tranches, and sold off in pieces. The Sunday fish stew of the financial markets!

The rating agencies were supposed to monitor the quality of these loans. It was their job to judge whether a bond would pay interest on schedule and the principal at maturity. At first glance, you would think when thousands of subprime mortgage loans were pooled together, they became a subprime rated security. However, if the securities were overcollateralized with more loans than the stated value, they received a high rating from the credit agencies. Theoretically, the odds were supposed to be 1 in 10,000 that top-rated AAA-rated security could go from AAA down to CCC in one year. Guess what? Many did![87] It was a powder keg waiting to explode.

The lead-up to the Liquidity Crisis was subtle. At first, it appeared the housing market had peaked and was suffering a correction. Then, several financial institutions went out of business. UBS, the colossal Swiss bank, closed Dillon Read Capital Management after a $123 million loss on May 4, 2007. Bear Stearns Asset Management collapsed in June. Then, on August 7, BNP Paribas froze two of their

[87] On August 21, 2007, S&P downgraded two sets of residential MBSs from AAA down to CCC+ and CCC.

money market funds.[88] One week later, Sentinel Capital Management, a highly-leveraged Chicago money market fund, went bust.

When the crisis struck, it started in the Commercial Paper market. Commercial Paper is a short-term funding source for banks and corporations. The securities are very short-term, with maturities of less than 270 days. The market had grown considerably through a recent innovation: Asset-Backed Commercial Paper (ABCP). Banks created asset-backed conduits to help fund their loan portfolios. These were Special Purpose Vehicles (SPVs)[89] that bought short-term assets from the bank, and issued ABCP for funding. The banks unloaded all kinds of debt – car loans, home equity loans, credit card loans – into their SPVs. Back in 2007, Commercial Paper was a $3 trillion market.

At the beginning of August 2007, investors suddenly got spooked. The market knew many banks and SPVs were over-leveraged with risky debts. The problem was they didn't know who. The result was that the whole Commercial Paper market shut down. ABCP, which accounted for about half of the entire market, stopped trading. By the middle of August, the amount of Commercial Paper outstanding fell by $244.1 billion. That's $244.1 billion of funding that issuers had to find elsewhere, often taping their back-up funding lines at the banks.

---

[88] They both resumed trading on August 30, 2007.
[89] Sometimes called a Special Purpose Entity (SPE).

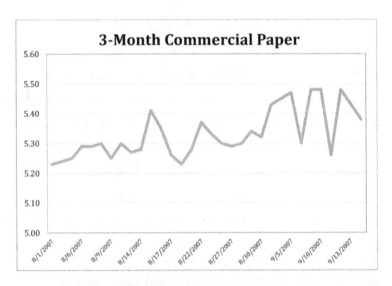

*Federal Reserve Bank of St. Louis https://fred.stlouisfed.org/*

One of the first affected was Countrywide Financial, the big California subprime underwriter. When they couldn't sell their Commercial Paper, they received a rescue package from a consortium of banks. By the end of August, the entire Commercial Paper market had shrunk by almost $1 trillion.

At the beginning of the crisis, the fed funds target rate stood at 5.50% – relatively high by today's standards. When the crisis struck, the Fed didn't immediately cut rates. Instead, they had a different approach. This time, they specifically allowed the fed funds rate to deviate from its target rate and chose to flood the market with liquidity. The Fed injected $24 billion into the Repo market on August 10, followed by $38 billion and another $17.25 billion a few days later. It was the biggest liquidity injection since the September 11 crisis.

The Fed followed-up with a Discount Rate cut on August 17. Normally, Discount Rate cuts are the toothless giant of the Fed's policy tools. This time around, however, the Fed made a few changes.

First, they allowed ABCP to be deposited at the Discount Window, which was exactly what a lot of banks needed. Second, they actively encouraged the banks to use the Window. Up until then, the Discount Window had a stigma. Banks went there when they were in trouble and on their way to the graveyard. Now, it was different. By the end of August, the four largest banks in the U.S. went to the Discount Window for a total of $2 billion – $500 million each. It was a sign of support for the Fed and it gave cover for the banks that really needed the funding. Discount Window borrowings reached historic highs.

Six weeks later, the liquidity injections and Discount Rate cut were still not enough. The Fed cut the fed funds rate from 5.50% to 5.25% on September 29, and then cut it again to 5.00% on October 15. Normally, 50 basis points in rate cuts would still be considered a weak response from the Fed. However, given that it was a liquidity crisis, the Fed continued to emphasize liquidity over lower interest rates.

When the crisis began, the Repo market didn't experience much of a Flight-To-Quality. There were no significant increases in short positions and there were few fails. Yes, there were wider bid/offer spreads, but that was more related to uncertainty than a disruption in the functioning of the market. That all changed when the Fed cut the Discount Rate. High demand for Treasury collateral then pushed General Collateral rates to their lowest level to date. On August 22, Repo General Collateral traded at 277 basis points below fed funds.

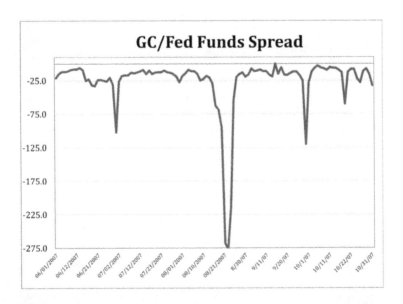

Just a few days later, all of the cash came back into the market and it appeared the crisis was over. The Fed continued to add liquidity through the end of September, so they clearly believed there was still some crisis left in the market. In the end, they were right, September quarter-end was volatile and funding was illiquid.

One victim of the Liquidity Crisis was LIBOR.[90] You could say that the beginning of the end of LIBOR started here. Yes, just like in the Commercial Paper market, spreads widened for bank CDs. And just like Commercial Paper, banks had problems selling their CDs. But there's one difference between the two markets: CD rates are tied to LIBOR. Or, more accurately, LIBOR is tied to bank CD rates.

When the Commercial Paper market was struggling, the bank CD market also shut down. Corporate treasurers and money market funds stopped buying CDs. When investors were unsure which banks were holding illiquid subprime debt, they just stopped buying. With those

---

[90] London Inter-Bank Offered Rate.

buyers gone from the market, nothing traded. Even when small trades occurred, no one bought maturities longer than a week.

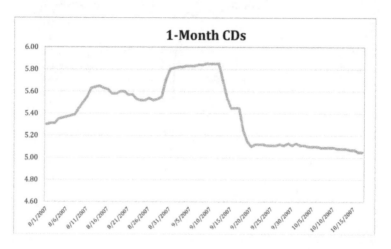

*Federal Reserve Bank of St. Louis https://fred.stlouisfed.org/*

If you look at the historical data,[91] it appears CD rates were high, but not out of line with a crisis. The truth is that there were no LIBOR rates at all because banks were not selling their CDs. Think of it this way, in a free market, when no one wants to buy a product, the recourse is to sweeten the deal. If the bank needs to raise cash, all they have to do is offer a higher rate. That's how markets work. But not during a crisis. Because bank CDs (and LIBOR) are a barometer of the health of the banking system, if a bank offers rates that are too high, it gives the impression that the bank is desperate for cash. And desperation is not the image a financial institution wants during a crisis!

---

[91] Even the previous Commercial Paper graph is incorrect. The data was fudged by the surveyors. Three Month Commercial Paper did not trade for most of August and September.

Back in August 2007, when banks submitted the rates they paid to issue CDs to the British Bankers Association, it was also a public admission of the bank's financial health. Given that none of the banks wanted to submit the rates where their CDs might actually trade, they submitted their posted rates. These were the rates they offered on CDs, kind of like saying, "Here's where we would like to sell our CDs," though no CDs ever traded there.

Once the depth of the crisis was past and buyers returned to the market, questions arose about LIBOR, and people were puzzled as to why LIBOR barely moved during the crisis. Six months later, the *Wall Street Journal* began looking into the inconsistencies and published an article on April 16. They suggested banks may "have been low-balling their borrowing rates to avoid looking desperate for cash."[92] Right then and there was the beginning of the end of LIBOR.

Over the next few months, there was still crisis left in the markets. Repo General Collateral was trading well below fed funds, and the market for credit products was pretty thin. When General Collateral dropped to 175 basis points below fed funds in January 2008, it meant something was amiss. Was there another Flight-To-Quality? Or was it some kind of mini-collateral shortage? The Fed immediately cut the fed funds rate by another 75 basis points and added additional emergency liquidity. The strange part was that there was no headline news. No one was in trouble. The market just moved back into crisis mode.

---

[92] For more information on the LIBOR rigging scandal, see my book, *Rogue Traders*.

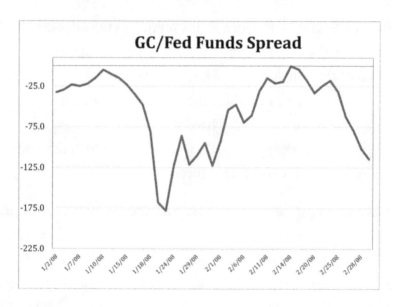

Then, just like that, it appeared the crisis was over. Again. Overnight rates returned to normal and cash came back into the market. The General Collateral/fed funds spread was almost back to zero. It seemed the rate cut had satisfied the markets. However, behind the scenes, banks were reducing their exposure to hedge funds, mortgage finance companies, and anyone with leveraged MBS positions. Cash investors, in turn, were reducing their exposure to the banks.

On March 12, 2008, after rumors of a liquidity crunch, Bear Stearns' CEO Alan Schwartz appeared on CNBC to assure the market they had plenty of liquidity. Once the market knew some investors thought Bear was having liquidity problems, it didn't take long for that "plenty of liquidity" to dry up. Two days later, JP Morgan, backed by the Fed, provided an emergency loan to Bear. JP agreed to provide financing as necessary for 28 days, but required Bear to have a funding plan thereafter. It gave Bear some breathing room, but not much.

At this point, the entire Repo market was in shambles. There was extreme volatility across the entire market. It was almost like quarter-end window dressing had started early. The premium came back for Treasury collateral. Repo rates for every on-the-run issue dropped to zero. There was a massive disruption in the settlement system and a large increase in fails. Something was amiss and cash was leaving the market.

There was confusion in the market about the cause of the Bear Stearns funding problems. One after another, Bear's Repo funding counterparties did not roll their loans and many hedge funds moved their accounts to other Prime Brokers.[93] That led to speculation that Bear's Treasury, agency, and agency mortgage-backed securities positions were causing the funding problems. Though Bear was highly leveraged, they were still a member of FICC. As a member in good standing, they continued to have access to the inter-dealer Repo market. Their funding problems did not come from the Treasurys, agencies, or agency mortgages. It came from illiquid securities – asset-back securities (ABSs), CDOs, private label MBSs, etc. When Repo counterparties refuse to fund these securities, there are few other places to go. It was over for Bear.

Under pressure from both the U.S. Treasury and the Federal Reserve, JP Morgan agreed to buy Bear for $236 million, or $2 a share. That was far less than the $30 a share and market value of $3.54 billion that Bear Stearns was worth just a few days earlier. There's a famous picture of a two-dollar bill taped to the door of the Bear Stearns Midtown office building. Two dollars a share was actually less

---

[93] This is more important than it appears. Prime Brokerage accounts generate a lot of cheap funding for banks.

than their Midtown office building was worth. After speculation that Bear Stearns shareholders would reject the low-ball price, JP increased the price in order to get the deal done.

In the end, JP Morgan picked up a great Prime Brokerage business for pennies on the dollar. However, given the eventual collapse of the mortgage market and the legal issues that came with Bear, they ultimately regretted the purchase.

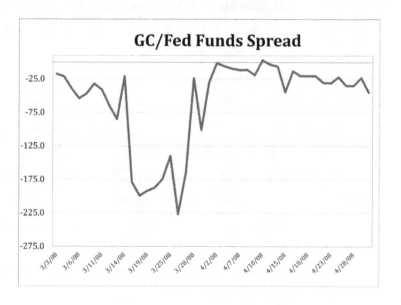

Leading into March quarter-end, once again there was a massive Flight-To-Quality and a shortage of Treasury collateral. The crisis finally broke in April. At that point, Bear Stearns was sold, quarter-end was past, and Treasurys came back into the market. General Collateral went from trading at 45 basis points below fed funds at the end of April to trading above fed funds by the end of May.

In hindsight, the Bear Stearns collapse was just a warmup for events later that year. Could it be that early quarter-end window dressing was the cause of the liquidity drain at Bear Stearns? Could the Flight-To-Quality be one of the causes of their collapse? Or did investors pull liquidity from the market because of Bear Stearns? Once again, for a period of time, it seemed the crisis was over. Yet again. However, a much larger crisis was on the horizon.

# THE FINANCIAL CRISIS

# 2008

The history books usually start the Financial Crisis on the day Lehman Brothers filed for bankruptcy.[94] That was the day when the financial markets went into crisis, but there were many events leading up to it.

Throughout 2008, the mortgage market continued to deteriorate, and Lehman's financial condition deteriorated along with it. Lehman was carrying billions of dollars' worth of illiquid mortgage-backed securities, and there was no way to get rid of them. In June, their clearing bank, JP Morgan Chase, issued a margin call on their Tri-Party accounts. The securities in the accounts weren't plain vanilla securities like U.S. Treasurys and agency mortgages; many of them had very illiquid paper. JP Morgan wasn't the cash investor in the transactions, but they were the custodial bank that was holding the collateral – the eponymous third party. Not only was it JP's obligation to value the collateral correctly, but also to protect the cash investors and themselves. In June, JP substantially marked down the value of the positions, requiring Lehman to come up with $6 billion in margin. This was possibly the largest margin call in history, and it occurred just when Lehman was running out of money.

---

[94] I tried to keep this chapter tied to the Repo market as much as possible. For further readying, there are plenty of books about the Financial Crisis.

If quarter-end is a window into what's going on behind the scenes in the financial markets, June quarter-end of 2008 was a fortune teller! Spreads widened and cash left the market. Mortgage-backed securities and credit products were difficult to finance, and General Collateral dropped to 63 basis points below Fed Funds. Behind the scenes, deep problems were brewing.

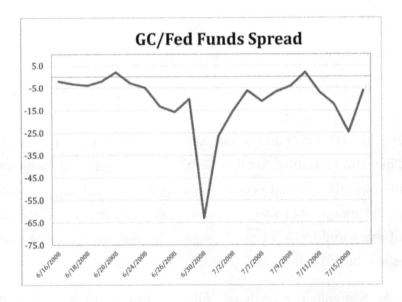

One of those problems began to surface in July. Investor interest in Fannie Mae and Freddie Mac securities was waning, and fewer cash investors were accepting their paper in the Repo market. This time it was not just the CMOs, IOs, and POs that investors were avoiding; now it was the plain vanilla paper like pass-throughs too. When Fannie and Freddie stock prices continued to decline, the U.S. government stepped in and nationalized them.

At the end of July, Merrill Lynch[95] announced the sale $30.6 billion in CDOs at .218 cents on the dollar. These securities weren't even the bottom of the barrel tranches. They were originally super senior tranches, many once rated AAA. Merrill had acquired some of them to facilitate underwriting deals.[96] Others were acquired when they liquidated hedge funds, like Bear Stearns Asset Management. In hindsight, though it seemed like they took a bath on the sales, they were lucky to get out of them when they did. The securities were completely worthless just two months later.

At the beginning of September, the mortgage market deteriorated even more. JP Morgan took another look at Lehman's Tri-Party collateral and didn't like what they saw. The values continued to decline, and JP wanted another $5 billion in margin. Lehman clearly didn't have the capital to cover this margin call. They argued with JP over the margin call and collateral valuations, and the discussions went back-and-forth for two weeks. In the end, Lehman never satisfied the full margin call.

As September progressed, funding was beginning to tighten throughout the entire financial system. There was an especially large cash crunch in Europe. European banks had trouble getting funded in pre-U.S. hours. Each day, U.S. dollar borrowing rates were high during early morning European hours, and then fell once the U.S. opened. There just weren't enough U.S. dollars in Europe. This stress added to the funding pressure and rate volatility in the U.S. market.

---

[95] There were plenty of liquidations, but this one was most interesting because of the link to BSAM.

[96] There's a good Wall Street maxim that says, "You should either be in the moving or storage business. Not both."

The big event finally occurred during the early morning hours of Monday, September 15. Lehman Brothers Holdings declared bankruptcy. Right from the start, no one waited to see the impact on the markets. The markets went straight into crisis mode. On the first day, fed funds traded between 3.00% and 10.00%, and General Collateral between 3.25% and 1.40%. In order to quell the panic, the Fed injected $70 billion of overnight liquidity into the Repo market.

The next day, fed funds were trading even higher - between 7.00% and 10.00%. The Fed began the day with a $20 billion, 28-day term Repo operation, but as the day wore on, it was clear the operation was too small. They came back later with a $50 billion overnight operation. After two days of $70 billion liquidity injections, it seemed like that was the right number. These were the largest liquidity injections into the Repo market ever.

General Collateral and fed funds continued to trade volatile all week. The fed funds target rate was temporarily a thing of the past. There was just no way to hold the rate in place with massive amounts of cash and securities moving in and out of the financial system every day.

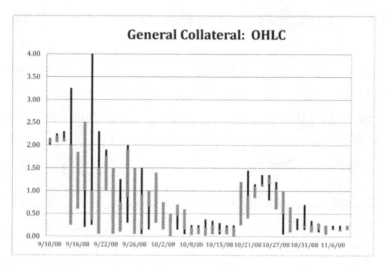

While funding U.S. Treasurys was tough, credit products were even more difficult. Even though Fannie Mae and Freddie Mac were nationalized and guaranteed by the U.S. government, their securities traded like high-yield bonds – securities that could go bankrupt at any time! On September 18, when General Collateral was trading 1.25%, agency MBS collateral was trading at 3.25% – a 200 basis point spread! The next day, when General Collateral opened the day at 1.50%, fed funds were at 2.00%, and agency MBS collateral was at 3.00%. Spreads were incredibly wide.

One glimmer of success was the central clearing counterparty FICC. Though Lehman caused financial havoc across the globe, unwinding Lehman's Repo book was not an issue. Because Lehman Brothers *Holdings* had filed for bankruptcy, the broker-dealer, Lehman Brothers, Inc., was in good standing with FICC. The broker-dealer wound down its Repo positions in the inter-dealer broker market. By the end of October 2008, FICC announced they had successfully closed out all of Lehman's positions. FICC participants suffered no losses, and no default funds were used. Imagine if there was no FICC? The Repo market would have been a mess. Or even more of a mess than it was. Think of all the Repo transactions that would have been liquidated.

Over in Europe, LCH.Clearnet[97] was also a success. After Lehman declared bankruptcy, they wound down Lehman's positions and did not suffer a loss or call on their default fund. Even in Europe, the unwinding of Lehman's Repo transactions was, in fact, fairly orderly.

During the crisis, there was an exodus of both cash and securities from the market because many customers stopped trading with the Street. When a customer is unsure who might go bankrupt next, they just stop trading with everyone. That meant very few securities were coming into the market to cover shorts, and fails were increasing. When so many Treasurys were packed away in investor portfolios, it caused securities shortages everywhere. Traders were unable to cover short positions.

In order to help relieve the blockage, the Fed announced an expansion of the SOMA securities lending facility. They increased the maximum number of securities each Primary Dealer could borrow to $1 billion and reduced the minimum borrowing fee from 50 basis points to 10 basis points. This allowed more securities to move out of the Fed's portfolio and into the Repo market. However, the fail situation continued to get worse.

---

[97] The European central clearing counterparty.

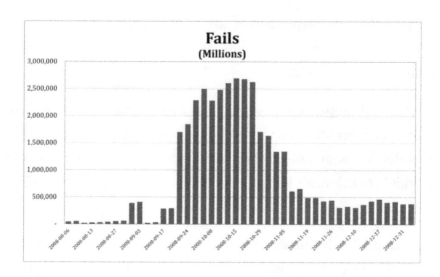

When fails begin to compound, it becomes a circular problem. Securities were failing, so end-user portfolios refused to loan their securities. Because those portfolios were not lending, there were fewer securities available to cover shorts, and therefore more fails.

On October 15, the total number of fails hit an all-time high of $5.06 trillion[98]. Many securities went dead fail. Traders bid for them at zero each day, but there were no offers and nothing settled. At this time, there were three categories of Specials:

1. All bids and no offers. The security was zero bid and there were no offers. Anyone long figured there was no reason to loan the securities since they wouldn't come back the next day anyway.

2. Traded at zero, but didn't clear. Dealers financed their long positions at 0%, but the settlements didn't clear.

---

[98] The $5.06 trillion is the combined Fails-To-Receive and Fails-To-Deliver.

3. Traded at 0% and sometimes cleared.

It was a mess!

As quarter-end approached, the Fed completely lost control of the fed funds market. On the day of quarter-end, the fed funds rate opened at 5.50%. Keep in mind, this was when the fed funds target rate was 2.00%. Ironically, the fed funds effective rate (EFFR)[99] ended that day at 2.03%. The Fed Funds rate looked good on paper, but there was a world of volatility in between perception and reality. General Collateral traded between 1.00% and .15%, and averaged .50%. September 30, 2008, was the biggest Flight-To-Quality of all time. General Collateral traded as low as 500 basis points below fed funds.

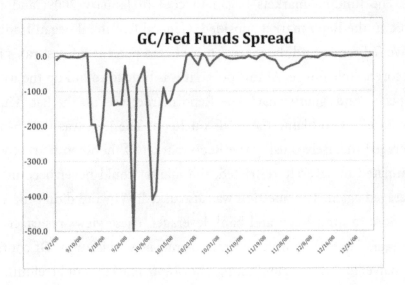

In October, the Fed finally began cutting rates. Because the easing cycle had already started in 2007, the target rate was already relatively low at 2.00%. On October 8, the Fed cut 50 basis points to 1.50%, then

---

[99] Average rate.

another 50 basis points to 1.00% on October 29. Finally, on December 16, they cut 100 basis points down to zero. This ushered in the first Zero Interest Rate Policy (ZIRP), with the fed funds target range set at 0% to .25%.

In addition to the Repo operations and rate cuts, the Fed introduced many liquidity programs. There could be books written just about the Fed's response to the crisis. And there are! All total, it's estimated that the Fed committed $7.77 trillion to the market, which included both actual loans and guarantees. In later years, the Fed emphasized that all of the loans were collateralized in some kind of way.

The funding markets began to cool in January 2009, and the panic in the Repo market subsided. General Collateral began trading above fed funds, and the market priced zero percent interest rates for the foreseeable future. At this point, it was time to round up the usual suspects. And, guess what? The Repo market was on the list. There was an effort to blame the crisis on Repo. The idea was that banks leveraged themselves using the Repo market. If the Repo market was eliminated or severely restricted, the market could never become so leveraged again. The question was also asked: Why did didn't the Fed do more to limit Repo and bank leverage? These views resurfaced a few years later when it came time to craft new legislation. Of course, it's naïve to believe eliminating the Repo market would eliminate financial leverage. It's like blaming a car crash on the gasoline that powers the engine. In the end, the Financial Crisis ultimately ushered in new bank regulations that would have a huge impact on the Repo market just a few years later.

# NEW FEDERAL RESERVE

It's an understatement to say the financial markets changed since the Federal Reserve was created. For years, Federal Reserve policy, the Treasury market, and the Repo market were sleepy corners of the financial world. Markets grew, they became more complex, more leveraged, and new financial companies supplanted banks. The financial system became global, filled with banking conglomerates, foreign banks, hedge funds, derivatives, mortgages, securitizations, and the list goes on and on. On top of that, the Treasury market grew into the trillions. It's no surprise that an institution that was created in 1913 had difficulty handling the financial markets of the 21st century. Clearly, the Fed needed some updates.

Most of these updates came during and after the Financial Crisis. Some came and went,[100] but along the way, four important changes remained:

1. Quantitative Easing (Large Scale Asset Purchases)

2. Interest on Reserve Balances (IORB)

3. Reverse-Repo Facility (RRP)

4. Standing Repo Facility (SRF)

---

[100] I left out several Fed programs that are irrelevant today and not necessarily Repo-related, like the Term Deposit Facility (TDF), Term Securities Lending Facility (TSLF), Treasury Supplementary Financing Program (SFP), and Primary Dealer Credit Facility (PDCF).

With these new facilities, the concept of managing monetary policy changed along with them. In the past, the Fed had managed short-term interest rates through operations. The Fed set an overnight fed funds rate. If rates were soft, they drained liquidity. When there was funding pressure, they added liquidity. Pretty simple. The new Federal Reserve manages interest rates through facilities. The facilities place a ceiling and a floor on the market. When combined, they create a corridor system.

## 1. Quantitative Easing (Large Scale Asset Purchases)

The market likes to call it QE. Fed officials often call it Large Scale Asset Purchases (LSAP). What's the difference? Technically, the goal of QE is to expand the central bank's liabilities by injecting cash into the banking system. LSAP is about expanding the asset side of the balance sheet: buying securities for the System Open Market Account (SOMA). Of course, whether it's called QE or LSAP, it doesn't really matter. They both inject liquidity into the financial system.

When the Fed embarks on a QE program, they go into the secondary market[101] and purchase U.S. Treasury or federal agency securities. The purchases remove securities from the market and inject cash. With fewer securities in the market, interest rates, theoretically, move lower.[102] Once the crisis is over and the QE program ends – in theory – the Fed sells the securities back into the market. In theory.

The concept of QE originated as a way to add liquidity after interest rates were already at zero. In the past, central banks couldn't

---

[101] The Fed is restricted from buying new Treasury securities at auction due to legal constraints related to directly financing the government.

[102] A pessimist might look at the operation differently. Perhaps the Fed is buying securities to prevent interest rates from spiking higher because of all of the new government issuance.

ease monetary conditions after rates had bottomed-out.[103] These days, if interest rates are at zero and the economy is still weak, there's another tool: flood the system with more liquidity through bond purchases.

The Bank of Japan (BOJ) originated the concept in the 1990s. They needed to stimulate a stagnating economy. The concept came to the U.S. in 2002, when the future Fed chairman, Ben Bernanke, first described QE: "If the central bank had exhausted all traditional policy tools and overnight rates were already at zero, the Fed could use QE to prevent deflation." During the Financial Crisis, the Fed chairman got his chance. When the Fed began the first QE program[104], they purchased $600 billion agency MBS.[105] After a series of programs, the Fed's System Open Market Account (SOMA) grew from $480 billion pre-crisis to a peak of $4.24 trillion in April 2017. Then, after the COVID crisis, the SOMA portfolio peaked again at $8.9 trillion in April 2022.

## 2. Interest on Reserve Balances (IORB)

During the depths of the Financial Crisis, the Fed lobbied Congress to allow them to pay interest on the bank reserves held at the Fed, the so-called Reserve Requirements. In the past, the cash deposited at the Fed didn't earn any interest. In November 2008, the Fed wanted to get the overnight fed funds rate back to its target. The target was set at 1.00%, while the fed funds rate was trading at .25% each day, a full 75 basis points under. The Fed figured if they paid an interest rate equal to the fed funds target rate, banks would move excess reserves out of the

---

[103] Yes, theoretically, the central bank can push rates into the negatives, but that creates different problems.
[104] November 25, 2008
[105] They later expanded QE1.

market and into the Fed. The exodus of cash would drain the fed funds market and bring the daily fed funds rate back to target.

The new rule was passed by Congress and the Interest On Reserves (IOR) and the Interest On Excess Reserves (IOER)[106] were born. Though the idea was supposed to be a temporary fix, the Fed realized it was a useful new tool to manage the fed funds rate. The effectiveness of the tool depends on the movement of excess reserves. Required reserves are stuck at the Fed; they cannot be withdrawn. When the Fed began paying interest on reserves, they also paid banks to leave extra cash at the Fed, what they called excess reserves. Over time, the Fed realized that if the fed funds rate needed tweaking, they could move the IOER higher or lower. If the IOER was high in relation to other overnight rates, banks moved excess reserves to the Fed. That drained liquidity from the market and nudged overnight rates higher. If the Fed moved the IOER lower, liquidity left the Fed and the fed funds rate moved lower.

Adjusting the IORB became even more important when the Fed switched from a fed funds target *rate* to a target *range*. Once there was a range, there was the question of where the daily fed funds rate should trade within the range. The actual fed funds rate can, theoretically, trade anywhere within the range. In practice, the Fed likes the fed funds rate right in the middle. It's never been specifically stated, but it's implied. The Fed changes the IORB to keep the daily fed funds rate in the middle of the range, but they always call it a technical adjustment.

---

[106] The two interest rates were eventually combined into what's called Interest on Reserve Balances (IORB).

## 3. Reverse-Repo Facility(RRP)

The Fed's Reverse-Repo Program was originally called the Fixed-Rate Reverse-Repo Facility (FRRF). These days it's sometimes called the RRP or RRP Window, or even the RRP Facility. Its function is simple: Market participants deliver cash to the Fed and receive U.S. Treasurys as collateral in a Tri-Party account. The Fed borrows cash and drains liquidity from the market.

Just like the IORB, the RRP rate is set by the FOMC. Whereas changes to the IORB affect the fed funds market, changes in the RRP affects Repo rates. Historically, the Fed set the RRP rate at either the bottom of the fed funds target range or up to 10 basis points above the bottom. Over time, the RRP evolved to become the tool to keep General Collateral from dropping below the target range. If General Collateral drops to the bottom of the target range, the RRP is an automatic market mechanism to drain liquidity.

The RRP began as a surprise. Back in 2013, the Fed's first round of ZIRP had been running for years. When the FOMC minutes from the July 30-31 meeting were released, there was a big new development: The FOMC was discussing a Fixed-Rate Reverse-Repo Facility. Surprisingly, there was no public discussion by Fed officials prior to the announcement.

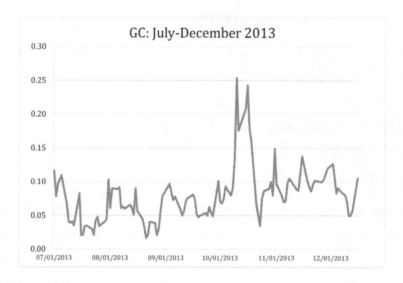

When the RRP facility was officially announced, it was billed as a tool to help the Fed drain reserves once they began the upcoming tightening cycle. In reality, that wasn't quite correct. Back in the summer of 2013, one of the unintended consequences of QE was beginning to show. Overnight Repo rates were approaching zero. There would be problems in the financial system if rates flat-lined at zero or even dropped into the negatives. It wasn't good Fed policy. The real reason for the RRP facility was to have a mechanism to keep Repo rates from dropping to zero or below.

Once the program was launched, the Fed opened it up to a list of approved counterparties. This was a big change from past Fed programs that were only open to Primary Dealers. The expanded counterparty list included banks, money market funds (MMFs), and the GSEs. When the program was launched, the counterparty limit was only $1 billion. No one counterparty could invest more than $1 billion with the Fed. That's almost comical today. The $1 billion eventually became $5 billion, then $7 billion, then $10 billion. Fast-forward to 2022 and the counterparty limit is $160 billion. How else could the Fed accommodate over $2 trillion at the RRP?

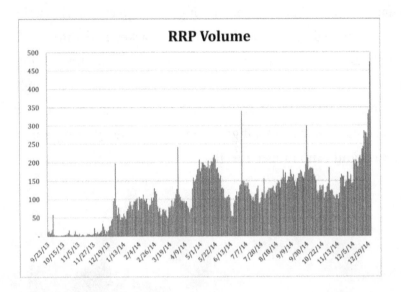

These days, trillions of dollars of overnight cash goes into the RRP facility each day. Because large cash investors have the option of investing at either the Fed or in the Repo market, their choice depends on the rate. The Fed uses the RRP rate to move Repo rates higher or lower. For example, back in June 2021, the market was awash in cash due to the long-running QE program. Overnight Repo rates were trading at 0% and occasionally trading negative. The Fed raised the RRP rate from zero to .05%, added more RRP counterparties, and increased the amount of cash each RRP counterparty could invest. The rate adjustment lifted both overnight rates and the entire short-end of the yield curve by 5 basis points.

Over time, volume at the RRP increases for three reasons. First, when there's downward pressure on market rates. Soft funding means there's too much liquidity in the financial system and the RRP is there to absorb it. Second, RRP volume increases during a crisis when there's risk aversion. Why leave your money at a bank when you can leave it at the AAA-rated Federal Reserve? There was even talk when the facility was launched that it might exasperate a crisis. As cash investors moved cash out of the Repo market and into the Fed, it would drain liquidity that was badly needed in the financial system. Lastly, once the Fed has purchased too many securities through a QE program, the excess cash ends up at the RRP. Rule of thumb: When RRP volume is increasing, it generally means the QE program has run its course and is no longer effective.

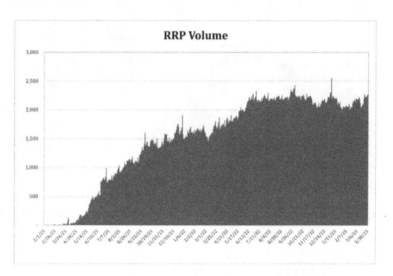

Unfortunately, the RRP facility came with an unintended consequence. It became the number-one window dressing tool for the market. Years ago, when cash investors like MMFs were turned away when banks shrank their Repo books on quarter-end, those investors had nowhere to go. These days, the RRP facility allows cash investors to go to the Fed with their cash when banks close them down.

# 4. Standing Repo Facility (SRF)

The Fed's use of Repo *operations* stood dormant for a long period of time. During the years of financial crisis, QE programs, and ZIRP, there was really no need to temporarily drain securities from the market. However, that all changed once the 2017-2019 Balance Sheet Runoff began. Treasurys were coming back into the market; when they combined with large net new Treasury issuance, the dynamics of the market changed. As more securities came into the market, the market evolved from having an abundance of cash to having a cash deficiency. The first clue came during the 2018 year-end. That day, overnight Repo rates spiked to 7.25%. It was a complete surprise to the market, but there were no further rate spikes over the next few months, so the concern passed. Then, overnight rates suddenly spiked again in September 2019. The Fed quickly dusted off the overnight Repo operations manual and put them back in place.

Once the panic passed, there was pressure on the Fed to establish a Repo facility that was similar to the RRP, but in reverse.[107] In July 2021, the Fed announced the Standing Repurchase Agreement Facility (SRF). It's important to note that this new program is a facility and not an operation. Though the Fed can certainly do Repo operations, the new program is a standing facility. Under the SRF, Primary Dealers deliver securities to the Fed in exchange for cash. The SRF rate is set by the FOMC at the top of the fed funds target range.

Whether the Fed was planning it or not, all of the new facilities combined ended up creating a corridor system for the Repo market.[108]

---

[107] Yes, the reverse of the Reverse-Repo!

[108] Someone could argue there's a fed funds corridor system with the IORB at the top. However, there is really no automatic system to drain liquidity from the fed funds market when rates get too low.

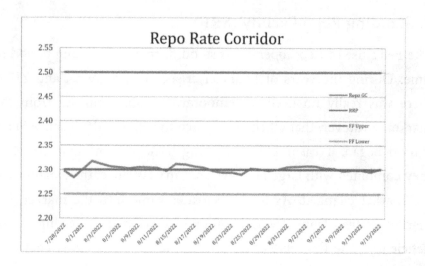

The Standing Repo Facility sits at the top of the fed funds target range, and the Reverse-Repo Program sits at the bottom. The SRF removes collateral from the market and the RRP removes cash. The RRP is tried and tested. During two periods of time in 2013 and in 2021 – 2022, it prevented overnight rates from dropping to 0% or below.

The SRF is not yet tested and there's no guarantee it will hold Repo rates within the target range. Given that only Primary Dealers can access the facility, it means support for the market is dependent on their balance sheets. If there's significant funding pressure, rates can still trade above the target range. That means the true ceiling might be 5 to 10 basis points above the top of the range. In some situations, like quarter-end and year-end, there could be no ceiling because Primary Dealers have balance sheet constraints. We shall see.

# TRI-PARTY REFORM

Back in late 2008, during the height of the Financial Crisis, I remember sitting at my trading desk and listening to CNBC in the background. Treasury Secretary Henry Paulson was giving one of his regular press conferences, and I heard him say something like, "and Tri-Party Repo is a threat to the entire financial system." Wait … What? Did I hear that correctly? That was the first time many of us in the Repo market ever heard of the unacceptable risks of Tri-Party Repo.

My next question was: What's so risky about Tri-Party Repo? It's a collateralized loan. One party provides cash, one party provides collateral, and the clearing bank holds it all. Wasn't Tri-Party created back in the 1980s to solve for the risks associated with Repo? Now Tri-Party is too risky?

The size of the Tri-Party market peaked at $2.8 trillion right before the Financial Crisis, and dropped to about $1.34 trillion in 2010.[109] The market had actually shrunk since the crisis, but what changed was the collateral. Tri-Party then consisted of dollar and non-dollar currencies, and it migrated away from Treasurys and agencies to high-yield corporate bonds, CMOs, private-label mortgages, and CDOs, just to name a few. The Financial Crisis really awoke regulators as to the cracks that developed in the market.

---

[109] It has since grown to $3.93 trillion.

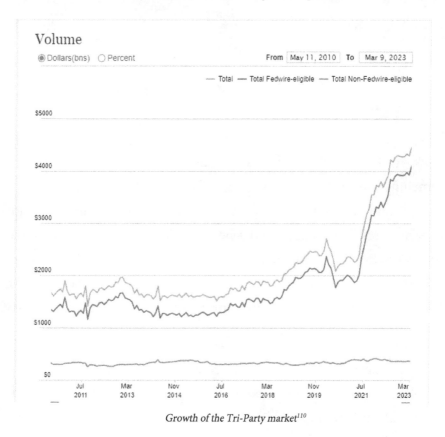

*Growth of the Tri-Party market[110]*

The first criticism of Tri-Party goes back to the age-old criticism of banking: lending long and borrowing short. What's the saying about the banking business of yesteryear? It was called a 3-6-3 business. Borrow money at 3, lend money at 6, and be on the golf course at 3. These days the financial markets are filled with shadow banks, broker-dealers, mortgage companies, and REITs that are all lending long and borrowing short. A broker-dealer might own a mortgage-backed security with an average life of 7 years and borrow money overnight in the Repo market to fund it. If you ever have to go on CNBC and explain that you have plenty of liquidity, you might not have that

[110] https://www.newyorkfed.org/data-and-statistics/data-visualization/tri-party-repo#interactive/volume/collateral_value

liquidity for long! If the broker-dealer went bust, the cash investor or the clearing bank might get stuck with the securities.

That brings us to the second concern: The cash providers didn't have the resources to liquidate the collateral if the bank or broker-dealer defaulted. That was a valid concern. Cash providers are made up of MMFs, insurance companies, corporate treasurers, state and local governments, and securities lending groups. Given that most are financial companies, they have the resources to liquidate Treasurys, agencies, and agency mortgages – all liquid securities[111] with deep markets. The question was whether they could liquidate the exotic securities, like CMOs, CDOs, and ABSs.[112] Liquidation of these instruments can take days or weeks, and oftentimes one Tri-Party liquidation depresses asset prices and leads to other liquidations.

Then, there was a technical problem with Tri-Party. Most Tri-Party transactions were booked overnight. But what's the definition of overnight? You might assume an overnight trade constitutes a transaction that lasts for 24 hours, but that wasn't the case. The system had evolved so that the clearing bank was holding the collateral for about 27% of the time. That was due to "the unwind."

The unwind was a function of the FedWire settlement system. The FedWire opens at 8:30 AM and closes at 3:00 PM.[113] Market participants settling U.S. Treasurys, federal agencies, and agency MBSs must deliver and receive securities during that period of time.

---

[111] Corporate bonds, CMOs, CDOs, ABSs, and municipal bonds made up about $360 billion of all Tri-Party in September 2022.

[112] From a free market viewpoint: If you don't have the resources to liquidate a certain type of security, then don't accept it as collateral! But regulators don't look at it that way. They're concerned with contagion and the overall financial system during a crisis.

[113] The FedWire technically stays open longer for what they call "customer time" and "reversal time," and for when the settlement deadline is sometimes extended.

And here's the problem: Cash investors returned the securities from their Tri-Party accounts at 8:30 AM each morning. That was the unwind. Given all the securities moving in and out of a securities dealer during the day, dealers rarely allocated the new day's Tri-Party collateral until the afternoon. That left a period of 6 ½ hours when the cash investors had their cash back, but the new collateral was not yet allocated. The clearing bank was effectively funding the collateral for 6 ½ hours each day.[114]

The 6 ½ hour period might not seem significant, but consider what happens if the securities dealer went bankrupt during those hours. It meant the clearing bank was stuck with the collateral, not the cash provider. The clearing bank was covering a risk they couldn't control, nor were they being compensated for it.

That meant the two clearing banks, JP Morgan Chase and Bank of New York, were extending the dealer community a huge amount of intraday credit. Then, when JP Morgan[115] gave up the clearing business, it left BONY as the only Tri-Party show in town. All of a sudden, BONY was even more systemically important.

Looking at all of those issues, it's no surprise that the Fed was concerned that the Tri-Party market that could destabilize the financial system. In 2009, the Fed appointed a Tri-Party Repo infrastructure task force to make recommendations and propose changes. The task force was made up of representatives of all of the major participants in the industry, including the cash investors (MMFs), collateral providers (banks and securities dealers), and the

---

[114] Not to mention that the cash providers were paid an interest rate for a full day when they were technically only lending cash for 73% of the day. Small details make a big difference with large sums of money.

[115] Pretty much right after MF Global blew up.

two major clearing banks, JP Morgan Chase and The Bank of New York. They were charged with making the Tri-Party system more resilient. Initially, the task force produced a roadmap to address the intraday credit extension. They pressed the clearing banks to add technology to change the settlement process and eliminate the automatic unwind. Naturally, the clearing banks liked the part about increasing the daylight overdraft fees to incentivize the securities dealers to get their settlements processed faster.

After four years, the clearing banks installed new technology and shortened the daily unwind. Collateral providers issued better trade confirmations and improved trade matching, and the largest dealers installed systems to reduce intraday credit. It appeared that most of the Fed's concerns had been addressed. At least that's what we thought.

However, the task force recommendations didn't satisfy the Fed. The task force was trying to tweak the existing system, while the Fed was looking for broad reform and perhaps an overhaul of the entire system. The Fed expected higher margin requirements, a plan to handle a dealer default, and a much greater intraday credit reduction. In the end, no particular group was willing to accept radical change. No one would voluntarily agree to increase their share of the credit risk. So the Fed disbanded the task force at the end of 2011.

In February of 2012, the Fed informed the market they were considering placing restrictions on the Tri-Party market. For much of 2012, the Fed asked dealer banks to voluntarily reduce their use of Tri-Party financing.

Then, one year later, Bill Dudley, the President of the New York Fed, gave a speech that was highly critical of the industry's reforms. In fact, he made it clear the industry had a significant amount of work to do. Though some progress was made on intraday credit, no progress was made on the fire sale issue. In fact, Dudley outlined three actions the Fed would take if the industry did not address the fire sale issue quickly:

1. The Fed might restrict Tri-Party collateral to the Fed's Open Market Operations (OMO)-eligible securities. That way, in case there was a dealer default, the Fed had the ability to step in and provide funding.

2. The Fed wanted a collateral liquidation mechanism established by Repo market participants. This would remove the liquidation process from the cash investors. Basically, some kind of Tri-Party central clearing counterparty (CCP).

3. If the market didn't create the collateral liquidation mechanism, the Fed might use regulatory oversight to declare Tri-Party an unstable source of funding for banks and require a collateral liquidation mechanism anyway.

Dudley's speech summed up the Fed's position: Create a CCP for Tri-Party on your own or we'll force you!

As it turned out, Tri-Party reform was really about shifting risk. And no one wanted to accept more risk. The initial proposal in 2009 was to eliminate the intraday credit extension by the clearing banks. Before the change, much of the liquidation risk was sitting at the clearing banks. When intraday credit extension was drastically reduced, the risk shifted from the clearing banks to the cash providers. Then, if the dealer community set up a vehicle to handle liquidations, the fire sale risk shifted indirectly to the dealer community. The reforms were really proposals to shift the risk from one set of market participants to another. Every time they covered-up the prairie dog hole, the prairie dog popped its head up a few yards away.[116]

In the end, the Fed got some of the things they wanted, but not everything. Over the next few years, the clearing bank made great progress in narrowing the unwind window. The market pushed the idea that moving some Tri-Party from the clearing bank into GCF Repo as a partial reform. GCF Repo is the equivalent of Tri-Party, except it's between FICC members and settles in FICC. Given that FICC holds the cash and collateral and FICC has the resources to value, margin, and liquidate the collateral, moving more Tri-Party into FICC seemed like a good idea.

However, over the years, the use of GCF Repo actually decreased. GCF Repo volume averaged around $325 billion a day in 2011 and now it only averages around only $100 billion. Then there's another problem. Only government securities like U.S. Treasurys, agencies, and agency mortgages are eligible for GCF Repo. There are no CMBs, CMOs, ABSs, corporates, equities, or foreign securities that are eligible. These are the securities that might actually cause a fire sale. Remember, Bear Stearns and Lehman didn't go down because they couldn't fund their government securities.

The idea of a CCP for Tri-Party never went anywhere. The Fed really wanted to remove the Tri-Party function from the clearing bank

---

[116] Is fire sale risk the great white whale of the financial system?

and create a utility as a special purpose vehicle. That would have completely changed the plumbing of the system. But perhaps a better solution is to have more clearing banks that offer Tri-Party services. Way back when, there were many clearing banks. Most of them disappeared through consolidation and mergers. The fact that one bank accounts for 100% of clearing and Tri-Party activity is a greater systemic risk than government securities Tri-Party.

# NEW REGULATION

When the new banking regulations rolled through the financial markets, the Repo market was not exempt. Banks continued to be the center of the Repo market, though their balance sheets were restricted. Under Dodd-Frank and Basel III, there were leverage ratios, capital charges, and a small chip in the Automatic Stay provision. As the new regulations kicked-in, banks evaluated their Repo businesses, the use of balance sheets, and, in many cases, reallocated assets based on revenue. Many Repo matched-books were scaled back, and some were even eliminated.

The new regulations stretched across geographies, leaving different regulations for different bank subsidiaries. Dodd-Frank covered the U.S. and foreign banks that operated in the U.S. Since the U.S. never joined Basel I or Basel II, they were never required to follow those regulations, but U.S. banks were required to follow Basel III. Both the U.S. and Europe have the same leverage ratios, though each has additional rules. Basel III has regulatory capital charges for Repo and Dodd-Frank has the Supplementary Leverage Ratio (SLR). These opened the Repo market up to big changes.

From the beginning, there were whispers of a leverage ratio. A leverage ratio is supposed to be a general limit on a bank's balance sheet. Given all the creative ways of netting assets, the ratios are supposed to be an absolute limit on the size of a bank. The Basel Committee originally proposed a 3% leverage ratio, which was not a hard lift for the U.S. banks, nor most of the foreign banks. A leverage ratio of 3% means there must be 3% of capital reserved against the bank's assets. At 3%, a bank can leverage itself 33-times-to-one.[117] That's one dollar in capital for every 33.3 dollars in assets.

The leverage ratios hit the Repo businesses the hardest. Think of a leverage ratio as limiting the size of a bank's playing field. Instead of a bank being able to grow its assets when opportunities arise, the leverage ratio fixes the size of the bank's assets. The bank's businesses needed to fit within the playing field. Businesses with a great return on capital but a low return on assets, like Repo, were no longer preferable.

The U.S. banks got a double-dose of new regulation. They were required to follow both Dodd-Frank and Basel III. Luckily, the Dodd-Frank leverage ratio is the same as the Basel III, however, Dodd-Frank added an extra limit on the largest banks, the so-called Systemically Important Financial Institutions (SIFIs). They have an extra leverage ratio: the SLR. From the beginning, it was rumored the FDIC might push the SLR up to 6%, but in the end, the FDIC settled at 5%. This keeps the largest banks leveraged at only 20-to-one.[118]

It's no surprise that the largest banks hate the SLR. If there's a liquidity issue, panic, or sell-off in the bond market, the first thing they propose is eliminating the SLR. When the bond market broke-down during the COVID crisis in March 2020, the Fed suspended the SLR from April 2020 to March 2021. For a year, banks had fewer balance sheet restrictions and, no surprise, they liked it!

---

[117] $1/.03 = 33.333$

[118] $1/.05 = 20$

When it came time to reinstate the SLR in March 2021, the banks fought back hard to keep the suspension. Bank economists and analysts predicted bond market sell-offs and a loss of liquidity. Just when it looked like the Fed was leaning toward continuing the suspension, a letter from Senator Elizabeth Warren put an end to it. For many in Washington, the SLR was an integral part of Dodd-Frank. Rolling back the SLR was like rolling back Dodd-Frank. There's strong political resistance to rolling back any part of the post-Financial Crisis banking legislation. As of now, the issue is still not settled. As the size of the Treasury market grows, there will be future calls to eliminate the SLR.

The leverage ratios changed the Repo business. Looking at the numbers, let's assume it costs $3 million in capital for every $100 million in assets. Using a 10%[119] ROE means those assets cost a bank $300,000 a year. As a back-of-the-envelope calculation, the $300,000 is the equivalent of 10 basis points on a $100 million Repo transaction annually. Therefore, the cost of doing Repo at a bank is approximately 10 basis points.[120] Banks must build 10 basis points into their Repo trades in order to make them economical. However, given that a bank can net positions, the real capital cost is substantially less.

The original Basel III proposed a gross calculation. A gross leverage ratio would have completely gutted the Repo businesses at Basel III banks. Luckily, the net ratio was adopted because it makes financial sense. If a Repo counterparty defaults, the securities borrowed and loaned are liquidated. The risk is the spread between

---

[119] The cost of a Repo asset is greater if a bank requires a 12% or 15% ROE. It's less if the bank accepts a lower ROE.

[120] This does not include the Basel III regulatory capital costs for Repo, which are too complicated for this book!

the long and short positions, not the gross positions. Overall, the leverage ratios make Repo more expensive, but the banks are clearly still in the business!

Repo transactions have been exempt from the Automatic Stay provision of the U.S. bankruptcy code since 1985. If a counterparty goes into default, Repo transactions can be immediately liquidated. This is the heart and soul of the Repo market. Dodd-Frank chipped away at it, but just a little. In July 2013, a report from the Securities and Exchange Commission (SEC) put part of the Automatic Stay exemption in doubt. A footnote in the report stated that certain exemptions for qualified financial contracts[121] are subject to Automatic Stay. An entity which is a party to a Repo transaction with a "covered financial company may not exercise any termination rights" until 5:00 p.m. on the day after the FDIC appoints a receiver. It means that the Automatic Stay exemption is delayed until the day after the FDIC takes over. This will leave the Repo counterparties sweating the movements in the market until they get a green light from the FDIC to start liquidating.

All-in-all, the new regulations made bank balance sheets more expensive. Assets have a higher marginal cost. If a bank wants to grow, it's constrained by the leverage ratio. The bank can either raise capital or shed some assets. If the bank is cutting assets to make room for a new business, the low ROA assets like Repo are often the first to go.

Once the new regulations began filtering into the market, the banks launched internal reviews of their business lines in order to

---

[121] Which include Repo

make sure the individual units generated an acceptable return-on-assets. The Repo desks managed down their customer positions as best they could, and customers with large gross positions were often forced out. If extra balance sheet was available, customers paid exorbitant Repo rates.

For internal customers, banks allocated a fixed amount of balance sheet to each Prime Brokerage (PB) customer. The banks looked at the customers' revenue across all of the product lines, and each client received an asset allocation that made financial sense.

With limited balance sheet available, the Repo desks discontinued much of their market-making activity, and most curtailed proprietary Repo trading. Many Repo desks moved away from Treasury and agency Repo into higher yielding products, like corporate bonds and private label MBS. This is one of the unintended consequences of the leverage ratios. The cost of balance sheet for Treasury Repo with a five basis point spread is about the same as corporate bonds with a 25 basis point spread. Not surprisingly, bank Repo desks shed low-yielding assets in favor of more speculative, high-yielding assets.

Along with the new regulations came incentives to book trades with certain types of customers. Customers with large gross positions and small net positions are considered great customers. Central counterparties (CCPs), exchanges, central banks, and quasi-government entities like the IADB and the World Bank are even better because they're exempt from Basel III regulatory capital charges.

Though it's been the trend for over 30 years, the Repo market continued to evolved away from the dealer-to-customer model. Many customers joined FICC, and many cash investors now have direct access to the Fed's RRP facility. Ultimately, this should reduce the volatility in the market because there are fewer middlemen for each Repo transaction.

Many market participants expected the Repo market to shrink. Considering the additional regulation and capital requirements, Repo transactions are more expensive. At first, it appeared that the Repo market was shrinking, when fundamentally it was not. Back then, no one ever imagined the trillion-dollar government deficits year after year. To this day, the Repo market continues to grow.

Many in the Repo market also expected bid/offer spreads to widen. This was supposed to be another consequence of the regulatory costs. If banks limited their market-making activity, spreads should widen because there is less liquidity. Over the years, bid/offer spreads did widen at times, but not due to regulation. As the size of the market grew, volatility also increased, and that was the primary driver of the wider spreads. Beginning in 2015, banks were intermediating much less in the Repo market and liquidity issues started to appear, especially at quarter-end and month-end.

Of course, where there's a regulation, there's usually a loophole or an exemption. If there's an economic need, the market usually finds a way. As banks reduced the size of their Repo books, many customers looked outside of the banks for Repo financing. The new banking regulation created a whole new cottage industry in the Repo market: the balance sheet providers. A substantial amount of Repo market activity moved to U.S. broker-dealers because they have regulatory advantages due to their exclusion from Dodd-Frank and Basel III regulations.

# MF Global

MF Global had a spectacular rise and fall. It grew out of a small futures broker into a major fixed-income trading firm, and then experienced a spectacular collapse. It's an especially good story because it has so many connections to the Repo market: They blew up because of an over-sized Repo-To-Maturity trade, and their collapse caused a fire sale. When the dust settled, there was $1.6 billion in customer seg funds missing. In fact, a whole book could be written about their rise and fall of MF Global.[122] Though it was a Repo trade that put them out of business, their demise was set in motion by the European Debt Crisis.

As the economies in Europe slowed down after the Financial Crisis, many countries found their tax revenues were no longer able to cover their debt burden. Years of free spending and debt accumulation had finally caught up to them. Greece was the first to feel the effects of the slow-down. In 2010, when Greece teetered on default, the IMF and the European Union stepped in to arrange a bailout to the tune of €110 billion.[123] Though Greece was saved for the time being, there was little expectation that the bailout was anything but temporary.

---

[122] In fact, there was a book written about it: *The Money Noose* by Scott E.D. Skyrm, available on Amazon.
[123] Two years later, in February 2012, Greece received a second bailout of €130 billion.

Once the market lost trust in Greece, investors worried about which other countries might have similar problems. An acronym referred to this collection of faltering economies: "PIIGS," which included the mostly southern European countries of Portugal, Ireland, Italy, Greece, and Spain.

Portugal has not been thought of as a world economic power, at least not for the past 400 years. They have a long history of nationalizing their industries, which has hindered economic development. In November 2010, Portugal began to feel the effects of the debt crisis that was wracking the rest of Europe. The Portuguese unemployment rate crept up into the teens, and the federal budget deficit continued to climb.

In December 2010, Fitch cut Portugal's debt rating to A+. The yield on long-term Portuguese bonds shot up to 465 basis points above Germany. As the situation continued to deteriorate, the government applied to the European Union for a financial bailout, and the EU granted Portugal a €78 billion package. However, yields on short-term Portuguese bonds still continued to climb, trading at 900 basis points over Germany. On July 5, 2011, Moody's cut the rating on Portugal to junk status, and their bond yields reached over 15%.

Ireland had an incredibly good run from 1995 to 2007, earning it the nickname "Celtic Tiger." When the housing bubble burst – set off by the Financial Crisis – Ireland was hard hit. Despite the best efforts of the government to stabilize the financial system, on August 24, 2010, Standard and Poor's cut the country's credit rating to AA-. When the financial situation grew worse, the government bailed out the domestic banks and borrowed money to finance the purchases. By

December 2010, Irish bonds with maturities between 12 and 18 months were yielding over 6.00%, compared to 0.65% for German bonds.

For much of the twentieth century, Italy's economy was marked by economic stagnation and recession. Though Italy is Europe's third largest economy, it has always been caught in the same economic malaise as the other southern Europeans. Before the Euro, Italy's Lira consistently lost value due to inflation, government over-spending, an inflexible labor market, and a generally difficult business climate.

Citing both "Italy's weakening economic growth prospects" and the lack of the government's "ability to respond decisively to events," Standard and Poor's downgraded Italy's credit rating to single-A in 2010. Italian bond prices were sent plummeting. Italy didn't need a bailout, but investors were cautious and interest rates remained high.

Before joining the Euro zone, Spain was surprisingly a source of cheap manufacturing in Europe. Sometimes called a manufacturing miracle in the 1990s, Spain was competitive because of its cheap currency, the peseta. Upon joining the Euro zone, they lost all of their competitive advantages and their manufacturing base slowly disappeared. The first cracks appeared when Spain's credit rating was downgraded by Fitch in May 2010, and then again by Moody's in September. It was the first time in Spain's history that they had been rated anything other than AAA. Spanish short-term debt increased to 150 basis points above Germany. Then, on June 25, 2011, Spain's access to the debt markets all but collapsed and the yields on their short-term bonds shot up above 12%.

While the collective wisdom at MF Global was to stay away from Greek debt, they saw plenty of opportunity in the high yields of the European periphery. There was a substantial amount of yield in the short-term debt of Portugal, Ireland, Italy, and Spain. Here were single-A and double-A-rated sovereign bonds trading at abnormally high yields.

Owning the bonds looked even better for short holding periods – something like 12 months or less. In December 2010, the short-term debt of Ireland was trading at 6.00%, Spain at 3.32%, Italy at 2.25%, and Portugal at 4.50%. Yes, there was default risk, but the short maturity dates made the risk seem insignificantly small. Now, suppose you could borrow money close to the risk-free rate, such as the equivalent of German-issued bonds, for 12 months in order to finance the purchases? Something like buying $100 million of Spanish bonds for a year with a yield of 3.32% and borrowing money at 1.00% to pay for the purchase. That's a profit of 2.32% or $2,320,000. Let's say you could increase the size of the trade tenfold to $1 billion. That's a profit of $23,200,000. Not bad. MF Global saw a huge opportunity, and it looked like they would make some easy money.

In the past, Repo-To-Maturity trades always involved U.S. Treasury and federal agency securities.[124] These securities are fully backed by the U.S. government, and the credit is about as risk-free as it gets. For accounting and risk purposes, selling a risk-free security or Repo'ing it to maturity was considered almost the same thing.

In order for MF Global to run up the kind of size they needed, they booked the Repo portion of the trades in the European Central

---

[124] Such as Freddie Mac and Fannie Mae.

Clearing Counterparty – LCH.Clearnet. If MF Global wanted to own $1 billion of European debt, all they needed to do was meet the LCH.Clearnet margin requirements. On a $1 billion debt portfolio, the margin requirement was about 3%, or $30 million. As long as MF Global had enough cash to meet the margin calls, the securities would eventually mature and generate a nice profit, assuming none of the countries defaulted.

As 2011 rolled on, the original $1 billion trade became $5 billion, then $7 billion, then $9.75 billion. Given the size of the trade at that point, the MF Global Board of Directors had to approve each increase in size. By the beginning of June, the firm had ratcheted it up to $11.5 billion. That was an incredible amount of leverage for a small futures broker like MF Global. Luckily, the trades were considered off-balance sheet, as long as their account firm was on board with treating a Repo-To-Maturity with non-risk-free securities as true sales.

As the size of the positions grew, the firm began to feel a strain on their liquidity. The margin requirement up until that point was never much more than $100 million. With a European debt crisis looming on the horizon, the prices of the bonds of the periphery countries – specifically Ireland and Portugal – began to decline en masse. A falling market and more price volatility meant higher margin requirements.

When the possibility of a Greek default became a real thing in June, LCH.Clearnet began taking larger haircuts on both Greek and periphery bonds. Once yields passed the magic 450-basis-point spread above Germany, a 15% margin rate was automatically imposed.

When the Board agreed to increase the position size to $11.5 billion, the firm was pledging about $170 million in margin. By the end of June, the situation deteriorated and MF Global was posting an astounding $550 million in margin to LCH.Clearnet. The trades became a severe drain on their liquidity, and no one could do anything about it.

The downfall of the Repo-To-Maturity trade came when their accounting firm and FINRA began to question the off-balance sheet status and regulatory capital requirements of the portfolio. The decision was handed down that MF Global's sale in the Repo-To-Maturity really didn't qualify as true, at least insofar as the accountants were concerned. When that happened, $11.5 billion in European sovereign bonds magically reappeared on their balance sheet. Then, the dominos began to fall further. When the trades reappeared, FINRA expected the firm to take a regulatory net capital charge. The capital charge led to a restatement of the financial statements. When MF Global posted a quarterly loss two months later, panic set in and the collapse began.

As pandemonium swept through the MF Global offices, their funding began to quickly disappear. Margin calls poured in and there wasn't enough of the firm's own capital to meet the funding needs. They needed to do something drastic. And they did. In their normal day-to-day operations, it wasn't uncommon for the company to dip into customer seg fund[125] money, usually taking $50 million here and there, but it was always returned by the end of the day.[126] It was, in the minds of MF Global personnel, acceptable to dip into the customer funds, just as long as it was repaid by the end of the day. On

---

[125] Segregated funds. Customer money is NEVER allowed to be mixed with a broker-dealer's own capital. The funds must always remain segregated.

[126] There were perhaps years of regulatory reports that were run at the end of the day that showed everything was in compliance and that no one knew customer funds had been used during the day.

Wednesday, October 26, 2011, more than $300 million was needed to finance the firm, but there was nothing left to return at the end of the day. As the days continued and MF Global lost more funding, more customer funds were used to cover the deficiencies. The missing funds shot up to $1.6 billion before everything was shut-down.

Looking back, many mistakes were made at MF Global. Banks have checks and balances for their traders to monitor and limit risk. At MF Global, there were very few such controls. In fact, the subject of risk management was largely ignored. The policies and procedures for handling customer funds were clearly lax, and the firm's own trading was minimally supervised.

As it turned out, the Repo-To-Maturity trades weren't really to maturity. LCH.Clearnet didn't accept Repo trades that ended on the security's maturity date. The closest they would accept was two days before maturity. In this instance, the term Repo-To-Maturity really wasn't to maturity at all. Regardless, there was default risk assumed by MF Global during those last two days. The off-legs of the trades were clearly not true sales. Of course, once they're not a true sale, they're not off-balance-sheet, and the dominos started to fall.

MF Global is remembered for the $1.6 billion customer seg funds that went missing. The largest fallacy of the whole MF Global affair is that the $1.6 billion in customer money was essentially stolen. Plenty of people were left with the impression that the people at MF Global stole the funds and nobody was brought to justice.[127] As the MF Global bankruptcy attorney stated in court on October 31, 2011, "The money is all accounted for." After an investigation, we learned the money was

---

[127] The culpability of Jon Corzine is a different discussion.

really just "misplaced."[128] As MF Global slipped into bankruptcy, their clearing banks, central clearing counterparties, and funding counterparties all grabbed as much margin as they possible could. Not that I blame them. The bankruptcies of Bear Stearns, Lehman Brothers, and AIG were still fresh in everyone's minds. The $1.6 billion in missing money was miraculously found at the CME, DTCC, FICC, LCH.Clearnet, JP Morgan Chase, MF Global's UK office, BONY London, Citibank London, and many of their Repo counterparties. In September 2013, the MF Global Trustee announced that they had returned 98% of the missing money, and the rest was all eventually fully paid back.

Before MF Global actually declared bankruptcy, the market smelled blood in the water. They knew MF Global would soon be liquidating, and there was plenty of speculative selling in front of the liquidation. After bankruptcy was declared, LCH.Clearnet assumed control and arranged an auction of the sovereign periphery debt. For one of the buyers, George Soros, the purchase was extremely lucrative. In total, he purchased approximately $2 billion worth of the Repo-To-Maturity securities, paying approximately 89 cents on the dollar for the Italian bonds, compared to the market price of 94 cents. It was estimated that Soros made a $140 million profit in a very short period of time.

There is, of course, no way of knowing the full extent of the losses that were due to the fire sale. Looking at the numbers, we can surmise the approximate damage done to MF Global's bottom line. For starters, the firm took a $7.3 million loss on the sale of $600 million worth of Repo-To-Maturity positions before the bankruptcy. The sale

---

[128] Not to understate the illegality of using the customer funds in the first place!

of Commercial Paper to Goldman Sachs for $1.33 billion had resulted in a loss of $15 million. Soros had paid $2 billion for a portion of the Repo-To-Maturity portfolio, costing MF Global another $140 million, with the remainder of the Repo-To-Maturity positions selling at a 10% discount, which adds another $280 million to the loss ledger. Moving on, we come to the $418 million worth of corporate bonds that the firm held, which were sold for $384 million, a loss of about $34 million. An additional $600 million worth of relatively illiquid securities were on the books, which we can conservatively assume a 10% discount, meaning the firm lost another $60 million. Assuming a negligible loss or even a slight profit was realized on the sale of the remaining assets in the firm's holdings – which included several billion dollars in federal agencies and U.S. Treasurys – the total cost of unwinding MF Global's trading positions in a one-week fire sale topped out at over $500 million.

In the end, the Repo-To-Maturity trades did not cause the losses. All of the bonds in the Repo-To-Maturity portfolio matured and none of the bonds defaulted. In fact, about 50% would have matured by the end of 2011, just two months after the collapse. The Repo-To-Maturity trades did not lose money, but they did drain the firm's liquidity, and caused the restatement of the financial statements, which added to the liquidity crisis, and eventually caused the fire sale which resulted in, at least, a $500 million loss.

# DEBT CEILING

Like it or not, there's a debt ceiling crisis every few years. In the past, there were some heated battles, with the worst coming in November 1997, July 2011, and November 2013. As it happens, the United States is one of the few countries that maintains a legal limit on the size of its debt. The debt limit is passed by Congress and must be occasionally increased before the Treasury can issue new debt. Though politicians generally find it easy to spend, many get sticker shock when it comes time to vote on increasing the size of the debt. Every few years, the federal government approaches its debt limit and a political compromise must be reached to increase it. Sometimes we get close to the date when the government runs out of borrowing authority without a resolution. That's when the politics of the debt ceiling spill over into the financial markets. It sometimes becomes a crisis.

The drop-dead date is never the date when the Treasury runs out of cash. Initially, it's the date when the Treasury is unable to continue to borrow. Sounds like the same thing? They're different. When the government reaches its debt limit, it cannot issue more debt, but that's just the beginning. There's still cash on-hand, tax revenue coming in, and the ability to shift internal government accounts to generate cash.

During this time, Treasury officials will offer doom and gloom scenarios, crying that the government will shut down and a catastrophe is at hand. Of course, they're supposed to do that. It's their job. The CBO[129] will estimate that the Treasury will run out of funds within a week or two. Economists will put the real date a little further out. In fact, the Treasury always has contingency plans to extend the drop-dead date further than they'll admit. The Treasury Secretary will underestimate how long the government can continue to operate under what are referred to as "extraordinary measures." Treasury Secretary Robert Rubin was the best at finding new money and juggling accounts.

A default of the entire U.S. Treasury market is highly unlikely. It's almost impossible, in fact. The real risk is a "technical default." In more practical terms, the risk is the market's *expectation* of a technical default. So far, there has never been an actual technical default, because a compromise was always reached.

There's a big difference between a default and a technical default. Officially, there's no cross-default in the U.S. Treasury market because the U.S. Treasury never included such a provision in its Uniform Offering Circular. If one Treasury security misses a coupon payment or is not paid at maturity, other Treasury securities are not legally in default. A technical default means that only the securities which did not mature or make a coupon payment are in default.

Let's say the Treasury doesn't have enough money to mature some Treasurys on the maturity date and make coupon payments. The Treasury Market Practices Group (TMPG)[130] made recommendations to the Fed back in 2011 to deal with the situation. The main goal of the Treasury market is to avoid having matured

---

[129] Congressional Budget Office. A non-partisan government group that generates estimates and projections that are friendly to Democrats.

[130] "Operational Plans for Various Contingencies for Treasury Debt Payments"; Treasury Market Practices Group; 2011, 2013, 2021.

Treasury securities frozen in the FedWire system. Technically, a security becomes non-transferable once its maturity date is reached. Unless something is done with that security by 7:00 PM the evening before, it becomes non-transferable the next day.

The TMPG recommended that all Treasurys that cannot be matured[131] have their maturity date extended one day forward. In other words, the Treasury should keep rolling the maturity date forward each day until the securities are paid off. If the Treasury is unable to mature the March 6 Treasury Bill, then the bill's maturity date is extended to March 7, then to March 8, and so on. This solution is operational within the FedWire system and within the market's trade processing systems.

Coupon payments are a slightly different story. There's a choice to be made. The coupon payments could be held for the holder of record[132] or they could be attached to the defaulted securities. In the first scenario, if the Treasury misses a coupon payment, the receiver would have a money wire fail from the Treasury. The underlying security continues to accrue interest for the next coupon payment, so the missed payment doesn't affect the security going forward. In the end, it's a matter of how long the investor waits before they get paid their coupon.

Keep in mind, the TMPG recommendations were never implemented. The recommendations were designed only to mitigate market disruptions, not eliminate them. It's also important to remember that there's no compensation for investors who are left

---

[131] Because there's not enough money at the U.S. Treasury.
[132] Like a money wire fail.

holding technically defaulted Treasurys because back interest would require an act of Congress.

As long as there's a mechanism to settle defaulted Treasurys, there must be a way to price them. Remember, a technical default is not about whether investors *will* get their money back, it's a matter of *when*. To put it mildly, a defaulted security carries uncertainty for a few days or a few weeks.

A technically defaulted Treasury should be priced[133] based on a term repo Rate with an uncertainty and illiquidity discount. The price of the security should be adjusted for the cost of the Repo financing while the security is in default. There's always a market for term Repo, but the problem is the uncertainty; you don't know how many days to finance the security. In addition, the liquidity factor is a wild card. Bid/offered spreads will be wide.

There's also a limited number of buyers. Most investors are not allowed to own defaulted securities under any circumstance. If the question is whether Treasurys with missed coupon payments can be pledged to an exchange, a clearing bank, in customer seg funds, or processed at a central clearing counterparty, then the answer is yes. However, those same investors are unlikely to accept a defaulted Treasury as Repo collateral.

Let's be clear: Neither the Treasury market nor the Repo market will become inoperable during a technical default. Believe me, that's been suggested by doom and gloom market participants many times in the past. The market disruption is limited to the very short-end of

---

[133] OK, there are two formulas in the book! Price = 100 – (Repo rate * number of days in default / 360) – illiquidity discount.

the market – usually those securities which mature or pay a coupon within the coming weeks. Basically, many investors just don't want to hold a security that matures during the crisis. Money Market Funds, corporate treasurers, central banks, and other portfolios will sell their Treasury bills and short coupons.

Large investment funds will, at some point, publicly announce that they have no exposure to any Treasurys affected by the debt ceiling. That generally means they just sold all of their short-term securities the day before the announcement. Evidently, SEC Rule 2a-7[134] does not specifically prohibit MMFs from owning Treasury securities which are in default.

The crisis affects the Repo market in a different way. There's a fear of receiving a defaulted security as collateral. If a cash investor is given a security that matures or pays a coupon and the debt ceiling is not raised, they might not be paid. Instead of policing every security they're allocated as collateral, some cash investors just exit the Repo market entirely.

In the inter-dealer Repo market, General Collateral buyers also worry they'll receive securities with coupon payments or short maturities. In order to avoid receiving another dealer's potentially defaulted collateral, the term General Collateral markets trade with the notation NIC, or "no intervening coupon." This signifies that the collateral borrower will not accept securities affected by a possible default.

---

[134] The rule that governs MMF investments.

Of course, the best solution for a debt ceiling crisis is a political compromise. However, in case of a long, drawn-out conflict, there are some powers that the Treasury and Fed have:

1. Keep Accruing Interest - The Treasury can announce that Treasurys close to a scheduled coupon payment date will keep accruing coupon interest until the next payment date and make a double coupon payment then. This would clean up the missed coupon payment issue.

2. The Fed could purchase all of the defaulted Treasurys. There's nothing in the Federal Reserve Act that prohibits them from doing this. The securities still qualify for purchase under Section 14 of the Federal Reserve Act because they are still guaranteed by the U.S. government. The Fed could sell existing securities in the SOMA portfolio and buy all of the Treasurys which are close to maturity.

3. The Fed could allow an expanded use of Repo operations and the Standing Repo Facility (SRF). They could expand the eligible counterparty list, so more market participants could submit maturing and/or coupon paying securities for financing.

# History

## 1985

This is a little before my time, but in 1985, James Baker, the Secretary of the Treasury under Ronald Reagan, faced a debt ceiling face-off between the President and Congress. Before the debt ceiling was reached, he shifted money out of the Social Security trust fund and was able to continue to pay the government's bills. A compromise was eventually reached and a precedent was set.

## November 1997

The crisis in November 1997 was one of the biggest show-downs ever. Problems began on November 1, 1997, when the details of the quarterly refunding were announced. Congress had passed a continuing resolution to keep the government funded through November 13, but there was no way to settle the newly announced securities settling on November 15 without a higher debt ceiling. Throughout the first two weeks of November, the market was waiting for the debt ceiling to be raised, while the auctions for the 3 Month Bills, 6 Month Bills, Cash Management Bills, 10 Year Notes, and 30 Year Bonds were postponed.

Repo market discussions centered around the specific Treasury securities scheduled to pay a coupon which needed a debt ceiling increase. Questions were raised as to whether Reverse-Repo counterparties who didn't receive coupon payments were required to pay coupon payments to their Repo counterparties. If the Treasury didn't pay the coupon, would one side of the Repo trade still owe the coupon to other side? Officially, coupon payments were governed by the issuance rules of the U.S. Treasury, whereas coupon payments between Repo counterparties were governed by the Master Repurchase Agreement. In 1997, the market determined that coupons must still be paid between Repo market participants, even if the security holder didn't receive the coupon from the Treasury.

Before the $4.9 trillion debt ceiling was reached, Robert Rubin, the Treasury Secretary under President Clinton, shifted $61.3 billion from two government employee trust funds out of U.S. Treasurys and into cash. These moves postponed the debt ceiling cliff for another three months. Then, again in January, while the debt ceiling fight was still raging, Rubin announced he could shift $82.6 billion out of Federal Financing Bank and into various government trust funds. The move allowed the Treasury to issue more debt. Naturally, Rubin's maneuvers did not sit well with Congress. Though a compromise was reached, the blueprint for Treasury accounting maneuvers was greatly enhanced.

## June 2002/October 2004

In June 2002, the announcement of the 2 Year Note auction was delayed, pending an increase in the debt ceiling. The ceiling was raised soon thereafter, and there were no market disruptions. In October 2004, the market was worried the debt ceiling limit would be reached in November, but the limit was increased again with no disruption.

## July/August 2011

The next big debt ceiling crisis arrived in July 2011. It was the largest disruption to date. This time, much of the anxiety centered on holding technically defaulted Treasury securities. The market was clearly more educated on the implications of a technical default than it was in the past.

Though there were relatively few bills, notes, and bonds maturing in August, fear spread through the Repo market. At the time, the fed funds target range was set close to zero, which meant there was little cost associated with holding cash out of the market. Investors began pulling cash out of the market. Just when overnight rates hit their peak on August 1, the Senate ratified a debt ceiling compromise.

Over the next few days, General Collateral rates moved back into their normal range, but many cash investors still left large cash deposits at their clearing bank. For the customers, there was little opportunity cost in receiving no interest. However, there was a cost for the clearing bank. Customer cash was technically a deposit, which had a regulatory cost. The Bank of New York immediately announced a holding fee on large deposits of idle cash. Zero rates are one thing, but charging fees on top of no interest is another. Cash flowed back into the Repo market and rates returned to normal.

## October 2013

This debt ceiling crisis lasted longer than most, about six days in total. As we approached the last day of borrowing authority, even before the extraordinary measures kicked in, there were cries about the entire U.S. Treasury market defaulting and an ensuing panic. Many investors were anxious there would be a full-blown debt default, which would lead to a global financial crisis. In reality, a technical default wasn't even pending for weeks. However, the cries of panic spooked politicians enough to extract a political deal.

The worst part of any debt ceiling crisis is the fear that's peddled. Political posturing makes the crisis appear worse than it is. Politicians are irresponsible during these times, creating more public anxiety than is warranted. Certainly, it's a bad precedent for any issuer to miss a payment, and missed principal and interest payments would affect the future liquidity of the Treasury market. I hope that we have experienced our last debt ceiling crisis, but I doubt it.

# QUANTITATIVE EASING (QE)

To date, the Fed has enacted four[135] full rounds of Quantitative Easing (QE) that grew the Securities Open Market Account (SOMA) portfolio from $924 billion before the Financial Crisis to $8.9 trillion in April 2022. The Fed now uses QE as a monetary policy tool to provide liquidity to the financial system. From the beginning, it seemed like QE was nothing short of revolutionary. It allowed the government to stimulate the economy during a crisis without the negative impact of large debt issuance hanging over the market.

## Domestic Securities Holdings

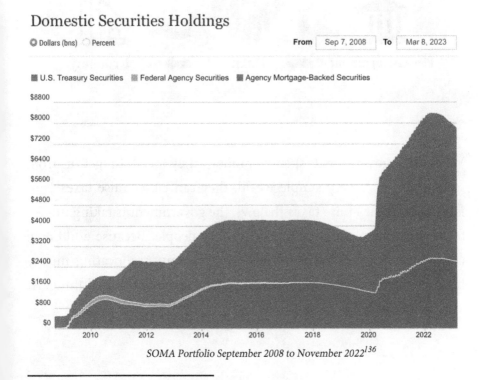

*SOMA Portfolio September 2008 to November 2022[136]*

---

[135] Five if you count QE3+.

[136] https://www.newyorkfed.org/data-and-statistics/data-visualization/system-open-market-account-portfolio

Let's say the government needs to increase spending during an economic downturn. Perhaps it's for increased unemployment benefits, stimulus money, or any range of new programs. This government money goes into the economy and ultimately stimulates economic activity. In the illustration [below], the government sends cash to the public who, in turn, spend it on goods and services. This is a very Keynesian economic view. When economic activity declines, the government fills the void with increased spending.

When the government spends money, they need to get it from somewhere. In a very simple world, they can either raise taxes[137] or issue debt. If they raise taxes [below], the government is taking money from some people and giving it to other people. Because additional consumption is needed to restart the economy, reallocating money from savings to consumption is generally considered a good thing. At least temporarily.

---

[137] I'm not getting into the different kinds of taxes or who pays more or less in taxes. This is a simple discussion and I'm just a Repo guy!

**Tax Payers** ➡ **US Government**

There's also another way to pay for the spending: It's the buy-now-and-pay-later plan. Instead of raising taxes, the government can issue debt [below]. Under this option, new Treasury securities are sold to the public to pay for the spending. When investors purchase the securities, they are reallocating funds from other investments[138] into U.S. Treasurys. Here, money that was previously invested is reallocated to consumption. Once again, increased consumption is needed during a downturn, so reallocating money from investment to consumption is again a good thing. Theoretically, the government pays back the debt when the economy is healthy and tax revenues are high.

**Public** ➡ **Bond Holders** ➡ **US Government**

---

[138] Often called "crowding out."

For most of this country's history, increased government spending meant either more taxes or more debt. There was always an immediate cost to bear. Either money was reallocated from savers to consumers or reallocated from investors to consumers. Recently, the Federal Reserve changed this equation.

**Federal Reserve** ➡ **Bond Holders** ➡ **US Government**

When there's an economic downturn and government spending is high, the Fed can now use a QE program to purchase government debt. Instead of the financial system being forced to absorb Treasury issuance and reallocate money from investment to consumption, the Fed can buy the debt through money creation.

Let's look at the mechanics. It all starts when the government issues new Treasury securities that are purchased by the public. The buyers are banks, pension funds, insurance companies, broker-dealers, hedge funds, etc. The newly-issued securities trade in the secondary market, and they may be sitting in end-user portfolios for years before the Fed shows any interest in them.

When the Fed announces a QE operation, Primary Dealers[139] offer securities to the Fed. The Primary Dealer might own the securities outright, purchase them from a client, or obtain them in the inter-dealer market. The Fed analyzes the securities and buys the securities with the lowest price. On the settlement day, the securities are sent to the Fed's SOMA account. As securities go into the Fed's account, cash goes out.[140] It's that easy. In the end, securities are removed and cash is injected into the market.

## QE1

The first QE program began on November 25, 2008, when the Fed announced they would buy $600 billion agency MBSs. At the time, the financial system was in the depths of crisis, mortgage spreads were wide, and the market was illiquid. The first round of QE was for a specific dollar amount, and proceeds were not reinvested when the securities matured or paid coupon.

The Fed expanded QE1 on March 18, 2009, to add another $1.75 trillion,[141] which included Treasurys. Once QE1 ended in June 2010, the Fed's balance sheet stood at $2.1 trillion. They had driven interest rates lower and added liquidity to the financial system.

## QE2

The first hints of a second QE program came at the Jackson Hole conference in August 2010. Reading the tea leaves and speeches at the

---

[139] Most Primary Dealers are broker-dealers and subsidiaries of banks.

[140] Just in case the Fed runs out of money, they can issue themselves a Deferred Asset – which is like an IOU - and pay themselves back with future income.

[141] The second round of QE1 is sometimes referred to as QE2. I consider it an expansion of QE1, and therefore part of the original buying program.

conference, it became clear the Fed was worried about deflation. And what's a good way to stop deflation? An inflationary program!

On November 3, 2010, the Fed announced they would purchase between $850 billion and $900 billion over the next eight months - about $110 billion a month. The real net increase in the SOMA portfolio was only about $600 billion, because the $850 billion included reinvesting the proceeds from maturing securities and coupon payments. Once again, there was a specified amount and timeframe. QE2 lasted from November 2010 through June 2011. When it was over, the Fed had run the SOMA portfolio up to $2.64 trillion.

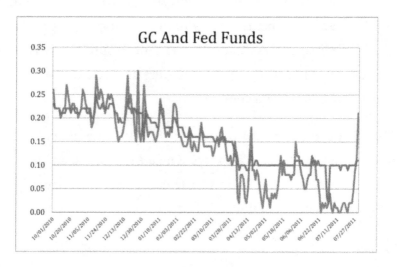

*GC and Fed Funds October 2010 to July 2011*

When the program began, General Collateral was averaging at .22%. When it ended, General Collateral was down to .03%. QE2 was the first program to have a clear impact on the Repo market. For every $100 billion a month in QE purchases, General Collateral rates moved about 2.7 basis points lower.

QE2 also illustrated the diminishing returns of a QE program. Where QE1 added much needed liquidity into the post-Financial Crisis market, it was not the same for QE2. The stated goal of the QE2 was to bring long-term U.S. Treasury yields lower. QE2 clearly pushed up asset prices and made it easier to finance the budget deficit. While the impact on long-term interest rates can be debated, there was a very clear and real impact on short-term rates. By removing so many Treasurys from the market, the Fed ended up reducing the supply of Treasurys and creating a collateral shortage.

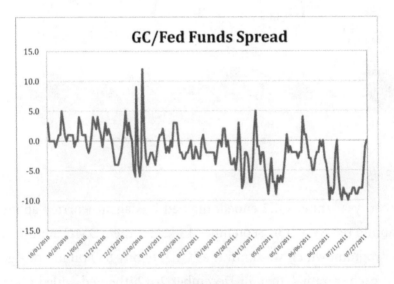

*GC/Fed Funds Spread October 2010 to July 2011*

After QE2 ended in July 2011, most of the positive effects were reversed. Over the next 16 months, the market had to absorb about $100 billion a month in net new Treasury issuance. In the end, Treasury issuance brought short-term rates back to the same place where they had started. By December 2012, General Collateral rates were trading between .23% and .25%. General Collateral had moved from 7 basis points below Fed funds back to 7 basis points above fed funds.

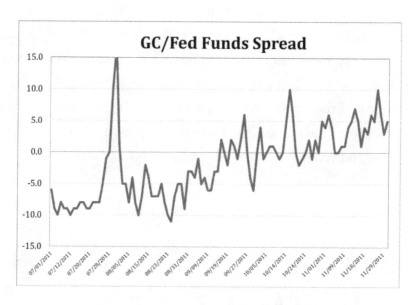

*GC/Fed Funds Spread July 2011 to November 2011*

## QE3[142]

Just two years after QE2 ended, the Fed was again worried about the economic recovery. On September 13, 2012, the FOMC announced a new program, which was known as QE3, to buy $40 billion of Agency MBSs each month. Then, in December 2012, the Fed added a second parallel program to buy $45 billion U.S. Treasurys each month. At first, the second program was dubbed QE3+.[143] Both of the QE3 programs were open-ended, so the market affectionately dubbed them "QE Infinity."

By the time QE3 ended, the SOMA portfolio stood at $4.22 trillion. During the program, General Collateral moved from .24%

---

[142] October 2012 to the end of 2014.

[143] QE3+ was also dubbed QE4 for a while.

down to .05%. Agency MBS collateral, which was trading at 14 basis points above fed funds, moved to 3 basis points below fed funds. As a rough estimate, every $85 billion in purchases moved General Collateral down an average of 2.6 basis points each month.

## QE4

With the SOMA portfolio extremely large and the economic recovery gaining strength, it was finally time to unwind QE. The Fed's initiated its first large-scale Balance Sheet Runoff from 2017 to 2019. After eighteen months, the portfolio was down to $3.55 trillion, and it seemed like everything was running smoothly. Then, the Repo market blew up. The cause of the Repo crisis is still in debate, but overall, there was clearly too much collateral in the market that was creating bottlenecks of cash and bank reserves.

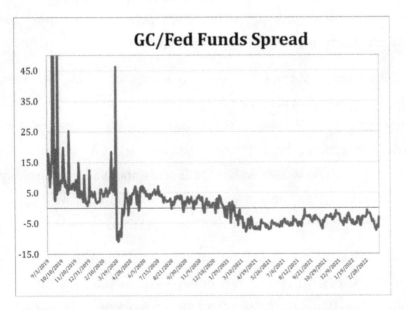

*GC/Fed Funds Spread September 2019 to March 2022*[144]

---

[144] The upper range of the graph doesn't show the full extent of the Repo blow up in September 2019.

QE4 began right after the Repo Market Crisis, with small-scale Fed buying. Six months later, when the COVID crisis hit, market liquidity was poor and collateral supply was heavy. When Treasury and Agency MBS spreads widened, several hedge funds and REITs were exposed, and wide-scale fire sales seemed possible. One of the first things the Fed did was to ramp up QE purchases. The Fed purchased nearly $1.5 trillion Treasurys in the span of one month from March to April. They continued buying at a pace of $120 billion a month thereafter. Buying slowed when they first tapered in November 2021, and then it completely ended in March 2022. At that point, the Fed had accumulated the largest balance sheet ever – $8.9 trillion.

There was a paper presented at the Fed's Jackson Hole conference in August 2013 that concluded that QE is not an effective tool for reviving the economy. That's a little disappointing, given how QE is now a fully integrated part of monetary policy. On the other hand, there are plenty of academic papers which extol the virtues of QE.

The stated goal of a QE program is always something like "market stability," "to provide liquidity," or "to support the smooth functioning ..." However, these days, there's a pretty strong correlation between large Treasury issuance and QE programs. That leaves the question as to whether QE is really about adding liquidity to the financial system or just to smooth over the negative impact of large Treasury issuance. Or are they the same thing?

QE1 was clearly good for the financial markets. During the Financial Crisis, there was not enough liquidity for the market to properly function. QE1 helped thaw frozen markets. QE2 was similar, but a little different. It lifted asset prices and was effective in supporting the agency MBS market. There's not much to say about

QE3, except that it drove short-term interest rates lower. In the beginning, QE4 helped supply liquidity after the Repo crisis and during the COVID crisis.

For some reason, QE4 went on for far too long. During that time, we learned that there's a point when the market no longer needs the Fed's liquidity. Toward the end of QE4, the Fed had removed too much collateral and injected too much cash. When the financial markets were saturated with liquidity, they sent the cash right back to the Fed via the RRP facility. Of course, hindsight is 20/20, but the Fed should have ended QE4 in April 2021. That's when RRP volume began climbing with each successive round of Fed buying. Rule of thumb: When RRP volume increases during QE, the program is no longer effective.

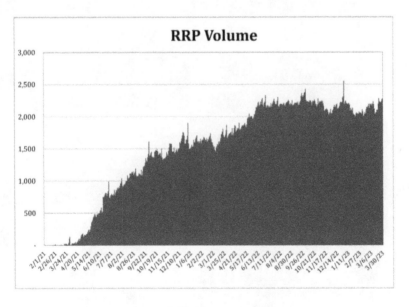

*RRP Volume 2021-2022*

There's an important part of QE that's constantly overlooked: It's unwind. The SOMA portfolio can't increase forever, so the Fed is supposed to unwind as much as possible when the market is stable and the economy is no longer in crisis. Unwinding means removing liquidity and increasing supply in the bond market. The one time the Fed tried Balance Sheet Runoff from 2017 to 2019, the Repo market blew up. The Fed clearly has a problem unwinding QE. If they're unable to unwind a monetary policy, that's a problem.

# BALANCE SHEET RUNOFF

Fed's balance sheet reached a massive $8.9 trillion in April 2022. Think of it, The Fed owned 28%[145] of the entire $31.5 trillion U.S. government debt outstanding. They had the largest balance sheet ever accumulated in financial history. But the buying was the easy part, the problem was unwinding it.

Because Quantitative Tightening (QT) sounds like the opposite of Quantitative Easing, it's often presumed that the Fed shrinks the SOMA portfolio through QT. However, that's not the case. The Fed doesn't like to move so fast when removing liquidity, so they prefer the slower pace of Balance Sheet Runoff.

Balance Sheet Runoff means that when the securities from the SOMA portfolio mature, the Fed doesn't reinvest the proceeds. When there's Balance Sheet Runoff, the Fed picks a fixed dollar amount to let mature each month. They usually start small and let the size of the runoff increase on a fixed schedule. If the Fed wanted a more aggressive policy, they would use QT, where they outright sell securities on a regular schedule.

The mechanics of Balance Sheet Runoff are simple. When securities mature, the Treasury transfers funds into the Fed's SOMA account. Since the Fed doesn't buy new securities to replace those maturing, the cash stays at the Fed. If "money creation" occurs when the Fed buys securities in a QE program, Balance Sheet Runoff is the opposite. It could even be called "money destruction," because liquidity is removed from the financial system.

---

[145] The SOMA portfolio includes both Treasurys and agency MBS.

Over at the Treasury, the debt doesn't just disappear. When the Treasury sends cash to the Fed, they need to get the funds from somewhere. The Treasury issues new securities to pay-off those that are maturing. Here's the important part: The new securities are purchased by private investors. It's no longer government money funding government securities. Private investors must either invest idle cash or sell other investments to buy the new Treasurys. This means for each successive round of Balance Sheet Runoff, more Treasurys are deposited into the market and investors must pay for them.

So far, there were only two large-scale Balance Sheet Runoff operations. The first one ran from 2017 to 2019 and the second one began in June 2022.

## Domestic Securities Holdings

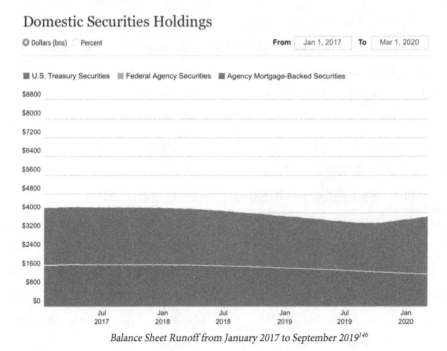

*Balance Sheet Runoff from January 2017 to September 2019[146]*

---

[146] https://www.newyorkfed.org/data-and-statistics/data-visualization/system-open-market-account-portfolio

The first Balance Sheet Runoff didn't quite go so well. The Fed shrunk the SOMA portfolio from a peak of $4.22 trillion down to $3.55 trillion – a total of about $670 billion. From 2017 through 2018, the market absorbed the securities without any problems. During that period, the General Collateral rate slowly moved from the bottom of the fed funds target range to the top. By the end of 2018, General Collateral was trading well above the target range.

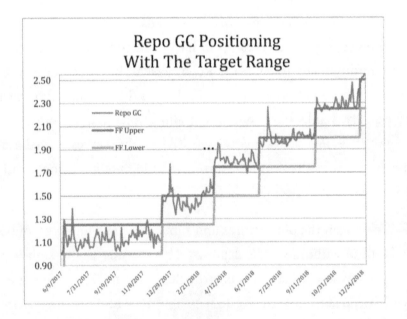

*Repo Rates During Balance Sheet Runoff: 2017-2018*

Then, things went sideways at the end of the 2018. During 2018 year-end, General Collateral spiked to 7.25%. Since rates didn't spike again for the next few months, the event was attributed to just something that occasionally happens on year-end. However, year-end 2018 was the harbinger of things to come. Nine months later, on September 17, 2019, General Collateral spiked again to 9.25%. The problems in the Repo market in September 2019 went down in the history books as the Repo Market Panic. Here's how it began:

Market commentators generally attribute the cause of the Repo Market Panic to "declining bank reserves." While collateral was accumulating in the Repo market, bank reserves were also declining. Total bank reserve balances peaked at around $2.8 trillion in 2014 and were down to about $1.7 trillion in 2019. Yes, bank reserves were on the decline, but there were no significant changes in or around September 2019.

The decline in bank reserves didn't cause the Repo panic, but the dwindling supply of reserves could have created a smaller cushion of extra liquidity ready to enter the Repo market. In other words, excess bank reserves don't come out of the Fed and into the Repo market very quickly. Banks have investment allocations that are often made by committee. Perhaps some rate sensitive bank reserves moved out of the Fed, but most bank reserves are not fluid enough to move out of the Fed on short notice.

We've seen the old pictures and films of people lining up outside of a bank to withdraw their deposits. Think of the Depression in the 1930s. Knowing that a bank is struggling and might not be able to pay-off depositors means the first people to withdraw are the most likely to get their money back. These days, banks are not as susceptible to the classic "run on the bank" because they have longer term funding in place. However, other types of financial institutions do not have the same requirements and are more susceptible to overnight funding risk.

The Repo market opens at 7:00 AM EST and closes at 3:00 PM. Cash comes into the Repo market throughout the day. Some cash investors invest when the market opens, some enter mid-morning, and many West Coast funds don't arrive until the early afternoon.

Cash borrowers (hedge funds, REITs, broker-dealers) rush to finance their positions between 7:00 AM and 8:30 AM. That's because most Prime Brokers require their hedge fund clients to book their trades by 8:30 AM. Whereas cash investors enter the market all day long, the bulk of the cash borrowers need to finance their positions between 7:00 AM and 8:30 AM.

Cracks in the system started to appear on December 31, 2018 year-end. On that day, General Collateral opened at 2.93% and a panic ensued. Rates backed-up all the way to 7.25% before finally closing at 4.00% at the end of the day. The Repo market had not seen such rate volatility in years. It was a real eye opener. The fact that the Fed didn't intervene was an even larger shock. Over the next several months, there was increased rate volatility and small rate spikes on January month-end, March quarter-end, and June quarter-end. The Fed talked about a permanent RP[147] Facility, but nothing happened.

Fast forward to Monday, September 16 and the market was expecting mild funding pressure that day:

1. $19 billion in net new Treasury issuance (more securities in the market).

2. Tax date (cash leaving the market for the Treasury).

3. Money Market Fund cash decreased from the previous week by about $20 billion (less cash in the market).

4. Bond market sell-off the previous week (generally adds collateral into the Repo market).

---

[147] RP = Repo. The Fed borrows collateral from Primary Dealers and injects cash into the market.

All of these things are a normal part of the Repo market. Cash and securities come in and out of the market and the market finds a clearing price. In fact, on Monday, September 16, the General Collateral opened only a little higher than normal at 2.33%. The market was expecting a little funding pressure, but nothing extreme.

On Monday, September 16 – the day before the official Repo Market Panic – General Collateral rates moved higher in the afternoon, trading as high as 8.00%. It didn't have a large impact on the overall market because little volume traded. Mild rate spikes can occur at the end of the day due to the dislocation of cash and collateral. However, this one was different, the volatility carried into the next day.

On Tuesday, September 17, bids were thin. That is, when a bid was hit, the sellers had much more collateral to sell than the buyers were willing to buy. When bids were hit, the market backed-up immediately. 3.00% traded, 3.50% traded, then 4.00%, then 4.50%, and so on. The total number of securities for sale overwhelmed the buyers. Everyone who was long collateral was in a rush to sell because rates were going higher. Everyone long cash didn't want to invest because rates were going higher. It was a modern day "run on the bank." The market peaked at 9.25%.

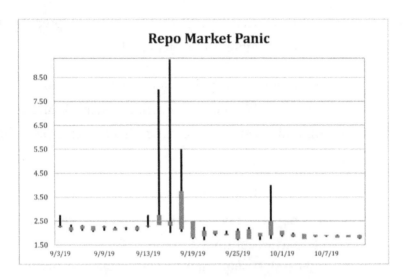

*General Collateral: Open, High, Low, Close*

At 9:15 AM, during the depth of the panic, the Fed realized they needed to inject cash and announced their first RP operation in years. It was successful. They pumped $53.15 billion into the market and rates recovered. The Fed's intervention drove overnight General Collateral down to 2.30%. Over the next two days, the Fed continued overnight RP operations each day at 8:15 AM and rates stabilized. On Friday, September 20, the Fed announced a daily schedule for RP operations that went through September quarter-end and into October. The three term operations eventually pumped $139 billion in the market. On the day of quarter-end, the Fed executed an overnight operation that added another $63.5 billion. Overall, the Fed pumped a total of $202.5 billion into the Repo market and the market was functioning smoothly again.

Additional thoughts:

- In September 2019, Fed had not yet created the Standing Repo Facility (SRF). In fact, they hadn't executed RP operations in years. The Fed was clearly not prepared for the impact of tighter monetary conditions.

- QE is a monetary policy tool that's here to stay. In September 2019, the Fed quickly ended Balance Sheet Runoff and restarted QE buying - inadvertently launching QE4.

- At no point during the Repo Market Panic did credit break down. The market didn't seize up and counterparties continued to trade. There was always a bid for collateral; though the bids kept moving higher.

- The Panic caused funding pressure and volatility in the Repo market for months. The event created a significant amount of market anxiety.

When breaking the Repo Market Panic down to its core, the rate spike was a direct result of Balance Sheet Runoff. Yes, there were other factors which contributed, but the underlying cause was the Fed adding securities to the market and removing liquidity.

That leads to the question: Given all of the potential problems with unwinding the SOMA portfolio, why unwind it at all? Why not just keep growing the SOMA portfolio forever? The answer is that there *must* be a cost for having a large balance sheet.

Under the "no free lunch"[148] school of economics, nothing comes for free. Any government program comes at a cost. There are often benefits today which must be paid down the road. QE injects liquidity into the economy and prevents government debt issuance from

---

[148] There's no official "no free lunch" theory in the economics text books, but there should be!

overwhelming the financial markets. The "cost" of QE is the massive amount of liquidity (cash) in the system.

The economist Milton Friedman launched the Monetarist approach in economic theory. "Helicopter Money," though often attributed to former Fed Chairman Ben Bernanke, was originally a Friedman idea. Without getting too much in the weeds, according to Friedman: *"Inflation is always and everywhere a monetary phenomenon."* If Friedman is even partly correct, then adding trillions of QE cash into the economy must drive up prices.

Just for argument's sake, let's assume that inflation *is* a monetary phenomenon. Maybe it's not 100%, maybe it's just 25%. Either way, increasing the supply of money has an effect on the price level. If you accept that some inflation is driven by QE and the size of the Fed's balance sheet, then the solution to inflation *must* involve shrinking the balance sheet.

The SOMA portfolio cannot grow forever, it must eventually shrink. The challenge for the Fed is how to minimize the negative impact of adding securities to the market as they shrink the size of the balance sheet. Theoretically, if the Fed waited long enough, the economy could grow into the right size to support the balance sheet. However, there's a problem between now and then. If they wait to shrink such a large balance sheet, it means there's extra liquidity sloshing around in the system which is causes inflation.

# Predictions

## General Collateral will move to the top of the fed funds target range and the SRF will be used every day.

It took a long time for the Fed to establish the Standing Repo Facility (SRF), but luckily, the Fed finally put a ceiling on overnight rates. Ironically, since the time the SRF became operational, no one has used it. It sits dormant because overnight rates are still at the bottom of the fed funds target range. It's just not economical for the market to use it. Once overnight rates move to the top of the target range, Primary Dealers will submit collateral into the SRF every day. For the time being, investors send their excess cash to the other facility, the RRP.

Think of the RRP as a giant holding tank of liquidity. It sits there as a storage facility for cash. As securities come into the market from Balance Sheet Runoff, cash will be pulled out of the RRP to finance them. Combine Balance Sheet Runoff with new Treasury issuance and a lot of securities are poised to enter the market. Eventually, the RRP facility will drain down to zero.

Once the RRP is out of cash, the Repo market will need to attract cash from other markets in order to pay for the securities coming in. At that point, overnight General Collateral rates will migrate from the bottom of the fed funds target range to the top, just like they did during the last round of Balance Sheet Runoff from 2017 to 2019.

When General Collateral hits the top of the target range, it will be trading at the same rate as the SRF. Once there's further pressure for General Collateral to move higher, Primary Dealers will submit collateral to the SRF.

## SOFR will replace fed funds as the Fed's monetary policy rate.

The federal funds rate was the most important overnight interest rate for many years. The problem is that it's less important today. In fact, it's outdated. It's shocking that the fed funds rate is still used to set monetary policy. It's really a relic of a bygone era. These days, it barely trades, and when it does, there are few counterparties.

Repo rates are more important to the financial system. They're more liquid, have thousands of market participants, and they represent trillions of dollars of transactions each day. In the past, it was impossible to discontinue using the fed funds rate because there was no viable replacement. Now that SOFR has been created to replace LIBOR, there's no reason it can't replace fed funds.

Replacing fed funds was even talked about at an FOMC meeting back in 2014. Many other central banks use a Repo rate as their policy rate. There was talk about a system with IOER at the top of the target range and the RRP rate at the bottom. That setup is not optimal, given that they are two different rates from two different markets. But that was before the Standing Repo Facility (SRF). Now, the Fed has a real upper bound (SRF) and lower bound (RRP) for Repo rates.

# The Treasury curve will cheapen relative to other yield curves

As more Treasurys and agencies are dumped into the market, it will push the Treasury yield curve higher relative to other yield curves. Think about the $95 billion of balance sheet runoff each month. That's a massive amount of Treasury and agency securities. Now consider new Treasury issuance, and that's even more supply. Assuming a government budget deficit of $1 trillion, there's another $83 billion a month in new securities. Combine the two together and we are looking at about $178 billion of securities coming into the market each month. That's $1 trillion more government securities in the market every six months. Two trillion every year. Four trillion after two years. Where's the cash coming from to pay for these securities?

The market needs to absorb these securities. Investment portfolios and central banks will be buyers. Maybe some corporate treasurers and some insurance companies. Not the Money Market Funds, since the duration of most of the securities is too long. That leaves the hedge funds. But the hedge funds only buy when there's a relative value opportunity. Spreads must then widen to make it economical to own Treasurys and finance them in the Repo market.

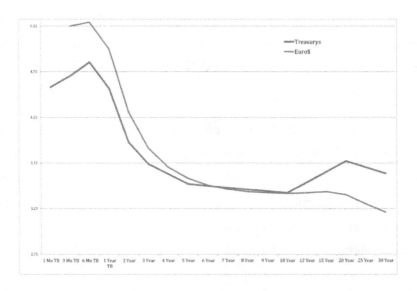

*Yield Curve: March 31, 2023*

Treasurys are rich to Eurodollars in the short end of the market, they're flat to Euros in the medium-term, and cheap to Euros in the long end. Over the next few years, the government bond market will return to a similar state as 2017-2019. That was the last time the market was supersaturated with government securities. Back then, every hedge fund owned as many Treasurys as they possibly could. They hedged their long positions with futures and swaps. At the same time, every REIT owned as many agency MBSs as they possibly could. There was a constant scramble for balance sheet. Everyone wanted more balance sheet because the wide spreads made fixed-income trading pretty easy.

## The Fed will either:

1. Continue Balance Sheet Runoff and control inflation

2. End Balance Sheet Runoff and let inflation run high

QE, by definition, is inflationary. QE was successfully used to provide liquidity to the market during a crisis or economic slowdown. In the last year of QE4, the Fed overused the tool and pumped too much liquidity into the system.

Since inflation is *at least* partially a monetary phenomenon, pumping of $5 trillion into the economy over the past few years must have had some effect on the price level. If you accept that even some of QE is driving some of the current inflation, then the solution to the inflation problem *must* include shrinking the balance sheet. That means inflation can't be solved without withdrawing liquidity from the financial system.

At the same time, as the Fed winds down the SOMA portfolio and adds securities back into the market, there's a tremendous risk lurking in the shadows. There's a risk that trillions of securities added to the market will break something. As of now, there's no official end to the runoff, but I expect it will continue until something breaks.

And herein lies the Fed's dilemma. If they run down the SOMA portfolio too much, they will break something. If they don't, we are stuck with inflation.

# ABOUT THE AUTHOR

Scott E.D. Skyrm is a leading figure in the Repo and securities finance markets. He is a highly regarded trader, salesman, desk manager, and "Repo economist." He is regularly quoted in the *Wall Street Journal*, *The Financial Times*, *Bloomberg News*, *Reuters*, and *Market News*.

Mr. Skyrm started his career at The Bank of Tokyo, worked at ING Barings, Société Générale, and Wedbush Securities. He is currently an Executive Vice President and manages the Repo desk at Curvature Securities, LLC – a broker-dealer dedicated to securities finance.

# ACKNOWLEDGEMENTS

I want to thank Andrew Spencer for a superb editing job, Stephen Malekian for proof reading, and Alexandra Romanova for help on book cover. And special thanks to Kristopher Gontzes.

www.ingramcontent.com/pod-product-compliance
Lightning Source LLC
Chambersburg PA
CBHW021706270125
20903CB00026B/389/J